Hobbes

Hobbes

Prince of Peace

Bernard Gert

Polity

First published in 2010 by Polity Press

Polity Press
65 Bridge Street
Cambridge CB2 1UR, UK

Polity Press
350 Main Street
Malden, MA 02148, USA

ISBN-13: 978-0-7456-4881-1
ISBN-13: 978-0-7456-4882-8(pb)

A catalogue record for this book is available from the British Library.

Typeset in 10.5 on 12 pt Palatino
by Toppan Best-set Premedia Limited
Printed and bound in Great Britain by MPG Books Group Limited, Bodmin, Cornwall

The publisher has used its best endeavours to ensure that the URLs for external websites referred to in this book are correct and active at the time of going to press. However, the publisher has no responsibility for the websites and can make no guarantee that a site will remain live or that the content is or will remain appropriate.

Every effort has been made to trace all copyright holders, but if any have been inadvertently overlooked the publisher will be pleased to include any necessary credits in any subsequent reprint or edition.

For further information on Polity, visit our website: www.politybooks.com

Contents

Preface

More than 45 years ago I finished my PhD dissertation on the *Moral and Political Philosophy of Thomas Hobbes*. More than 35 years ago I edited and wrote an introduction for a volume entitled *Man and Citizen*, which includes both *De Homine* (chapters 10–15) and all of *De Cive*. I have also written many articles about Hobbes and reviewed several books about him. More importantly, much of my own work on morality and human nature has been influenced by Hobbes. My own moral theory is a version of the natural law theory put forward by Hobbes in *De Cive* and *Leviathan*. The account of human nature that I am developing also owes much to Hobbes, in particular his account of reason, but also of the emotions and of pleasure and pain.

While working out my own views, I have been struck by how often, when I arrive at what I take to be an original point, my next reading of Hobbes shows me that he had made that same point centuries before me. Hobbes did not get everything right, but it is surprising how much he did get right. His views about human nature, though pessimistic, are not unduly so. He was among the few moral and political philosophers whose views take into account that people differ from one another in significant ways. It is ironic that he should be criticized for holding that all people are completely selfish, because he held that one could not make any universal empirical claims about the motivation of all people. He does hold that the nature of the passions is the same in all people, e.g., fear and hope, but not the object of these passions. He says, "I say the similitude of the *passions*, which are the same in all men, *desire, fear, hope,* &c, not the similitude of the objects of the passions, which are the things *desired, feared, hoped,* &c." (*Leviathan,* Introduction par. 3) Hobbes is doing philosophy; he is providing a philosophical analysis of the passions. He is not doing empirical psychology, making universal claims about the motivation of all people, for he realizes that people are different.

Hobbes acknowledges the extent and power of religious beliefs and realizes that they provide a continuing threat to civil peace. He is aware that the primary difference between religious beliefs and superstitious beliefs is that the former are generally looked on favorably whereas the latter are not. He realizes the importance of distinguishing morality from religion, and establishes a foundation for morality completely independent of religion. However, because he is aware of the impossibility of eliminating religious belief, he devotes an enormous amount of time and effort trying to show that Christianity, properly interpreted, supports his account of morality. He presents an interpretation of Christianity, the only religion that was relevant in seventeenth-century England, which is most compatible with his moral and political views. His views on religion are an area in which he holds a position held by many contemporary philosophers.

Hobbes's work on language anticipated many of the discoveries of philosophers of language of the twentieth century. He explicitly describes the performative use of language in the transferring of rights, as in promises. He is aware that the primary benefit of language is that it enables people to communicate with each other for practical purposes. He does not, as many philosophers do, consider the primary function of language to provide a description of the world. Even though Hobbes is considered a thoroughgoing materialist, he was not primarily interested in metaphysics, and often does not distinguish between different versions of materialism, e.g., reductive materialism and epiphenomenalism. He also was not greatly interested in epistemology and did not take skepticism seriously. His primary concern with epistemology and metaphysics is to discredit those religious views that he thought were responsible for civil unrest and war. This lack of interest in epistemology and metaphysics may explain why some philosophers do not consider him to be ranked with Locke, Berkeley, and Hume. But no one denies that he ranks with the very best of all time in political theory, and I would rank him in a similar way in moral theory.

My appreciation of the greatness of Hobbes's moral and political theories has led me to spend considerable time and effort correcting some of the traditional misinterpretations of his views. I am pleased that I have played some role in changing the most egregious of those misinterpretations, that Hobbes held psychological egoism, i.e., the view that self-interest is the only motive for human action. That misinterpretation was used as a basis for criticizing Hobbes, and so it was not difficult to persuade those scholars who recognized the philosophical power of Hobbes's views that it was indeed a misinterpretation. It is more difficult to persuade such scholars that the standard interpretations of his views about reason or rationality are also mistaken because their misinterpretations of this concept are not used as a basis for criticizing him. Indeed, Hobbes is often credited with anticipating Hume's account of rationality as solely instrumental. I hope, however, to be as successful in changing this misinterpretation as I was in changing the misinterpretation of his views about human nature. Removing these misconceptions of Hobbes's views of human nature and rationality makes it possible for Hobbes's moral and political theory to be read more straightforwardly and sympathetically, and their power and relevance to become more apparent.

The state of nature, the right of nature, and the law of nature are central to Hobbes's accounts of human nature, rationality, morality, and politics. It may seem that his account of these technical terms, which are no longer in general use, are of interest only to Hobbes scholars. It is true that understanding these concepts are essential to understanding Hobbes's moral and political theories, but understanding them is also helpful in a more general understanding of how human nature and rationality are related to moral and political theory. Hobbes's discussion of the state of nature, the right of nature, and the law of nature are central to his justification of morality and of the political theory that he puts forward. When all of these concepts are given their proper interpretations, it becomes clear why Hobbes is considered one of the greatest political philosophers of all time. It is my view that Hobbes's moral theory is superior to other theories, such as those of Kant and Mill, which are generally regarded in a more favorable light.

Hobbes wrote about human nature, morality, and politics over a long period of time. The account of human nature expressed in his earliest work, *The Elements of Law Natural and Politic* (at one time considered as two separate works, *Human Nature* and *De Corpore Politico*), might be taken as egoistic. This non-authorized and only privately circulated early work, which was a draft of *De Cive*, provides most of the support for the misinterpretation of Hobbes as a psychological egoist. *De Homine*, published in 1658 but not translated into English until 1972, cannot possibly be taken as supporting psychological egoism. I am concerned with Hobbes's mature views, which start with the publication of *De Cive* in 1642 when he was already over 50. His philosophical views did not change much after that time, although he made successive refinements. He did, however, become interested in having more political influence, which may explain why *Leviathan*, published in 1651 (the same year that the English translation of *De Cive* was published), was initially published in English rather than Latin. (It was published in Latin in 1668). Although *Leviathan* is a very long work, Hobbes wrote it to influence an audience wider than that of *De Cive*.

Philosophers are situated in a particular time and place and their writings are a response to the problems with which they are presented. Hobbes's moral and political theories were clearly influenced by the religious controversies and civil wars that England was embroiled in during the much of the seventeenth century. In the Author's Preface to the Reader in *De Cive*, he even says that it was the impending civil war that led him to write *De Cive*, the third part of a trilogy, before writing the two works that were to precede it, *De Corpore* and *De Homine*. The Thirty Years War started when Hobbes was 30, so he was aware that the problems caused by religious beliefs were not peculiar to England. He was also aware of the conflict between religion and science. When Hobbes was in his mid-40s, Galileo published *Dialogue Concerning the Two Chief World Systems* and was punished by the Inquisition for publishing it. Hobbes fled to France to escape the English Civil War, which broke out when he was 54, the same year that *De Cive* was published. It is not surprising that he was concerned with the evils caused by religious controversy and devoted increasing space in his political writings to discussing religion. Nor is it surprising that he thought that applying the new scientific method to moral and political philosophy might provide a way to establish peace and stability.

I am interested in Hobbes's views because I think that they are important and mostly correct. When they are not, I shall suggest modifications of his views to correct them. I am not the kind of philosophical scholar who treats the writings of his favorite philosopher as if they were sacred texts, so that they have to be interpreted in order to rule out any mistakes. Hobbes made mistakes. Most of them were in matters of detail, not in the general theory. However, even in stating his general theory, there are problems, usually due to Hobbes's tendency to hyperbole. I shall try to distinguish clearly between my interpretations of Hobbes's views and my clarifications and revisions of them. For example, Hobbes seems to hold that, absent appropriate religious beliefs, it is irrational to sacrifice your life to save others. He comes close to giving up this view in the fifth paragraph of A Review and Conclusion in *Leviathan*, when he adds a new law of nature, "*that every man is bound by nature, as much as in him lieth, to protect in war the authority by which he is himself protected in time of peace.*" However, in most of his writings he assumes the irrationality of sacrificing your life for others, and seems mistakenly to think that this position is an essential premise of his moral and political theory.

Despite centuries of being attacked on the basis of mistaken interpretations of his views, Hobbes has maintained his reputation as the leading English political philosopher. It is a fully deserved reputation. I hope to show also that he should be ranked as highly as a moral philosopher and even as a philosopher of human nature. There are many philosophers who are very impressive upon first reading, but who become somewhat less impressive with each successive reading. Hobbes, on the other hand, is one of those few philosophers who become more impressive on each successive reading. Although his writings were occasioned by what was happening around him, we do not read him today because of his immersion in the problems of his times. We read him because his solutions to those problems incorporate solutions to problems that every age faces. I hope that my account of his moral and political philosophy will make clear how impressive his account of human nature and his moral and political theories views are.

1

Hobbes's Life, Times, and General Philosophical Views

Hobbes's Life and Times

Hobbes lived in troubling times. In his Verse Autobiography, he says that he was born prematurely on April 5, 1588 because of his mother's fear of the impending arrival of the Spanish Armada sent to invade England. He refers to this event by saying, "my mother gave birth to twins: myself and fear." Somewhat surprisingly, Hobbes seems to be proud of being a fearful person. When he left England for France in 1640, he claims that he was among the first to flee the civil war. But since Hobbes held that the primary goal of reason is to avoid avoidable death, it may be that his claim that he was a timid person was a modest way of claiming that he was a rational person. However, his writing shows no hint of timidity. He put forward views that he knew were quite controversial, when to publish controversial views about politics or religion was far more dangerous than it is now in England and America. Even now, in many parts of the world publishing controversial views about politics or religion may result in imprisonment or even death, and England during Hobbes's lifetime was more like these parts of the world than present-day England. Both the Roman Catholic Church and Oxford University banned the reading of his books, and there was talk, not only of burning his books but also of burning Hobbes himself. Actually, a few years after Hobbes died, Oxford University did burn copies of *De Cive* and *Leviathan*.

Hobbes was intimately involved in the political and religious controversies of his time, so that a proper understanding of his moral, political, and religious views requires some understanding of these controversies. Queen Elizabeth died in 1603 when Hobbes was almost 15 and James VI of Scotland became James I of England. James died in 1625, and his son, Charles 1, became king. Charles I, like his father, believed in the divine right of kings, and was almost continuously in conflict with the Parliament of England, precipitating two civil wars. He was defeated by parliamentary forces in the first civil war (1642–5) and was asked to approve a constitutional monarchy, but he would not do so, and in the resulting second civil war (1648–9) he was defeated again. The monarchy was then abolished and the Commonwealth of England was established with Cromwell as its leader. In 1646, the son of Charles I, Charles II (1630–85), fled to Paris, and Hobbes, who had fled there himself in 1640, became his mathematical tutor for two years. They must have developed a close relationship, for after the restoration of the monarchy in 1660, when Charles II became king, Hobbes was welcomed to his court and provided with a small pension. This happened even though Hobbes had presented Cromwell with a copy of *Leviathan* when he returned to England in 1651.

Because the politically perilous times that Hobbes lived through were due in large part to religious conflicts, it is no surprise that in trying to fashion his political theory Hobbes pays far more attention to religion than is common for contemporary political philosophers in the west. However, in the Islamic world, where religion is taken as seriously today as it was in seventeenth-century England, Hobbes's concern with religion may be far more relevant. But although Hobbes was concerned with religion, religious beliefs play no essential role in his moral and political theories. He presents his views so that those for whom religion is important can take God as the source of morality, but he is quite clear that morality can be based solely on human nature and rationality. Although he defines the laws of nature, which incorporate the moral law, as the dictates of reason, he says that they can also be considered as the commands of God. He says this because he knows that most people are far more influenced by their religious beliefs than by philosophical arguments. It is because he wants to influence the way people behave that he sometimes writes in a way that can be interpreted as if the force of morality did depend on the laws of nature being the commands of God.

In Hobbes's time, neither atheism nor deism was a position that any person seeking to influence the way people should behave or how a commonwealth should be organized would put forward.

Indeed, if a person hoped to have any practical influence, he would also not put forward any non-Christian view. Hobbes lived in a Christian world, and all of the religious controversies were controversies between different branches of Christianity. In England these were Roman Catholicism, Anglicanism, and Presbyterianism, whereas on the continent the controversies were between Catholics and Protestants. Less than 10 years after Hobbes graduated from Magdalen Hall, Oxford, the Thirty Years War (1618–48) began on the continent. This war started as a religious controversy but later became more of a political war. It involved so much death and destruction that many felt the need to find a moral view that was independent of any particular religion and could command acceptance from all rational persons. Probably the most important writer putting forward such a view was Hugo Grotius. Although Grotius was born only five years before Hobbes, on April 10, 1583, his influential book, *On the Law of War and Peace* (1625) was published 15 years before Hobbes wrote the first draft of a book on moral and political philosophy. That draft, *The Elements of Law Natural and Politic*, which was clearly influenced by Grotius's book, was not written until 1640. Although Hobbes circulated it in manuscript, he realized that it had serious problems and did not have it published. Nonetheless, this first draft of a book continues to be taken by many commentators on Hobbes as presenting the clearest account of his views on human nature. This has resulted in a serious distortion of his considered and mature views on human nature and morality.

Hobbes's considered views on human nature and his developed moral and political theories are presented in *De Cive*, his first published book on moral and political philosophy. This book, written in Latin (1642, Notes and Preface added in 1647), was translated into English as *Philosophical Rudiments Concerning Government and Society* in 1651, the same year that the English edition of *Leviathan* was published. (The Latin version of *Leviathan* was published in 1668.) *De Cive* was supposed to be the third book of a trilogy; the first book was to be *De Corpore* (1655), which was devoted to an examination of language, scientific concepts, physics, and geometry. The second was *De Homine* (1658), most of the first nine chapters of which were devoted to optics, but the last six chapters, X–XV, provide an account of human nature that can serve as an introduction to the moral and political philosophy put forward in *De Cive*.

The combination of the translation by myself and colleagues of these chapters from *De Homine* and of the English translation of *De Cive* was published in a volume entitled *Man and Citizen* (1991

[1972]). These chapters from *De Homine* serve as a foundation for
De Cive in the same way as Part I: "Of Man" of *Leviathan* serves
as a foundation for Part II: "Of Commonwealth," so that *Man
and Citizen* provides another complete account of Hobbes's moral
and political theories, including his account of human nature. When
both of these accounts put forward the same views, we can be
confident that these are indeed Hobbes's considered views. This
book uses *Leviathan* and *Man and Citizen* as the primary sources
for Hobbes's account of human nature and for his moral and political theories.[1]

Hobbes published *De Cive* before he finished the two books of
his trilogy that were supposed to precede it because of his concern
about the impending civil war in England. Although Hobbes was
aware that most people acted on their emotions rather than their
reason, he exhibited the standard naïveté of philosophers, acting as
if philosophical arguments would affect people's behavior. He not
only wanted to discover the truth, he wanted to persuade others
that he had discovered it. He believed that if his discoveries were
universally accepted, there would be no more civil wars and people
would live together in peace and harmony. After praising the work
of the geometricians, he says:

> If the moral philosophers had as happily discharged their duty,
> I know not what could have been added by human industry to the
> completion of that happiness, which is consistent with human life.
> For were the nature of human actions as distinctly known as the
> nature of *quantity* in geometrical figures, the strength of *avarice* and
> *ambition*, which is sustained by the erroneous opinions of the vulgar
> as touching the nature of *right* and *wrong*, would presently faint and
> languish; and mankind should enjoy such an immortal peace, that
> unless it were for habitation, on supposition that the earth should
> grow too narrow for her inhabitants, there would hardly be left any
> pretence for war. (*D.C.* Ded., p. 91)

---

[1] In order to make it possible to check the reference no matter what edition of *Leviathan* or *De Cive* is being used, references to *Leviathan* are by chapter and paragraph
number and to *De Cive* and *De Homine* are by chapter and section number, except
for the Preface where paragraph numbers are given, but, because some paragraphs
are three pages long, pages numbers to *Man and Citizen* are also given. The Dedication is one long paragraph, so only page numbers to *Man and Citizen* are given.
References to other works of Hobbes, e.g., *De Corpore* and *The Elements of Law
Natural and Politic*, are also by chapter and section number. I will use *D.C.* for *De
Cive*, *L.* for *Leviathan*, and *D.H.* for *De Homine*.

It is true that great philosophers such as Hobbes do have an effect on society, but usually this effect takes place many decades, even centuries, after they have written. For example, Hobbes's view that morality is independent of religion is now the standard view of many educated people in English-speaking countries; however, almost no one in Hobbes's time accepted such a view. That is why Hobbes devotes more than a third of *Leviathan* trying to show that his moral and political theories are not only compatible with Christian Scripture but are also actually supported by Scripture. Although his works are now studied in colleges and universities, Hobbes did not write them as academic works. Despite its size, about 500 pages, *Leviathan* is a political tract, which is why Hobbes published it first in English rather than in Latin, in contrast with all the books of the trilogy, *De Corpore, De Homine*, and *De Cive*.

Many of Hobbes's views about human nature and the emotions were taken from Aristotle, especially his *Rhetoric*. Individual elements of his accounts of morality and politics are also not original, but were put forward by others who participated in the political and religious controversies that were current in his time. Hobbes's originality is in how he unites all of these elements into a powerful philosophical system. He wrote with the intention of influencing current events; however, philosophers do not now read Hobbes because of the role he played in the political and religious controversies of his time.

Like all great philosophers, Hobbes transcended his times. He constructs a philosophical system in which all of his moral and political views are derived from what he considers to be clear truths about human nature, language, morality, and rationality. He takes this system so seriously that he abandons positions that were held by most of his political allies; e.g., he denies the divine right of kings. Once he discovers what he takes to be obviously true premises, he follows out their implications regardless of where they lead. Of course, like most philosophers, he knows what results he wants, and this influences his choice of premises. However, unlike many philosophers, he never adopts a premise solely because he needs it to reach conclusions he wants. For example, John Rawls, in *A Theory of Justice*, rules out envy from the characteristics people have in the original position because only by doing so can he reach the conclusion that all rational persons will choose the two principles of justice that he wants as his conclusion.

Hobbes on Religion

Hobbes is so contemporary in so many of his philosophical views that it is easy to think of him as holding contemporary views in all matters. That would be a mistake. At the present time, most philosophers who are not officially associated with some religion usually do not believe in any traditional concept of God. Hume, in his *Dialogues Concerning Natural Religion* (1779), presents arguments against theism that have never been refuted, but he provides no positive alternative to explain all those features of world, especially the biological world, that seem to need an explanation. It is not until Darwin's *Origin of Species* (1859) and *Descent of Man* (1871) that a non-theistic explanation for these matters becomes more plausible than a theistic explanation, not only to philosophers but also to others. Hobbes wrote *De Cive* and *Leviathan* two centuries before Darwin and a century before Hume. He almost certainly believed that there was a being that created the world, but it was crucial to him that the miraculous stories in the Hebrew Bible and the Christian Scriptures be interpreted so that they were compatible with his philosophical views, especially his moral and political theory.

Just as almost all philosophers who wrote after Darwin accepted Darwin's natural selection account of the evolution of human beings, so almost all philosophers who wrote after Galileo's *Dialogue Concerning the Two Chief World Systems* (1632) accepted the Copernican system. Just as acceptance of Darwinian evolution is often taken as incompatible with orthodox Christian belief, so too was acceptance of the Copernican system. However, just as many contemporary Christians accept the Darwinian account of the origin of human beings, so many believing Christians during the seventeenth century accepted Galileo's views. It is tempting for contemporary philosophers to underestimate the importance of religious beliefs, for many of the most distinguished contemporary scientists do not believe in a theistic God. However, even the greatest scientists during the time of Hobbes, e.g., Galileo and Newton, believed in such a God. It is important not to forget the extraordinary impact that the Darwinian account has had on belief in any kind of theistic God. Even if Hobbes was a deist, it is crucial for understanding him to appreciate the importance that he attributes to Christian religious belief.

These common-sense observations about the influences on Hobbes simply acknowledge that Hobbes was a person of his time.

It would be a serious mistake to attribute to Hobbes views that no one could be expected to hold in seventeenth-century England, such as secular humanism. But Hobbes was a humanist in the sense that he was deeply influenced by his reading of classical sources such as Homer and Thucydides. His first published work was a translation of Thucydides' *History of the Peloponnesian War* (1629) and his excellent translations of Homer's Iliad and Odyssey were completed and published less than five years before he died in 1679. He knew all three classical languages, Greek, Latin, and Hebrew, and was clearly extremely proficient in both Greek and Latin. Given how much he borrowed from Aristotle's *Rhetoric* concerning the emotions, and that he translated Thucydides while in his 30s, it is likely that Hobbes's views about human nature, rationality, and morality were developed prior to his discovery of Euclid when he was 40 years old. Although he presents his views on human nature, morality, and politics as if they were derived from his metaphysics, it is fairly clear that the substance of his views on these topics was fixed by his humanistic readings and his own observations of the behavior of people.

Nonetheless, we do not now read Hobbes primarily because of the views that he holds about human nature, morality, and politics, but because of the way in which he argues for his views. Hobbes presents his moral and political theories as if he were putting forward scientific theories, combining very plausible definitions of such key terms as "justice," "morality," and "rationality" with common-sense observations about human nature. It is the systematic character of Hobbes's thought that makes his theories so powerful. But his theories are not quite as systematic as he sometimes seems to claim. He does think that an account of human nature is derivable from materialism, but he makes no effort to derive his account of any of the passions from his metaphysical materialism. Although his account of human nature is not derived from his materialism, but based on introspection and observation of the behavior of others, once he has that account, he develops his moral and political theories in a remarkably systematic way.

Hobbes holds a very contemporary sounding form of materialism, encountering some of the same problems that contemporary materialists have. Even though his metaphysics does not have any significant impact on his moral and political theories, he does have some interesting metaphysical views. It is worthwhile to provide a brief account of his materialism, partly because this plays a role in his attempt to reduce the influence of traditional religious beliefs that he considered dangerous. A similar reason makes it worthwhile to provide a brief account of epistemological views, for they also serve to diminish the plausibility of traditional religious views. Hobbes's account of language, reasoning, and science has a much wider interest. Hobbes has a sophisticated account of the uses of language, anticipating some of the discoveries attributed to contemporary philosophers. He regarded human beings' use of language as the primary activity that distinguished them from non-human animals. He also regarded language as an essential feature in the formation of a commonwealth.

Hobbes on Human Nature, Morality, and Justice

Before I present an account of Hobbes's views on language, reason, and science, and brief accounts of his metaphysics and epistemology, I shall briefly anticipate what will be the main topics of the following three chapters: human nature, morality, and justice. Hobbes's felt need to lessen the influence of religion colors his views on language, metaphysics, and epistemology as well as being a significant part of his moral and political theories. The amount of space that Hobbes devotes to religion and the interpretation of Scripture in both *De Cive* and *Leviathan* cannot be explained except by his conviction that religious beliefs were a constant and serious threat to the stability of a commonwealth. He believed that unless he could show that Christianity supported the moral and political philosophy that he was putting forward, his theories would have no practical influence at all. He was not writing for an academic audience: he was writing to influence those who ran the commonwealth. But he was first and foremost a philosopher, so he wanted his influence to be based on correct accounts of human nature, rationality, morality, and politics.

Hobbes adopts only those premises that he thinks even his opponents would grant. Once he has adopted these premises, he does not reject them because they lead to conclusions to which he would prefer they did not lead – e.g., that it is not unjust for atheists or deists not to obey the commands of God. He neither abandons these premises nor distorts them so they do lead to the desired conclusion. It is because he systematically builds his moral and political theories from very plausible accounts of human nature, language, morality, and rationality that we read him now. Many regard him as the greatest political philosopher writing in English. However, the standard interpretations of his views on human nature make it difficult to understand why he is so highly regarded. Until fairly recently, Hobbes was taken as putting forward an account of human nature that claims that all motives for human behavior are motives of self-interest. This sophomoric view, which is commonly known as psychological egoism, would make it impossible for Hobbes to hold any kind of plausible moral or political theory. Interpreting Hobbes as holding psychological egoism is also partly responsible for the claim that he holds that there is no morality in the state of nature, and that the sovereign, because he has the power to punish, determines what counts as morally right and wrong. However, when the serious misinterpretations of his views on human nature are corrected, it becomes possible to appreciate the force of his moral philosophy and to understand the sophistication of his political philosophy.

It is acknowledged by all that Hobbes's primary practical concern is to prevent civil war. Of course, he wants to provide the foundation for a commonwealth in which all citizens have "such things as are necessary for commodious living" (*L*. XIII, 14), but most of all he wants to avoid civil war. He even describes the moral virtues as those traits of character that are necessary for "peaceable, sociable, and comfortable living" (*L*. XV, 40). These moral virtues apply to everyone, citizens and sovereigns alike, but this creates a problem. If there is a universal morality that applies to sovereigns as well as to citizens, then citizens may take the immoral behavior of their sovereign as warranting punishment and hence as grounds for rebellion. Thus, putting forward a universal morality, contrary to his primary practical goal, preventing civil war, may actually lead to civil war. That a universal morality may lead citizens to civil war is a serious problem for Hobbes, because, from his own experience, he knows that sovereigns quite frequently do not exhibit the moral virtues, and in fact often act immorally.

In order to deal with this problem, Hobbes distinguishes between immoral behavior that warrants punishment and immoral behavior that does not. He also makes clear that only the sovereign is authorized to inflict punishment for immoral behavior and that citizens are not so authorized. Hobbes distinguishes between justice and the other moral virtues. Only unjust behavior warrants punishment and only sovereigns are authorized to punish because they are the persons to whom the citizens have given up their right to decide how they should behave. Although Hobbes can and does admit that sovereigns can behave immorally, he denies that they can behave unjustly. As a practical matter, Hobbes knows that if he is to have any influence on the way a commonwealth is governed, he has to persuade those who govern, that is, sovereigns. Sovereigns would certainly not be persuaded by a view that claims that citizens may punish sovereigns for their immoral behavior. Thus Hobbes's distinction between justice and the rest of morality serves a practical as well as a theoretical purpose. Overlooking this quite sophisticated distinction between justice and the other moral virtues results in commentators claiming that Hobbes holds that morality does not apply in the state of nature. They mistakenly interpret his remark, "To this war of every man against every man, this also is consequent: that nothing can be unjust" (*L.* XIII, 13) to mean that in the state of nature nothing can be immoral.

Although Hobbes's major interest is in moral and political theory, he is a systematic thinker, and his views about language, reasoning, and science have a significant impact on the presentation of his moral and political theory. His epistemological and metaphysical views, which are less developed, are used primarily as arguments against religious views that he regards as dangerous. Hobbes views religion as the one of the greatest, if not the greatest, threat to civil peace. As the amount of space that he devotes to biblical interpretation shows, he regards it as crucial that Christianity be interpreted in a way that is compatible with his moral and political theory. Hobbes knew that belief in some form or another of Christianity was a dominant factor in the political life of England (and of the other European countries), so he attempts to provide an interpretation of Christianity that removes it as a threat to civil peace. Although Hobbes uses his account of language and meaning in arguing against dangerous religious views, he also has a more positive view about language as necessary for scientific reasoning. On the other hand, his epistemological and metaphysical views are developed only as far as is necessary to support his arguments against the religious views that he regards as dangerous. For that he does not need the level of sophistication that might be expected of a thinker of Hobbes's caliber.

Hobbes on Language, Reasoning and Science

In order to make his views absolutely certain, Hobbes tries to provide a scientific basis for views that he had already acquired by experience. The following passage provides an analogy to what Hobbes thought about what he was doing:

> As much experience is prudence, so is much science sapience . . . But to make their difference appear more clearly, let us suppose one man endued with an excellent natural use and dexterity in handling his arms, and another to have added to that dexterity an acquired science of where he can offend or be offended by his adversary in every possible posture or guard; the ability of the former would be to the ability of the latter as prudence to sapience; both useful, but the latter infallible. (*L. V*, 21)

Hobbes thought that by providing a scientific or philosophical basis for views that he had acquired by experience, he would so strengthen them that they would be irrefutable. His accounts of language and reasoning do provide support for his moral and political views, but he also makes many important points about the nature of language that have nothing to do with his moral and political views. However, his accounts of epistemology and metaphysics have somewhat less value and were primarily used as weapons against those dangerous religious beliefs that he needed to discredit.

Hobbes devotes far more time and space to language, reasoning, and science than he does to epistemology and metaphysics. His interest in language goes far beyond its use as a weapon against dangerous religious beliefs. He considers the ability to use language to be the essential feature distinguishing human beings from all other animals. Without language, which is essential for transferring or giving up one's natural right to decide how to act, human beings could never form a commonwealth. Like Wittgenstein, Hobbes thinks that the most important use of language is practical, not theoretical. Nonetheless, Hobbes is impressed by the power of language to reach universal conclusions. Because language is essential to the forming of commonwealths, Hobbes thinks he can derive universal conclusions concerning the duties and rights of subjects and sovereigns from the way commonwealths are formed. It may have been his first reading of Euclid's *Elements* that so impressed him with the power of deductive reasoning.

> [Hobbes] was 40 years old before he looked on Geometry; which happened accidentally. Being in a Gentleman's Library, Euclid's Elements lay open, and 'twas the 47 *El. Libri* I. He read the Proposition. "By G——," sayd he (he would now and then swear an emphaticall Oath by way of emphasis), "*this is impossible!*" So, he reads the

Demonstration of it, which referred him back to such a Proposition; which proposition he read. That referred him back to another, which he also read. *Et sic deinceps* [and so on] that at last he was demonstratively convinced of that trueth. This made him in love with Geometry.[2]

According to Hobbes, geometry demonstrates how important speech is:

Seeing then that *truth* consisteth in the right ordering of names in our affirmations, a man that seeketh precise *truth* had need to remember what every name he uses stands for, and to place it accordingly, or else he will find himself entangled in words; as a bird in lime twigs, the more he struggles the more belimed. And therefore in geometry (which is the only science that it hath pleased God hitherto to bestow on mankind) men begin at settling the significations of their words; which settling their significations they call *definitions*, and place them in the beginning of their reckoning. (*L*. IV, 12)

Because Hobbes says, "*truth* consisteth in the right ordering of names in our affirmations," he has been accused of holding that we can make statements true simply by arbitrarily providing definitions that make the statements true. But this accusation is the result of not realizing that Hobbes holds that there can be right and wrong definitions. "So that in the right definitions of names lies the first use of speech, which is the acquisition of science; and in wrong or no definitions lies the first abuse, from which proceed all false and senseless tenets" (*L*. IV, 13). Right definitions of names or words are definitions that include the essential features of the thing named or referred to; they are what are sometimes called "real definitions." Although Hobbes limits the use of the word "true" to utterances in languages, this does not mean that he regards truth to be determined primarily by the use of language, as if considerations about the world independent of language played little or no role. Hobbes does hold that there is no natural relationship between words as sounds or marks on paper and the objects or properties they refer to. He agrees that it is arbitrary what sound or mark on paper is used as a name for an object or property. However, once a relationship between a word and the object or property that it refers to is established, then the truth of statements using that word is

[2] *Aubrey's Brief Lives*, ed. Oliver Lawson Dick. Ann Arbor: University of Michigan Press, 1962, p. 150.

determined by the real characteristics of the object or property. Language relates to the world by means of real definitions, that is, accurate descriptions of the essential features of the referents of the word being defined.

Hobbes knows that some names do not merely refer to things, but also indicate the attitude of the speaker toward those things. He says of such names that "they are of *inconstant* signification" and that they "can never be the true grounds of any ratiocination" (*L*. IV, 24). So Hobbes knows that names are not used merely to refer to objects or properties in the world, but also to express our attitudes about these objects or properties. Indeed, he realizes that language has more important uses than enabling one to make true statements about objects and properties in the world. His list of the main uses of language in *De Homine* (*D.H.* X, 3) is an improvement over that in *Leviathan*, although the latter shows his interest in aesthetics by including as one of the main uses of language, "to please and delight ourselves and others, by playing with our words, for pleasure or ornament, innocently" (*L*. IV, 3). In *De Homine* the first pre-eminent advantage of language is "that the power of numeral words enables man not only to count things, but also to measure them" (*D.H.* X, 3). Hobbes regards the benefits of having numeral words as enabling people to do so much that he says, "From these things the enormous advantages of human life have far surpassed the condition of other animals" (ibid.). The second advantage is "one may teach another, that is communicate his knowledge to another" (ibid.). But he does not limit this advantage to simple teaching, for he includes in this advantage, warning and advising. Then he concludes, "that we can command and understand commands is a benefit of speech, and truly the greatest" (ibid.). It is this use of language that is necessary for commonwealths to be maintained.

Hobbes does not explicitly mention the performative use of language, that is, using words to perform some action that we don't normally think of as a linguistic action – e.g., in the appropriate circumstances saying "I christen this ship *Leviathan*" is christening that ship. Currently, the most common example of the use of performative language is with regard to making promises. In the appropriate circumstances, saying "I promise" is promising. Hobbes's discussion of renouncing or transferring a right can be taken as equivalent to this common use of performative language. He says, "The way by which a man either simply renounceth or transferreth his right is a declaration . . . that he doth so renounce or transfer . . . And these signs are either words only, or actions only, or (as it happeneth most often) both words and actions" (*L.* XIV, 7). Given the importance of commands, Hobbes must regard the performative use of language as one of language's main advantages, for he counts as commands only those imperatives that are made by someone who has received the right that another person has renounced or transferred.

As is evident from the following quote, Hobbes realizes the importance of this performative use of language:

> And when a man hath in either manner abandoned or granted away his right, he is said to be OBLIGED or BOUND, not to hinder those to whom such right is granted or abandoned from the benefit of it; and [it is said] that he *ought*, and it is his DUTY, not to make void that voluntary act of his own, and that such hindrance is INJUSTICE and INJURY, as being *sine jure*, [without right] the right being before renounced or transferred. (*L.* XIV, 7)

Hobbes uses his account of this kind of performative use of language to explain why citizens are obliged to obey the laws of the commonwealth, that is, to obey the commands of the sovereign. Contemporary philosophers make a similar move when they try to explain why making a promise obliges the person making it to keep it.

Hobbes, like the later Wittgenstein, regards language primarily as a practical tool. The primary function of language is to enable us to interact with each other in useful ways, such as coordinating our activities. Although language allows us to provide true descriptions of the world, that is not its primary function. However, Hobbes was impressed by the fact that descriptive language enabled reasoning about the world, thus leading to science and increased power to achieve practical goals. For Hobbes, only pure referring words, that is, words that are used by everyone to refer to the same objects or properties in the world, can be used in science. To ensure that everyone is referring to the same objects or properties in the world, it is necessary to start with definitions. The right definitions of these words are descriptions of the essential features of the referents of these words, that is, the essential features of the objects and properties referred to. This account of definitions correctly describes most of the definitions of referring words that are presented in dictionaries, which simply provide a description of the essential features of the object or property being referred to.

Hobbes says that there are four general kinds of referring words because he holds that there are four different kinds of things that are subject to names. The first and most basic are names that refer to bodies of all kinds, *"living, sensible, rational, hot, cold, moved, quiet,* with all such names, the word matter, or body, is understood, all such being names of matter" (*L. IV,* 15). Hobbes distinguishes between names that refer to particular things, or, as he says:

> [S]ome are *proper,* and singular to one thing only, as *Peter, John, this man, this tree*; and some are *common* to many things, as *man, horse, tree,* every of which, though but one name, is nevertheless the name of diverse particular things, in respect of all which it is together it is called an *universal,* there being nothing in the world universal but names; for the things named are every one of them individual and singular. (*L. IV,* 6)

Hobbes is here putting forward a view called nominalism. He holds what might be called "resemblance nominalism." "One universal name is imposed on many things for their similitude in some quality or accident: and whereas a proper name bringeth to mind one thing only, universals recall any one of these many" (*L. IV,* 7). The word "living [body]" refers to all bodies with the property of being alive, no matter how much they differ in other respects.

Secondly, we can refer to the properties themselves, rather than to bodies having that property. We do this by simply making a small change in the words used. So "for *living* [we] put into account *life*; for *moved, motion*; for *hot, heat,* for *long, length,* and the like" (*L. IV,* 16). When we refer directly to these accidents or properties of bodies, Hobbes says the names are "called *names abstract,* because severed (not from matter, but) from the account of matter" (ibid.). This is how Hobbes deals with what are sometimes called abstract objects. If nominalism is taken as denying that, independent of language, there are any universals or abstract objects, then Hobbes is clearly a nominalist. But he is not really interested in metaphysical doctrines; he is primarily concerned with providing an account of language that allows for what he calls science.

The third kind of referring word contains those words that refer to what Hobbes calls "fancies" and that he regards as special kinds of properties of our own bodies. Hobbes accepts a materialist view and claims that what we call sensations or ideas are simply properties of our own bodies, some of which are the result of external bodies immediately acting on us. The contemporary materialist view would be that sensations or ideas are states of the brain. Why these properties of our bodies should be distinguished from other properties of bodies and have a category of names all to themselves, Hobbes does not explain. Perhaps it is because philosophers have often confused fancies, which are properties of the perceiver's body, with properties of the bodies being perceived. The most common example of this is that color properties like red and green are taken to be properties of the objects rather than properties of the perceiving person. However, Hobbes does not distinguish clearly between the names of fancies and the names of properties of bodies external to the person. He does not distinguish between "length" which refers to a property of external bodies, and "heat" which refers to a property of the perceiving body. He seems to use the same words, "heat," "color," and "sound," as names of both fancies and as names of properties of external bodies. However, he may distinguish different uses of these words – i.e., when we are concerned not with the property of an external object, but with the effect of that external object on us, then we are referring to fancies.

Fourth and last, Hobbes says that we "give names to *names* themselves and to *speeches*." He recognizes that we have words that refer to words such as *"general, universal, special, equivocal,"* and words that refer to sentences and longer stretches of language, such as *"affirmation, interrogation, commandment, narration, syllogisms, sermon, oration*, and many others" (*L.* IV, 18). Hobbes says that these four categories are the only kinds of *positive* names. Although he recognizes negative names, he does not regard them as referring to negative things; rather he regards them as "notes to signify that a word is not the name of the thing in question, as these words, *nothing, no man, infinite, indocible, three want four*, and the like; which are nevertheless of use in reckoning" (*L.* IV, 19). Hobbes does not use his account of names to generate any metaphysical positions; rather he provides a classification of names that is consistent with the materialism that he holds independent of his account of language.

Hobbes says, "all names are imposed to signify our conceptions, when we conceive the same things differently, we can hardly avoid different naming of them" (*L.* IV, 24). When he talks about giving different names to the same thing, he is distinguishing between people using a different name or word to refer to the same thing, e.g., a particular piece of behavior seen by all, but of which some approve, while others disapprove. As examples of this kind of inconstant signification, Hobbes uses "the names of virtues and vices; for one man calleth *wisdom*, what another calleth *fear*; and one *cruelty*, what another *justice*" (ibid.). This is why he distinguishes between words as signs and words as names. Hobbes regards words as signs of our thoughts, but as names of objects and properties in the world. He holds that signs and names are related because he regards our thoughts as being about objects and properties in the world.

Insofar as everyone has the same attitude toward the objects and properties in the world, they use the same names for them, but when they have different attitudes toward them, as they do with regard to virtues and vices, they do not call them by the same name. It is only when everyone uses the same names for objects and properties in the world that these names should be used in reasoning and science. Words are used as signs "when many use the same words to signify (by their connexion and order) one to another, what they conceive or think of each matter, and also what they desire, fear, or have any other passion for" (L. IV, 3). Although Hobbes claims that words name or refer to objects and properties in the world, they do not name or refer to those objects and properties as things independent of human experience. Rather, words refer to objects and properties only as they are conceived to be part of our common experience. It is when all human beings conceive of things in the same way that the names that they use to refer to these things can be used in science.

That human beings experience the world in the same way is necessary for the development of language. That they successfully use the same words to refer to various objects and properties in the world in giving advice, issuing commands, etc. confirms that people experience the world in the same ways. This uniformity of experience enables words that are signs of the thoughts of different individuals to be the name of a single object or property in the world. It is because definitions explicitly include those features that are common to all of the referents of that name that it is possible to reach universal conclusions. Definitions describe the essential features of the referents of the words being defined. When we create that which is referred to, as Hobbes thought we did with the shapes that are referred to by the words that are used in geometry, we are able to reason *a priori*. This is the original meaning of *a priori*, going from cause to effect. Hobbes held that since we create or cause the shapes that are referred to in geometry, we can be certain that their descriptions are correct. We know what we have to do to create those shapes, and because definitions are descriptions of the referents that include all and only their essential features, this allows us to generalize from particular cases and to draw universal conclusions.

> By this imposition of names, some of larger, some of stricter significa-
> tion, we turn the reckoning of the consequences of things imagined
> in the mind into a reckoning of the consequences of appellations. For
> example, a man that hath no use of speech at all (such as is born and
> remains perfectly deaf and dumb), if he sets before his eyes a triangle,
> and by it two right angles (such as are the corners of a square figure)
> he may by meditation compare and find that the three angles of that
> triangle are equal to those two right angles that stand by it. But if
> another triangle be shown him, different in shape from the former,
> he cannot know without a new labour, whether the three angles of
> that also be equal to the same. But he that hath the use of words . . .
> will boldly conclude universally that such equality of angles is in all
> triangles whatsoever, and register his invention in these general
> terms: *every triangle hath it three angles equal to two right angles* [Euclid,
> *Elements*, I, 32]. (L. IV, 9; see also *De Corp.* II, 9)

Hobbes does not make the absurd claim that by our use of language we create truths about the world. Rather he holds the very
plausible view that by providing "right definitions" or accurate
descriptions of the essential features of the referents of referring
terms, we can derive universal conclusions. It is interesting to note
that he defines science as conditional knowledge, "as when we
know that *if the figure shown be a circle, then any straight line through
the center shall divide it into two equal parts*" (L. IX, 1). He does not
view looking at a circle and seeing that it is a circle as scientific
knowledge. Nor does he seem to hold that the rightness of definitions is scientific knowledge either. But he also does not explicitly
claim it to be knowledge of fact, so it is not quite clear how he would
classify knowledge of the correctness of definitions. Contemporary
philosophers still have this problem. Those philosophers who distinguish between our knowledge of analytic truths and our knowledge of empirical truths do not seem to realize that our knowledge
of the former depends upon our knowledge of language. However,
this knowledge, which includes knowledge of the meaning of words
as well as of the grammar of sentences, is empirical.

In *De Corpore*, Hobbes provides a detailed discussion of definitions. He says: "[T]he names of things which are understood to be
able to have a cause ought to have that cause or method of generation in the definition, as for instance we define a circle to be a figure
generated from the rotation of a straight line in a plane and so on"

(*De Corp.* VI, 13; see also *D.H.* X, 5). Here he seems to be claiming, that the word "circle" refers to that figure which can be generated as he describes. This strongly suggests that these kinds of definitions depend upon empirical knowledge. It is quite likely that someone discovered that those figures that look like circles and satisfy all the geometrical theorems about circles could be generated in this way. It is quite clear that to be a circle it is not necessary that it be generated in that way, only that it could have been so generated.

Hobbes even discusses the definition of "definition." "How 'definition' itself ought to be defined can be understood from what has been said, namely, that it is a proposition, the predicate is the resolution of the subject, when it can be done, and is its explication, when it cannot be done" (*De Corp.* VI, 14). Resolution is possible only for composite names such as "square," where it is resolved into "equilateral," "quadrilateral," and "rectangular" (*De Corp.* VI, 15). Explication without resolution occurs when giving definitions of simple names, such as "matter" or "quantity." In these cases, it is necessary to provide some circumlocution that will guarantee that everyone is referring to the same thing by that name. Other definitions that are done by explication without resolution occur in what we would now call science. These are the scientific definitions of the various basic elements such as quark and meson, but they also seem to be based on empirical investigation.

The other kind of definition, that which consists of "the resolution of that name into its more universal parts," as when we define man by saying "A man is a body, animate, sentient, and rational," also requires empirical knowledge, but of a very different kind, namely, knowledge of the way words are used. Hobbes, like many contemporary philosophers, often seems to forget that knowledge of how words are used, or what they refer to, is something that must be learned. He continues in the next section to claim that "it is the nature of a definition that it defines, that is, that it determines the signification of the term defined and cuts it off from every signification other than what is contained in the definition" and "[t]hat it produces a universal notion of the thing defined, so that there is a certain universal picture, not for the eye, but for the mind" (*De Corp.* VI, 15).

Although Hobbes talks of right and wrong definitions (*L.* IV, 13), sometimes he seems to think that although definitions can be useful or useless, they cannot be correct or incorrect. Thus he says of a definition:

That it is not necessary to quarrel over whether a definition is to be admitted or not. For since only the issue between a teacher and pupil matters, if the pupil understands all the parts resolved in the definition of a thing defined and still does not want to accept the definition, all argument is then already at an end, for it is the same as if he did not want to learn. (*De Corp.* VI, 15)

This remark seems to apply only to the introduction of new terms. Hobbes does not say that people can define "just" and "unjust" in any way they want as long as they agree on the definition. Rather, he claims to be providing definitions of "just" and "unjust" that capture what these terms actually mean, that is, to refer to behavior that everyone would refer to as just. It would be pointless for Hobbes to provide definitions of "just" and "unjust" that did not capture what people ordinarily mean by these terms. He wants to explain the fact that people believe that they ought to be just, in the ordinary sense of that term. He is trying to show that when one is clear about the kind of behavior that everyone refers to as just, it will be obvious why everyone thinks people ought to be just. He must therefore define "just" and "unjust" so that they mean what people ordinarily mean by them.

Hobbes holds that the definitions of terms that refer to things that we create are better than definitions of terms that refer to things of which we do not know the cause. He seems to think that the certainty of the truths of geometry depends on this fact. He holds that "*a priori* demonstration [is] only of those things whose generation depends on the will of men themselves" (*D.H.* X, 4). Hobbes's use of "*a priori*" explains why we use that phrase, namely, that it comes from what is prior, the cause, and "*a posteriori*" means that it comes from what is later, namely, the effects. This use of *a priori* precedes the concept of *a priori* developed by Kant and which has become the standard use. It is interesting, however, to note the similarity between Kant's use of the phrases and Hobbes's. According to Hobbes, *a priori* demonstration yields knowledge that derives from our being the cause of what is known, and it is certain. On the other hand, "we can, deducing as far as possible the consequences of those qualities that we do see, demonstrate that such and such *could* have been their causes. This kind of demonstration is called *a posteriori*, and its science physics" (*D.H.* X, 5). This kind of knowledge is not certain. Kant holds that *a priori* knowledge derives from the nature of the human mind and is certain, whereas *a posteriori* knowledge is dependent on using our senses in order to discover features of the world, and is not certain. Hobbes's concept of *"a priori"* is not a useful way to distinguish knowledge about which we can be certain from knowledge about which we cannot be certain, for it is not clear why we should be certain of the consequences of that "whose generation depends on the will of men themselves." Nor is it clear that we can never be certain of the cause when we start with the effects.

Hobbes was encouraged in his belief that if we generated something ourselves, we could be certain of its consequences, because he viewed geometry as a science in which we generated the figures, and geometry was certain. He was further encouraged in this belief because, according to him, "politics and ethics (that is the science of *just* and *unjust*, of *equity* and *inequity*) can be demonstrated *a priori*: because we ourselves make the principles – that is, the causes of justice (namely laws and covenants) – whereby it is known what *justice* and *equity*, and their opposites, *injustice* and *inequity*, are" (*D.H. X*, 5). However, regardless of how he arrived at his view about the kinds of reasoning that were involved in geometry and politics, it is quite clear that he thought that he could demonstrate *a priori* certain truths in politics just as Euclid had demonstrated *a priori* certain truths in geometry.

Hobbes's Metaphysics

Hobbes was not completely single minded, but it is remarkable how much of what he writes about is related to his moral and political views. All of his considerable work on the interpretation of Scripture obviously is directly related to his political theory, as is his account of religion in general. His work on language is not quite as completely and directly related to his political theory, but some parts of it clearly are, particular when he talks about the most important uses of language. He also uses his sophisticated understanding of language to produce interpretations of the Scriptures that are more congenial to the moral and political theories he put forward. The close relationship of his account of religion to his moral and political views makes his views on topics that are related to various religious views indirectly related to his moral and political views. It is only in this way that Hobbes's views on metaphysics are related to his moral and political views.

Hobbes is an acknowledged proponent of materialism. His materialist view is so complete that he makes no exceptions even for

God. Since only bodies exist, God must be a body (*L.* IV, 21; see also Latin Appendix, III, 5, 6, pp. 540–2). But, because Hobbes says that nothing actually exists except bodies, this does not tell us anything about God except that he exists. Many contemporary philosophers would say that Hobbes is not expressing his view precisely enough, because, in addition to bodies, Hobbes acknowledges that there are properties and relationships. Hobbes would not have taken these objections seriously, for he would claim that talking about properties is talking about the properties of bodies and talking about relationships is talking about the relationship between bodies. He would not deny that there are different kinds of bodies (bodies with different properties) and that they interact with each other in different ways (bodies have different relationships). Although abstract names refer to properties, this is not because the properties can be severed from matter, but only "from the account of matter" (*L.* IV, 16). Hobbes's materialism claims only that talking about properties and relationships are ways of talking about bodies and that neither properties nor relationships can exist independent of bodies.

According to Hobbes, bodies move from place to place over time. To the objection that then there must also be space and time, it is not clear what he would say. It would be compatible with his view to claim that space and time are simply relationships between bodies and do not exist independently of them, but it would be implausible to suggest that Hobbes anticipated Einstein's theory of relativity whereby space and time depend on the existence of bodies. Hobbes did not explicitly put forward any views about space and time, so we have no evidence about what views he took concerning them.

Although Hobbes sincerely held a materialist view, he did not try to deal with the philosophical problems that arise from holding such a view. Materialism was important to Hobbes because it provided a way of denying various religious views such as the view that souls are immaterial and that they exist independently of bodies. Hobbes, following Aristotle, regards talk about souls, not as talk about some nonmaterial entities, but rather as ways of talking about living bodies. Contrary to the claims of some commentators, Hobbes never uses his materialism to support any specific claims about how human beings behave. Like modern-day sophisticated materialists, he does not deny the existence of beliefs, feelings, and sensations, but only claims that they can be viewed as features of a body. He did not know about the functions of the brain, so he does not attempt to redescribe beliefs, feelings, and sensations as mere brain states. However, given his state of knowledge of the body, he does make philosophically similar claims. "So that sense in all cases, is nothing else but original fancy, caused (as I have said) by the pressure, that is, by the motion, of external things upon our eyes, ears, and other organs thereunto ordained" (*L.* I, 4).

Some passages seem to indicate that Hobbes is a reductive materialist, for he says of pleasure: "As in sense that which is really within us is (as I have said before) only motion caused by the action of external objects" (*L.* VI, 9). But this remark is immediately followed by the parenthetical statement, "but in appearance, to the sight, light and colour, to the ear, sound, to the nostril, odour, &c.," where he seems to be holding epiphenomenalism. The passage continues with the same oscillation between reductive materialism and epiphenomenalism, "so when the action of the same object is continued from the eyes, ear, and other organs to the heart, the real effect is nothing but motion or endeavour, which consisteth in appetite or aversion, to or from the object moving. But the appearance or sense of that motion, is that we either call DELIGHT or TROUBLE OF MIND." In reading these passages, it is obvious that Hobbes does not distinguish between reductive materialism and epiphenomenalism; the important point is that only matter in motion has any causal power. For Hobbes, materialism is important because it denies that immaterial entities such as souls have any existence independent of bodies, or that they have any causal powers. In this context the difference between reductive materialism and epiphenomenalism makes no difference to Hobbes because both are incompatible with immaterial souls and other essential ingredients of what he regards as dangerous religious views.

Hobbes's materialism is simply a kind of scientific common sense; it is not worked out in any detail. Materialism is put forward against dualism, the view that the mind or soul can exist independent of any body. Dualism is a view supported by and supportive of dangerous religious views. Materialism is important to Hobbes because it is incompatible with dangerous religious views that support dualism. Hobbes does not distinguish between reductive materialism and epiphenomenalism, because both are incompatible with dualism. Even if he had distinguished between these two views, I do not think he would have viewed the difference as significant. The existence of "phantasms" that have no causal efficacy cannot be used to support any dangerous religious views, especially if these phantasms cannot even exist independent of material bodies.

Although Hobbes often makes claims that sound like reductive materialism, when he talks about the phantasms of sense and pleasure and pain, he sounds more like an epiphenomenalist. Like all other materialist philosophers, he never provides a satisfactory account of phantasms, fancies, or appearances, that is, an account of the fact that we are aware of something related to the motions of sense. He even seems to take conflicting positions in the same paragraph. He says:

> All which qualities called *sensible* are in the object that causeth them but so many several motions of the matter, by which it presseth our organs diversely. Neither in us that are pressed are they anything else but divers motions (for motion produceth nothing but motion). But their appearance to us is fancy, the same waking as dreaming. (L. I, 4)

Here Hobbes seems to be saying that sense is nothing but motion, but then talks about fancy as if it were something other than motion, namely the appearance of motion.

Later in the same paragraph, he says, "sense in all cases, is nothing but original fancy, caused (I have said) by the pressure, that is, by the motion, of external things upon our eyes, ear, and other organs thereunto ordained." Whether fancy is the appearance of motion, caused by motion, or whether appearances of motion are themselves simply motion, is not clear. He sometimes talks about appearances, fancy, or phantasms as caused by motion, but distinct from it, even though he also says they are nothing but motion. When talking about the phantasms of sense, he was quite inventive to say, "phantasms seem to be without, by reaction of the endeavour outwards, so pleasure and pain, by reason of the endeavour of the organ inwards, seem to be within" (*De Corp.* XXV, 12; see also *D.H.* XI, 1). However, Hobbes knows that this explanation of why sensible qualities seem to be located outside the body, while pleasure and pain seem to be inside, is simply speculation. It should be distinguished from what would now be classified as his philosophical views concerning the phantasms of sense and pleasure and pain, namely, that he viewed the phantasms of the senses, e.g., light and color, sound, and odor, to be the same kind of thing as pleasure and pain. All of these were endeavors of the organs of the body, either inward or outward, or else were the appearances of these endeavors.

Endeavor is a crucial concept for Hobbes. It is the bridge between imagination or sense and voluntary motion. He says, "imagination is the first internal beginning of all voluntary motion" (*L.* VI, 1). He then says, "The small beginnings of motion within the body of man, before they appear in walking, speaking, striking, and other visible actions, are commonly called ENDEAVOUR" (*L*. VI, 1). He admits that endeavor "is invisible, [and] the space it is moved in (for the shortness of it) insensible," but he goes on to say, "yet that doth not hinder that such motions are" (*L*. VI, 1). He then defines appetite and aversion in term of endeavor and defines all of the passions as species of appetite or aversion. That endeavor, and hence appetite and aversion, are invisible and insensible, makes it clear we do not know about our passions from observing these invisible motions of our body. Rather, his account of the passions is based upon introspection in the standard sense of "introspection."

He is clear that introspection, together with observation of the behavior of others, is the appropriate way to arrive at an account of human nature. Although he claims that there is a materialist account of mental phenomena, he never denies that mental phenomena are what all ordinary people take them to be. His materialism consists in claiming that mental phenomena, qua mental phenomena, have no causal powers. Only matter in motion has causal powers, but whether phantasms or appearances are simply some particular matter in motion, or are caused by that particular matter in motion, they are not independent of that matter in motion. It is acceptable to talk about the phantasms or appearances as causes even though, literally, they have no causal powers because they are appearances of motions that are causes. Insofar as a distinction is made between reductive materialism and epiphenomenalism, epistemologically Hobbes is clearly an epiphenomenalist rather than a reductive materialist. He ends his Introduction to *Leviathan* by saying of his account of human nature: "[W]hen I have set down my own reading orderly and perspicuously, the pains left another will be only to consider if he also find not the same in himself. For this kind of doctrine admitteth no other demonstration" (*L*. Intro, 4).

Hobbes's Epistemology

From a contemporary philosophical point of view, Hobbes takes epistemology even less seriously than he takes metaphysics. He does not think it necessary to prove that there is an external world, even though he holds that the objects in the external world do not have the properties that we sense them to have (*L*. I, 4). Hobbes's attitude is more like that of a present-day scientist than a present day philosopher. He recognizes that the world is not as we perceive it to be, but does not doubt there is an external world that causes all normal people in the same situations to have the same sensations as each other. As mentioned earlier, his account of why we think that there is an external world is inventive – "phantasms seem to be without, by reaction of the endeavour outwards, so pleasure and pain, by reason of the endeavour of the organ inwards, seem to be within" – but no longer even plausible (*De Corp*. CXXV, 12; see also *L*. I, 4 and *D.H*. XI, 1). Although Hobbes's account of perception is not a serious philosophical view, it allows him to accept the most sophisticated string theory of modern physics without having to change anything in his metaphysical account of the world.

Hobbes is not bothered by the fact that people sometimes have difficulty distinguishing between dreams and sense impressions caused by external objects (*L*. II, 5–8). He is aware that some philosophers claim that dreams lead to skepticism, but he is not troubled by this possibility.

> And hence it cometh to pass, that it is a hard matter, and by many thought to be impossible, to distinguish exactly between sense and dreaming. For my part, when I consider that in dreams I do not often, nor constantly, think of the same persons, places, objects, and actions that I do waking, nor remember so long a train of coherent thoughts dreaming as at other times, and because waking I often observe the absurdity of dreams, but never dream of the absurdities of my waking thoughts, I am well satisfied that being awake I know I dream not, though when I dream, I think myself awake. (*L*. II, 5)

Hobbes here takes a very common-sense view, but the contrast with Descartes is striking, although Hobbes admits that when he dreams he thinks that he is not dreaming. He bases his certainty about his ability to distinguish dreams from waking life by means of content. He does not even consider that, like Little Nemo of the classic comics pages, his dreams might form a coherent whole.

Hobbes is interested in the world as it appears to human beings. Just as he dismisses all religious claims about the nature of God, he is not interested in unknowable claims about what the world is like independent of human beings. Although he holds that everything is simply matter in motion, he makes no effort to describe what matter is or explain why it is that way. He thinks that we project onto the world colors and all of the other properties that children and naive adults regard as being intrinsic properties of that world, but he does not regard this as detracting from the objectivity of colors and other properties of objects. Objectivity rests upon the agreement of human beings in their descriptions of the world. If there are some few human beings who do not experience the world in the way that almost everyone else does, they suffer from some defect such as color-blindness. The objectivity of world, and the truth of statements about it, depends upon the way the world is experienced by most people. It is not affected at all by the presence of defective observers. This agreement of qualified persons also grounds the objectivity of psychology and morality. For Hobbes, as for Wittgenstein, agreement on what we experience, on how we use language, and in our attitudes is sufficient foundation for objectivity. Skepticism, either explicit or implicit, plays no role in Hobbes's account of the world or of human beings' place in that world.

Hobbes admits that the whole world could be annihilated and yet it seem to us that everything has remained the same; however, even this does not lead him to a skeptical view. It is interesting, although I do not know how important, that although Hobbes talks about the world being annihilated without our being aware of it, he does not claim that there may never have been any external world at all.

Hobbes's Common-sense Views

In Hobbes's time the distinction between philosophy and science was not as sharp as it is today. Although some contemporary philosophers now reject Wittgenstein's view that philosophy is independent of science, there still seems to be a clear distinction between the methods of science and those of philosophy. Hobbes thought of himself as a scientist as much as he thought of himself as a philosopher. He engaged in disputes with scientists, e.g., about the existence of a vacuum, as well as with philosophers, e.g., about a nonmaterial soul. He simply puts forward the kind of materialism that would be held by many scientists today, and does not worry about distinguishing reductive materialism from epiphenomenalism. Nor does he take skepticism seriously, even though he is aware of philosophical arguments, e.g., those of Descartes, which make the overcoming of skepticism their primary focus.

Hobbes's common-sense attitude toward the world and our knowledge of it is not limited to metaphysics and epistemology. Contrary to what used to be the standard interpretations of his views of human nature, Hobbes's views about human nature are also fairly similar to what I will call a scientific common-sense view of human nature. He recognizes that adult human beings differ from each other in significant ways. He regards most of those differences to be the result of different education and training, but he is also aware that there are significant innate differences. Some people are naturally smarter and stronger than others, but no one is so much smarter and stronger that on his own he could survive for long in the state of nature. Hobbes knows that children could not survive if they were not taken care of by their parents, and he also knows that families are unlikely to survive unless they band together with other families to form a small society. However, he holds that such a small society, where everyone in the society knows every other person, does not provide the model for the kind of society that can provide lasting protection to its citizens.

Hobbes does not claim that people in this kind of small society need a sovereign to keep them all in awe. Such a society, like a family, can come to agreement by informal methods without instituting a sovereign. But he claims that in a society large enough to provide lasting protection, many people in the society will be strangers to each other. In such a society of strangers there is a need for a strong sovereign. It is important for understanding Hobbes's point about the need for a strong sovereign that it arises only in a commonwealth big enough that most people are strangers to one another. This makes it clear that Hobbes is not putting forward some unusual account of human nature, but rather holds only the common-sense view that in a society composed of people who are strangers to one another, one cannot count on mutual good will to achieve the kind of stability that everyone wants. Even if everyone had the best will in the world, they would still need a sovereign to make laws that dictate to people how they should behave when uniformity of behavior is essential, but there is more than one way to achieve that uniformity, e.g., whether people should drive on the left-hand side of the road or the right-hand side. A large society needs a formal way to achieve uniformity; informal negotiation is not a realistic alternative.

In addition to the need to have some way of achieving uniformity, every large society needs a sovereign with the power to keep everyone in awe, because some people will not do what the law dictates unless there is such a sovereign. Every society big enough to have members who are strangers to one another has a police force to protect the vast majority of law-abiding citizens from the few citizens who are not sufficiently motivated to obey the law. Hobbes does not need, and does not put forward, any view of human beings that differs in any significant way from the view of human beings that is commonly held. He does not claim that most people, let alone all people, are egoistic; indeed, he seems to hold that most people are law-abiding. But he is aware that in any large group there will be some who are prepared to break the law when it serves their interests or the interests of their family or friends. None of this requires him to hold anything other than a common-sense view of human nature.

What may be different about Hobbes's account of human nature is the force he attributes to ideas, especially moral and religious ideas. It is tempting to think that Hobbes places such emphasis on moral and religious beliefs because he is a philosopher, and so exaggerates the power of ideas, However, it is important to remember that Hobbes was living in a time when religious ideas seemed to have extraordinary force. Only by thinking about the intensity of the religious beliefs of those who engage in suicide bombings can one get any idea of the ferocity of the wars between people with different religious views in Hobbes's time. And even now in America, some people are so motivated by their moral or religious views about abortion that they are prepared to kill the doctors who perform abortions. Regardless of why Hobbes thought that ideas had such force, it is clear that he did think that it was false religious and moral ideas that provided the greatest threat to the stability of the commonwealth. They provided such a great threat because ideas could lead to civil war. Individual self-interest, even though it may require a sovereign power to keep it from causing problems for law-abiding citizens, was not a possible cause of civil war. Indeed, in the Preface to *De Cive*, he explicitly cites false moral views as a cause of civil war.

Hobbes is surprisingly similar to Freud. Both are materialists and determinists, but in neither case does their materialism and determinism adversely affect their observations about human nature. On the contrary, although neither properly understands what is required by the scientific method, each is an extremely perceptive observer of human behavior. Their attempts to explain human behavior, although not scientifically sound, result in significant insights into human nature. Although both had great influence on the way we think about human beings, their views about human nature are far more complex than the views that are commonly attributed to them. Partly, this is due to their style of writing. Both of them are convinced of the importance of what they are saying and sometimes simplify what they write in order to be more persuasive. But neither of them either compromises or softens their views in order to gain wider acceptance. Their style of writing shows that it is important to them for their views to gain wide acceptance. Both of them claim that only widespread acceptance of their views can save humankind from much unnecessary suffering. They may be right.

2

Human Nature

Hobbes has served for both philosophers and political scientists as the paradigm case of someone who held an egoistic view of human nature. He supposedly held that all of the motives of all people were motives of self-interest. Until about 50 years ago this was the almost unanimous view. Hobbes does make some statements that, taken out of context, can be seen as supporting this interpretation of his account of human nature, but a careful reading of the texts makes clear that he does not hold this view. Hobbes is not completely consistent, but no one would interpret his last work on human nature, *De Homine*, published in 1658, as putting forward an egoistic view of human nature. This work, which was written in Latin, was not translated into English until 1972 and so had little influence on interpretations of Hobbes's views of human nature. Even after 1972 it is uncommon to see books on Hobbes that cite *De Homine*, perhaps because the views on human nature expressed there do not fit in with the standard interpretations. The only work of Hobbes that can be plausibly taken to support psychological egoism is his earliest work, *The Elements of Law*, which he never intended to be published. The first part of this book is called *Human Nature*, and it is cited quite frequently. This early work contains Hobbes's famous comparison of life to a race, where he says: "But this race we must suppose to have no other goal, nor other garland, but being foremost . . ." (IX, 21).

Psychological Egoism

De Cive and *Leviathan*, Hobbes's major works on moral and political theory, have been interpreted in light of his earlier work, *Human*

Nature, rather than in light of his latter work, *De Homine*. This has had the unfortunate result that Hobbes is taken to argue for an egoistic psychology that makes it impossible to provide an acceptable interpretation of either his moral theory or his political theory. Given this history, any attempt to provide an accurate account of Hobbes's view of human nature must begin by showing that any interpretation of Hobbes as accepting psychological egoism, the view that all of the actions of all people are motivated by self-interest, is mistaken. Hobbes, like every other philosopher, does make some statements that can be taken as supporting an egoistic interpretation of his account of human nature. However, these statements, taken in context, are almost always rhetorical exaggerations designed to support the particular point he is trying to make, e.g., that there are some inalienable rights. Hobbes makes many more statements that directly conflict with psychological egoism, and show him to have a far more plausible view of human nature. Further, given that his most important practical goal is to prevent civil war, it would be absurd for him to hold that the primary, let alone the sole, motivation of citizens is self-interest. No one holds that self-interest is the primary, let alone the sole, motivation for civil war. Hobbes explicitly says that among the most important causes of civil war are false moral views (*D.C.* Pref., 2), a view that is incompatible with an egoistic psychology.

It is difficult to find any clear arguments in favor of psychological egoism, because only those who are trying to refute psychological egoism provide accounts of it. No major philosopher defends psychological egoism. There is a good reason for this; psychological egoism is a silly view. If it were taken literally, it would mean that no parents ever sacrifice their own interests for those of their children, and no children ever sacrifice their own interests for those of their parents. It would also mean that no lovers ever sacrifice their own interests for the benefit of loved ones, or that no citizens ever sacrifice their own interests for their country. It would also mean that no one ever keeps a promise when that requires acting against their own self-interest, or ever refrains from hurting someone even though they could benefit by doing so. Taken literally, it even denies that anyone gives into temptation when they know that giving in to that temptation is contrary to their own best interests, e.g., smoking or binge drinking.

Hobbes is quite aware that people often sacrifice their own interests for their families and friends. He also constantly laments that most people are so moved by their emotions that they act in ways that they know are against their self-interest. Hobbes explicitly makes both of these points when he says that it is the closer relationship between the private and the public interest in a monarchy that explains why he prefers a monarchy to other forms of government. He holds that a person "is more (or no less) careful to procure the private interest of himself, his family, kindred, and friends, and for the most part if the public interest chance to cross the private, he prefers the private; for the passions of men are commonly more potent then their reason" (*L.* XIX, 4). Thus, even when Hobbes contrasts public and private interests, the private interests are not limited to those of self-interest, but include the interests of "family, kindred, and friends."

No one arguing for psychological egoism could sincerely urge people to keep their promises simply because they have promised, but Hobbes says: "More clearly I say thus; that a man is obliged by his contracts, that is, that he ought to perform for his promise sake; but that the law ties him being obliged, that is to say, it compels him to make good his promise for fear of the punishment appointed by the law" (*D.C.* XIV, 2, n.). Hobbes also distinguishes a just person from a guiltless one:

> He who hath done some just thing, is not therefore said to be a *just* person, but *guiltless*; and he that hath done some unjust thing, we do not therefore say he is an *unjust*, but *guilty* man. But when the words are applied to persons, to be *just* signifies as much as to be delighted in just dealing, to study how to do righteousness, or to endeavour in all things to do that which is just; and to be unjust is to neglect righteous dealing, or to think it to be measured not according to my contract, but some present benefit. (*D.C.* III, 5; see also *L.* XV, 10)

In *Leviathan* he continues: "That which gives to human action the relish of justice is a certain nobleness or gallantness of courage (rarely found) by which a man scorns to be beholden for the contentment of his life to fraud or breach of promise" (*L.* XV, 10; see also *D.C.* III, 5). So, although Hobbes holds that not many people have the courage to be just, he does not deny that some people do have that courage. Nonetheless, because psychological egoism is such a popular view among beginning students of philosophy, it is worthwhile to explain the confusions that lead them to accept this view and to mistakenly attribute it to Hobbes.

Materialism and Egoism

Hobbes has been accused of regarding men as machines, but he never compares men to machines. Rather, like Descartes, it is animals, not men, that he regards as machines. In the introduction to *Leviathan*, he asks: "Why may we not say that automata (engines that move themselves by springs and wheels as doth a watch) have an artificial life?" (Intro, 1). When he calls the heart a spring, the nerves strings, and joints wheels, he is talking about an artificial animal, not an artificial man. According to Hobbes, when "*Art* goes yet further, imitating the rational and most excellent work of nature, *man*," it is not a machine that art creates but "that great LEVIATHAN called COMMONWEALTH, or STATE" (ibid.). In this respect Hobbes follows Plato, which is not surprising as at this time he considered Plato to be "the best philosopher of the Greeks" (*L.* XLVI, 11). But Hobbes also owed a great deal to Aristotle, and Leo Strauss has shown that Hobbes's psychology owes more to Aristotle than it does to the new science of mechanics.[1]

As mentioned in the previous chapter, Hobbes wants to show that there is a plausible explanation of all of the features of human psychology, e.g., sense, imagination, dreams, appetites, aversions, and the passions or emotions, in terms of the motions in the body (*L.* VI, 9). He holds that a plausible explanation of voluntary motion is provided by the motions of sense interacting with the vital motion, those motions that are necessary for life, e.g., circulation of the blood. This interaction either helps or hinders the vital motion and so leads to either appetite or aversion. "This endeavour when it is toward something which causes it, is called APPETITE or DESIRE. . . . And when the endeavour is fromward something, it is generally called AVERSION" (*L.* VI, 2; see also *D.H.* XI, 1). Hobbes then goes on to use appetite and aversion to define the more common psychological terms that he will use in his analyses of particular passions.

In *Leviathan* Hobbes gives the following definitions: "*[A]ppetite*, with the opinion of obtaining, is called HOPE. The same, without such opinion, DESPAIR. *Aversion*, with opinion of hurt from the object, FEAR" (*L.* VI, 14–16). But according to his materialist account,

[1]Leo Strauss, *The Political Philosophy of Hobbes: Its Basis and Its Genesis*, trans. Elsa M. Sinclair. Chicago: University of Chicago Press, 1952 (first published in 1936 by The Clarendon Press, Oxford).

appetite and aversion are not available to introspection, for they are species of endeavor (see *L.* VI, 2) and endeavor is invisible and insensible (see *L.* VI, 1). If Hobbes were using his materialist account, he would have to hold that introspection cannot be used to discover what fear or hope or any other passion is. However, he claims that introspection is the method he uses to discover the nature of fear and hope and the other passions. Further, his materialist account provides no explanation of belief or opinion; hence on the materialist account introspection cannot distinguish between hope and despair. Hobbes, like modern-day materialists, is simply trying to show that a materialistic account of the passions is possible; he is not trying to provide such an account.

Although Hobbes claims that an account of human nature can be developed from materialism, he completely ignores his materialist account when providing his analyses of the complex psychological phenomena that he calls the passions. In fact, Hobbes explicitly claims, "whosoever looketh into himself and considereth what he doth, when he does think, opine, reason, hope, fear, &c and upon what grounds, he shall thereby read and know, what are the thoughts and passions of another upon the like occasions" (*L.* Intro, 3). At the end of the introduction to *Leviathan*, he makes an even stronger claim about the foundation for his doctrine about human nature:

> He that is to govern a whole nation must read in himself, not this or that particular man, but mankind, which though it is hard to do, harder than to learn any language or science, yet when I have set down my own reading orderly and perspicuously, the pain left another will be only to consider if he also find not the same in himself. For this kind of doctrine admitteth no other demonstration. (*L.* Intro, 4)

Although it is generally agreed that Hobbes's actual account of human nature is independent of his materialism, because some claim that his egoism stems from his materialism, it is worthwhile to make clear that his account of the passions is completely independent of his materialism. Hobbes regards introspection as the appropriate method for arriving at analyses of the passions, and observations of people's actions is the appropriate method for discovering the objects of the passions, "the similitude of the *passions*, which are the same in all men, *desire, fear, hope,* &c, not the similitude of the *objects* of the passions, which are the things *desired, feared, hoped*, &c; for these the constitution individual and particular education do so vary . . . are legible only to him that searcheth hearts" (ibid.). According to Hobbes, introspection can tell us what is involved in hoping and fearing, but it cannot tell us what things people hope for or fear. It is by looking at the actions of people that we can gain knowledge of the objects of their passions. Hobbes never claims that all human beings hope and fear the same thing, but rather realizes that people differ in the objects of their passions. Although his account of rationality entails that insofar as people are rational they desire to avoid death, pain, and disability, he constantly laments that most people often act irrationally.

Psychological Egoism versus Tautological Egoism

It is not easy to provide an account of psychological egoism for, though often explicitly attacked, it is a view that no philosopher explicitly defends. Psychological egoism is not the view that most actions of most people are motivated by self-interest; given that most of our actions do not even involve anyone else, that view presents no philosophical problems. Psychological egoism's philosophical interest rests upon its claim that every action of every person is motivated by self-interest. It is only when the claim is presented in this all-inclusive manner that it is correct to talk of psychological egoism or of an egoistic view of human nature. Hobbes does hold a pessimistic view of human nature, but his pessimism does not consist in the view that most people act in their own self-interest most of the time, but rather in the view that most people usually act on their emotions rather than on their reason.

If we take psychological egoism to entail that any sincere answer to the question "Why did you do that (voluntary) act?" would be "I thought it was in my best interest," then psychological egoism is so obviously false that it is pointless to discuss it. We often act in ways that we know to be contrary to our best interest. Giving in to temptation is a common phenomenon, e.g., going to a movie when we know we ought to be studying, taking a second helping when we know we ought to watch our weight. Hobbes explicitly says, "most men would rather lose their lives . . . than suffer slander" (*D.C.* III, 12; see also *L.* XV, 20), clearly indicating that he holds that acting contrary to one's self-interest, and even to one's self-preservation, is a common occurrence. Hobbes constantly laments that men's passions often lead them to act contrary to their best interests

(see *D.C.* III, 27, 32). Oddly, Bishop Butler is praised for his refuta-
tion of Hobbes by advancing these very same points as criticisms
of Hobbes.[2] Hobbes certainly cannot be held to be a psychological
egoist if this means that he holds that men always act from motives
of self-interest.

If psychological egoism is to be at all plausible, it must include
acting on individual passions – ambition, lust, etc. – as well as
acting out of self-interest. As striking as this enlargement seems, it
does not affect the main point of psychological egoism, which is to
deny the existence of certain kinds of motives. Although psychological egoism is phrased positively, i.e., holding that people act
only from motives of self-interest, its point is most clearly expressed
negatively, that no one ever acts in order to benefit others, or because
they believe a certain course of action to be morally right. Aware-
ness of this makes it clear why psychological egoism is relatively
immune to the kinds of criticisms put forward above. To point
out that to act because of hunger, thirst, or ambition is not to act
on a motive of self-interest persuades no one to give up believing
in psychological egoism. Failing to distinguish acting on one's
emotions from acting to further one's self-interest may add further
confusions to an already confused position, but making this distinction does not free one from the temptation of psychological egoism.
No one who accepts psychological egoism gives it up after recognizing the distinction between hunger and the motive of self-
interest. Students who are persuaded by psychological egoism do
not deny that people act on their passions; they deny that anyone
acts from a motive of genuine benevolence, or because of the belief
that the action is morally right.

Recognizing the point of psychological egoism leads to the formulation at which those students defending psychological egoism
usually end up: *people always act in order to satisfy their own desires.*
Defenders of psychological egoism like this formulation because it
seems to allow them to provide forceful replies to serious criticisms.
They do not realize that the supposed force of these replies depends
on not realizing the ambiguity of the phrase "their own desires"
and switching from one interpretation of this phrase to another. To
support psychological egoism, the phrase "their own desires" must
be interpreted as being opposed to both "their moral sense" and
"the desires of someone else." Only when "their own desires" is
interpreted in this way is the result a psychological egoism that

---

[2] In *Five Sermons*. New York, 1950, p. 24, n. 5.

denies that there are any benevolent actions or that there are any actions done because the person believes it is the morally right thing to do. Only when interpreted in this way is psychological egoism a view about human nature that undermines the very possibility of morality.

However, "their own desires" can also be interpreted so that it is not opposed to either "their moral sense" or "the desires of someone else." On this interpretation people can have desires to satisfy the desires of others, or desires to do what they believe is morally right. This interpretation of "their own desires" does not result in psychological egoism or any other view of human nature. Rather it is simply playing around with words to state a view that sounds like psychological egoism, but says nothing at all about human nature. I call this view "tautological egoism," i.e., a view that is true by definition, viz., a voluntary action is one that is caused by desire. It has no empirical consequences and results in no predictions about how people will behave when confronted with a choice between their own interests and helping others or doing what is morally right. The claim that tautological egoism says something about human nature is similar to the claim that "Everyone casts his own shadow" says something about optics, or physics, or any other empirical science. The claim that no one can cast anyone else's shadow is a tautology that depends solely on the way that we use the phrase "casting a shadow." We only count someone as casting a shadow when the shadow that is cast is the shadow of the person by whom it is cast.

Tautological egoism is a direct consequence of Hobbes's definitions of "voluntary act" and "will": "For a *voluntary act* is that, which proceedeth from the *will*, and no other" (*L.* VI, 53); "*Will* therefore *is the last appetite in deliberating*" (ibid.). Thus for Hobbes it is simply a matter of definition that all voluntary acts of all people are based on their own desires. However, this in no way limits what the objects of those desires are. The following definition of benevolence shows that Hobbes realizes that tautological egoism does not deny that people can act on the desires of others: "Desire of good to another. BENEVOLENCE" (*L.* VI, 22). His definition of indignation shows that he holds that people can be motivated by their moral sense: "*Anger* for great hurt done to another, when we conceive the same to be done by injury, INDIGNATION" (*L.* VI, 21). These definitions show that Hobbes holds that people sometimes desire to benefit others and that people's moral sense sometimes leads them to act. These definitions are not taken out of context in

the way that Hobbes's statements that seem to support psychological egoism are. However, tautological egoism, a view which
Hobbes clearly holds, does sound like psychological egoism, and
so is easily confused with it. Tautological egoism, however, although
it says that people always act to satisfy their own desires, does not
put any limit on the objects of people's desires. As shown by the
definitions of benevolence and indignation, it is perfectly compatible with acting on the desires of another and with acting on one's
moral sense.

Hobbes's tautological egoism is made more complex and confusing by his definition of "good." According to Hobbes, "whatsoever
is the object of any man's appetite or desire, that it is which he for
his part calleth good" (*L.* VI, 7). Thus, when, in the course of arguing
that some rights are inalienable, Hobbes says, "of the voluntary acts
of every man, the object is some good to himself" (*L.* XIV, 8), he is
not ruling out either benevolent actions or actions done because of
one's moral sense. This complex structure has not only confused
Hobbes's commentators, but also seems to have sometimes confused Hobbes himself. So the traditional view of Hobbes as arguing
for psychological egoism has not been manufactured out of whole
cloth. Nonetheless, no one reading Hobbes's published works carefully and without preconceptions would ever conclude that he
argues for psychological egoism. Indeed, it is hard to imagine any
serious philosopher arguing for psychological egoism, or to take
seriously any philosopher who does argue for psychological egoism.

Human Beings as Natural Animals versus
Human Beings as Citizens

Another reason why Hobbes is accused of arguing for psychological egoism is that one of his most important distinctions – that
between human beings as natural animals and human beings as
citizens or civilized beings – has been almost completely neglected.
Human beings as civilized beings are the human beings that actually exist, born into a family and brought up by their parents in a
functioning society. Human beings as natural beings are an abstraction; they are not the kind of beings that ever existed. They are best
described in this passage: "Let us return again to the state of nature,
and consider men as if but even now sprung out of the earth, and
suddenly (like mushrooms) come to full maturity, without all kinds
of engagement to each other" (*D.C.* VIII, 1; see also (*D.C.* I, 10).

Hobbes never thought that there were human beings like this, although he did think that there must have been a time when human beings lived in small families or groups of families that were too small to provide protection from attacks by others. Hobbes realized that although members of these small groups or families were often not concerned with anyone outside of their group or family, they were concerned with members of their group or family. So, even in any actual state close to a state of nature, Hobbes did not put forward psychological egoism as an account of human nature.

The importance of the distinction between human beings as natural animals and human beings as civilized beings can be seen from Hobbes's remark, "To speak impartially, both sayings are very true; *that man to man is a kind of God; and that man to man is an arrant wolf.* The first is true, if we compare citizens among themselves; and the second, if we compare cities" (*D.C.* Ded., p. 89). Hobbes is claiming that civilized human beings do not act toward each other as cities act toward each other. He does hold that human beings as natural animals do act to those outside of their group like cities act toward each other. Though obviously an abstraction, human beings as natural animals, not modified in any way by education or discipline, are exemplified by young children. "Unless you give children all they ask for, they are peevish, and cry, aye and strike their parents sometimes, and all this they have from nature" (*D.C.* Pref., 3, p. 100). Note that Hobbes is not claiming that psychological egoism is true of children; rather he is claiming that children naturally act on their emotions or passions before they have been brought up to act on their reason. It may be natural for human beings to behave like arrant wolves, but citizens, i.e., civilized human beings, will not behave in this way if they have been properly trained and brought up.

The importance of education and training is made most explicitly when Hobbes explains why he denies the common opinion "that man is a creature born fit for society" (*D.C.* I, 2). In his explanation, which is contained in a footnote to this denial, he admits that his claim seems false since all human beings do live in society. Hobbes does not deny "that men (even nature compelling) desire to come together" (*D.C.* I, 2, n), but he points out that "civil societies are not mere meetings, but bonds, to the making whereof faith and compacts are necessary" and children are not yet capable of entering into compacts. "Manifest therefore it is, that all men, because they are born in infancy, are born unapt for society." Hobbes is not simply stating the truism that human beings are not born apt for society because they are born infants and infants are incapable of meeting the requirements necessary for society. The point of the passage is that "Many also (perhaps most men) either through defect of mind, or want of education, remain unfit during the whole course of their lives; yet have they, infants as well as those of riper years, a human nature; wherefore man is made fit for society not by nature, but by education" (ibid.).

Hobbes is claiming that for people who do not suffer from a defect of mind it is not nature, but education that makes them fit for society. Education can change people so that they do not act on their passions when these passions conflict with reason, especially the laws of nature. Hobbes calls the emotions "perturbations because they frequently obstruct right reasoning. They obstruct right reasoning in this, that they militate against the real good and in favour of the apparent and most immediate good, which frequently turns out to be evil when everything associated with it hath been considered" (*D.H.* XII, 1). Hobbes recognizes the significant power of the passions, so he knows that it is not a simple matter for education to shape children into good citizens. But he seems to have the optimistic view that proper training and education would be sufficient to make most people into good citizens.

However, Hobbes thinks that most people have not received proper training and education; on the contrary, he thinks that many have received the wrong kind of education. "Therefore, among all peoples' religion and doctrine, which everyone hath been taught from their early years, so shackle them forever that they hate and revile dissenters" (*D.H.* XIII, 3). This passage makes clear that Hobbes knows that the wrong kind of education and training, especially bad moral or religious training, can have terrible consequences. He laments, "How many throats hath this false position cut, that a prince for some causes may by certain men be disposed! And what bloodshed hath not this erroneous doctrine caused, that kings are not superior to, but administrators for the multitude!" (*D.C.* Pref., 2, pp. 96–7). These passages make it clear that Hobbes thinks that civil wars arise from people acting on their incorrect moral views, not from motives of self-interest. If Hobbes believes in psychological egoism, he should hold that human nature is responsible for the faults of civil society, but what he actually holds is that when societies fail, "the fault is not in men as they are the *matter*, but as they are the *makers* and orderers of them" (*L.* XXIX, 1).

Hobbes's lack of concern about the character of human beings as natural beings is explained by the importance that he gives to education: "Unless thereafter we will say that men are naturally evil, because they receive not their education and use of reason from nature, we must needs acknowledge that men may derive desire, fear, anger, and other passions from nature, and yet not impute the evil effects of those unto nature" (*D.C.* Pref., 3, p. 101). Children are free from guilt, but adults are not "when nature ought to be better governed through good education and experience" (*D.C.* Pref., 3, p. 100).

In *Leviathan* the unaptness of man for society is discussed again:

> And to consider the contrariety of men's opinions, and manners, in general, it is, they say, impossible to entertain a constant civil amity with all those, with whom the business of the world constrains us to converse: which business consisteth almost in nothing else but a perpetual contention of honour, riches, and authority. (*L.* Rev. and Con., 3)

Hobbes's answer to the claim that the nature of man is incompatible with civil amity is just what we should now expect: "To which I answer, that these are indeed great difficulties, but not impossibilities: for by education, and discipline, they may be, and are sometimes reconciled" (*L.* Rev and Con., 4). Hobbes's continues his reply to those who hold that his account of human nature prevents him from having a moral theory: "Nor is there any repugnancy between fearing the laws, and not fearing a public enemy; nor between abstaining from injury, and pardoning it in others. There is therefore no such inconsistence of human nature, with civil duties, as some think" (ibid.).

To those who regard Hobbes as holding psychological egoism, it is, of course, impossible to think of him as claiming that the opinion of the rightness or wrongness of an action has any effect upon the actions of people (*D.C.* Ded., p. 91). But in the Preface to the Reader, in *De Cive*, Hobbes explicitly laments the lack of a true moral philosophy and says that mistaken doctrines of what is right and wrong have been responsible for a great amount of bloodshed (*D.C.* Pref., 2, pp. 96–7). One of the reasons he offers for the necessity of a coercive power is that men may be misled in their opinion of good and evil, right and wrong (ibid.; see also *L.* XXX, 3). He even claims that it was in order to correct these mistakes that he wrote *De Cive* before writing the two books of the trilogy, *De Corpore* and *De*

Homine, that should have come first (*D.C.* Pref., 7, p. 103). Further, he insists that the sovereign teach citizens why it is their duty to obey him, i.e., that they have covenanted, in order to keep their obedience, and holds that such teaching is of more importance than "terror of legal punishment" (*L.* XXX, 4).

Hobbes believed that human nature was malleable, that people could be trained, educated, and disciplined into good citizens. Granted, this conditioning must take into account the strong passions that most human beings have, but still, through such training human beings could become quite different from what they originally were. Hobbes points out that children "have no other rule of good and evil manners, but the correction they receive from their parents and masters . . . [and] children are constant to their rule" (*L.* XI, 21). And in *De Homine* he gives a detailed analysis of how character is formed: "Dispositions, that is, men's inclinations toward certain things, arise from a six-fold source: namely from the constitution of the body, from experience, from habit, from the goods of fortune, from the opinion one hath of oneself, and from authorities. When these things change, then dispositions change also" (*D.H.* XIII, 1).

From this list of character-forming forces, Hobbes gives special importance to the influence of authorities:

> From authorities. Moreover, I call authorities anyone in any subject whose precept or example is followed, because one hath been led thereto by belief in their wisdom. From them, if good, the dispositions of youths are well formed, and deformed, if deformed; they are teachers, or fathers, or anyone whomsoever that youths hear commonly praised for wisdom; for they revere those who are praised, and they imitate those whom they think worthy. Whence it may be understood, first, not only, how much fathers, teachers, and tutors of youths must imbue the minds of youths with precepts which are good and true, but also how much they must bear themselves justly and in a righteous manner in their presence, for the dispositions of youths are not less, but much more disposed to bad habits by example, than they are to good habits by precept. (*D.H.* XIII, 7)

Here Hobbes shows a clear understanding of the way in which character is formed, noting the importance of good precepts, but aware of the far greater importance of good examples.

Hobbes's view of human nature may sound a little too pessimistic, but given the incredible amount of cruelty and violence throughout the history of humankind, he may actually have been more

optimistic than is warranted. For example, the following is his definition of cruelty: "*Contempt,* or little sense of the calamity of others
is that which men call CRUELTY, proceeding from security of their
own fortune" (*L.* VI, 47). This sounds more like a definition of "cal-
lousness" than a definition of "cruelty." Why Hobbes offers this as
a definition of "cruelty" is explained by the next sentence: "For, that
any man should take pleasure in other men's great harms without
other end of his own I do not conceive it possible" (ibid.). Taking
pleasure in the harm suffered by others, or what we would call
malevolence or sadism, is simply inconceivable to Hobbes. Contrary to the claims of those who accuse Hobbes of holding a too
pessimistic account of human nature, he may hold too optimistic
an account. He explicitly denies that there is such a passion as
malevolence or desire to harm another while explicitly acknowledging benevolence as "Desire of good to another" (*L.* VI, 22). He
admits that various passions may lead one person to harm another,
but he always thinks that one must provide an explanation for why
one person harms another, or goes to events, e.g., hangings, where
harm is being done to others. It is somewhat ironic that it is in his
attempts to explain away malevolence that Hobbes makes many of
those statements that seem most egoistic.

He seems to think that if human nature were understood it would
be possible to design a state that would enable people to live in
perpetual peace:

> For were the nature of human actions as distinctly known as the
> nature of *quantity* in geometrical figures, the strength of avarice and
> ambition, which is sustained by the erroneous opinions of the vulgar
> as touching the nature of right and wrong, would presently faint and
> languish; and mankind would enjoy such an immortal peace, that
> unless it were for habitation, on supposition that the earth should
> grow too narrow for its inhabitants, there would hardly be left any
> pretence for war. (*D.C.* Ded., p. 91)

His claim that there should be no built-in restraints on the power
of the sovereign and his preference for a monarchical form of sovereignty are based as much on an unjustified optimism about the
nature of persons who might be sovereigns as on his pessimistic
account of the nature of the citizens.

Hobbes recognizes that "the estate of man can never be without
some incommodity or other" (*L.* XXVIII, 18). But he thinks "that
the greatest that in any form of government can possibly happen

to the people in general is scarce sensible, in respect of the miseries and horrible calamities that accompany a civil war" (ibid.). Looking at the problems created by the overthrow of Saddam Hussein in Iraq suggests that Hobbes may be right. However, looking at the miseries caused by ideological sovereigns such as Hitler and Pol Pot suggests that Hobbes did not appreciate the truth of Lord Acton's saying, "Power corrupts; absolute power, absolutely." Although Hobbes continually laments that most people act on their passions rather than their reason, and that false moral views often lead people astray, he does not seem to appreciate that sovereigns have these same faults. He is so concerned to avoid civil war, which was the primary threat to peace in his time, that he does not seem to give sufficient consideration to the harms that can come from having no limits on the authority and power of the sovereign.

Self-Preservation

In addition to the factors already discussed, the traditional view of Hobbes as a psychological egoist has been supported by the fact that reason dictates self-preservation plays such a central role in Hobbes's moral and political theory. However, Hobbes's claim that it is rationally required to avoid an avoidable death cannot be used to support the view that he argues for psychological egoism. That he holds that avoiding death is rationally required does not even support the view that he holds that all people act to avoid death, unless he also holds that all people always act rationally, which he clearly does not. That self-preservation is rationally required may seem to support rational egoism, i.e., the view that for an action to be rational it cannot be contrary to a person's self-interest. However, "it is never rational to act against one's own self-preservation" does not mean the same as "it is never rational to act against one's own self-interest." In *Tom Jones*, Fielding makes the following remark about Tom Jones's servant, Partridge: "For Partridge, though he had many imperfections, wanted not fidelity; and though fear would not suffer him to be hanged for his master, yet the world, I believe, could not have bribed him to desert his cause." Hobbes would consider Partridge to be rational, yet it is quite clear that Partridge acts on motives other than his own self-interest. That Hobbes argues that reason prohibits acting against one's self-preservation may be taken to show that he thought rational persons to be similar to Partridge, but this is far different from taking it to show that he held either psychological or rational egoism.

Both the laws of nature and the right of nature are grounded in the rational seeking of self-preservation (*D.C.* I, 7; II, 1; see also *L.* XIV, 4). But we have seen that Hobbes does not hold that people never act against their own self-preservation. The claim that Hobbes holds that everyone acts to avoid death is another result of failing to make the distinction between natural and civilized human beings. Even when claiming that the right to resist is an inalienable right, he says: "For man by nature chooseth the lesser evil, which is danger of death in resisting, rather than the greater, which is certain and present death in not resisting" (*L.* XIV, 29). The phrase "by nature" is important; ignoring it results in Hobbes holding that no person can ever act contrary to his own preservation, and we have seen that he explicitly says that some people do act contrary to their own preservation.

The distinction between what human beings naturally avoid and what actual human beings (those who have been subject to education and training, good or bad) avoid is also crucial in interpreting other passages, for example: "For every man is desirous of what is good for him, and shuns what is evil, but chiefly the chiefest of natural evils, which is death; and this he doth, by a certain impulsion of nature, no less than that whereby a stone moves downward" (*D.C.* I, 7). Only by distinguishing between natural evils, that is, evils to natural persons, and evils to civilized persons, can this statement of Hobbes be reconciled with some others. Examples of such statements are: "most men would rather lose their lives (that I say not, their peace) than suffer slander" (*D.C.* III, 12; see also *L.* XV, 20) and "a son will rather die, than live infamous, and hated of all the world" (*D.C.* VI, 13). An unavoidable contradiction arises if what is evil to a natural being is not distinguished from what is evil to a civilized being. It is, of course, not a conclusive argument against an interpretation that it results in inconsistencies and contradictions, but when a plausible interpretation avoids such harsh results, it is certainly to be preferred.

Passions

In the first sentence of the first chapter of *De Cive*, Hobbes says: "The faculties of human nature may be reduced unto four kinds: bodily strength, experience, reason, passion" (*D.C.* I, 1). He continues by saying that based on these faculties, he "will declare, in the first place, what manner of inclinations men who are endued with these faculties bear toward each other, and whether, and by what faculty they are born apt for society, and to preserve themselves against mutual violence" (ibid.). I take this to mean that Hobbes will ground his moral and political theory on these four kinds of characteristics that human beings have. He does not claim, indeed he denies, that all people have the same bodily strength, experience, reason, and passion. Rather, he claims that there is a limited range in each of these characteristics, and that this limited range can supports his moral and political theory. For example, Hobbes knows that some people are smarter and stronger than other people, but he also knows that in the state of nature, "there can be no security to any man, (how strong or wise soever he be) of living out the time which nature ordinarily alloweth men to live" (*L*. XIV, 4).

That the range of bodily strength is so limited that the weakest can kill the strongest (at least with confederates) is all that Hobbes needs to show that people with the rational desire to avoid death will try to form a society that will help preserve them against mutual violence. Hobbes does not need to claim, nor does he claim, that people are equal in bodily strength or in wisdom. Indeed, he is very cautious in making claims about characteristics that apply to all people. Rather, he is aware that people behave in quite different ways because they differ from each other, not only in their natural characteristics, but also in the way that they have been brought us. This is the point of the quote that was cited earlier: "Dispositions, that is, men's inclinations toward certain things, arise from a six-fold source: namely from the constitution of the body, from experience, from habit, from the goods of fortune, from the opinion one hath of oneself, and from authorities. When these things change, dispositions change also" (*D.H*. XIII, 1). Hobbes does not hold psychological egoism because he does not hold any view that claims that all people have the same objects of desire.

All that Hobbes needs for his political theory about the objects of desire is that the overwhelming majority of people are rational much of the time. He must also hold that people are close enough in strength and wisdom that no one is exempt from the dangers of living in the state of nature, that is, without some common power to keep them all in awe. He need not and does not claim that all people are equal in their natural or acquired skills and talents, only that they must be acknowledged as equals in the forming of a civil society. "If nature therefore have made men equal, that equality is to be acknowledged; or if nature have made men unequal, yet because men that think themselves equal will not enter into conditions of peace but upon equal terms, such equality must be admitted" (*L. XV*, 21). Because even the strongest and most wise need civil society, they must acknowledge others as equals. Hobbes uses this reasoning in arguing that pride is prohibited by a law of nature and hence is a moral vice.

Hobbes also knows that some people have more experience than others, but he holds that all of them have enough experience to know, "during the time men live without a common power to keep them all in awe, they are in a condition which is called war, and such a war as is of every man against every man" (*L. XIII*, 8). This is another example where Hobbes's rhetorical exaggerations, although they make for good reading, cannot be taken literally. He is not claiming that members of a family living together are all at constant war with each other; he acknowledges the natural affection of parents and children for each other. He is claiming only that, in the state of nature, no one will trust strangers, or even people that they do not know well. He claims that in such a state every person should know that this state of war would make "the life of man, solitary, poor, nasty, brutish, and short" (*L. XIII*, 9). This is one of the great rhetorical flourishes that Hobbes did not expect anyone to take so literally.

Hobbes certainly meant that the state of nature would be miserable, but he did not expect readers would take each word, e.g., "solitary," literally. This is shown by how he supports his claim about how miserable life in the state of nature would be. He points out that even in a civil state, a person, "when taking a journey, he arms himself, and seeks to go well accompanied; when going to sleep, he locks his doors; when even in his house, he locks his chests" (*L. XIII*, 10). He is not claiming that everyone guards himself against members of his family, only that they are all appropriately fearful of strangers. If everyone from his own experience knows that life, even in a civil state, is dangerous, then everyone has enough experience to know that to avoid an unacceptable level of mutual violence they need a common power to keep them all in awe.

Hobbes need not and does not claim that everyone has the same passions, that is, passions for the same kinds of objects. But he does claim that the passions that might lead to war are common enough that, in the absence of a common power, they would lead to war.

He says: "So that in the nature of man, we find three principle causes of quarrel; first, competition, secondly, diffidence, thirdly, glory." The next sentence is simply supposed to explicate the preceding one: "The first maketh men invade for gain; the second, for safety; and the third, for reputation" (*L.* XIII, 6, 7). This explication makes clear that Hobbes is not using "diffidence" in the way that he defines it in Chapter VI (20) of *Leviathan* as, "Constant *despair*, DIFFIDENCE of ourselves." (In general, as the quoted sentences show, the one-line definitions of the passions that Hobbes presents in Chapter VI of *Leviathan* should not be taken literally.) Hobbes is not claiming that all people act on all three of these passions; rather, he claims that even though only a few invade for gain or reputation, all others must act for safety. He is quite clear that different people act on different passions. He says: "For though the wicked may be fewer than the righteous, yet because we cannot distinguish them, there is a necessity of suspecting, heeding, anticipating, subjugating, self-defending, ever incident to the most honest and fairest conditioned" (*D.C.* Pref., 3).

Hobbes thinks that he has shown that, given the limited range of bodily strength, experience, and passion, all rational persons will desire peace. Insofar as they are rational and appreciate the miseries of the state of nature, they will agree to create a sovereign power to keep them all in awe. Having made clear the characteristics of bodily strength, experience, and passion that Hobbes thinks lead to war, it must be pointed out that he thinks that some passions lead to peace. He says: "The passions that lead to peace are fear of death, desire of such things as are necessary to commodious living, and a hope by their industry to obtain them" (*L.* XIII, 14). However, these passions lead to peace only when one realizes that the state of war makes death almost inevitable, makes it impossible to obtain those things as are necessary to commodious living, and so destroys the "hope by their industry to obtain them." After listing the passions that lead to peace, Hobbes says: "And reason suggesteth convenient articles of peace, upon which men may be drawn to agreement" (ibid.).

Reason

It is now necessary to make clear what Hobbes means by "reason." This is difficult because he seems to use the word in several different senses. In one sense, reason is simply the faculty of reasoning:

"For REASON, in this sense is nothing but *reckoning* . . . of the consequences of general names agreed upon for the marking and signifying of our thoughts" (*L. V*, 2). However, he is clear that "REASON, in this sense . . . is not, as sense and memory, born with us, nor gotten by experience only, as prudence is, but attained by industry, first in apt imposing of names . . . and that is it men call SCIENCE" (*L. V*, 17). Reason in this sense is not one of the faculties of human nature that Hobbes had mentioned earlier. So this is not the natural reason that dictates the laws of nature.

Hobbes sometimes distinguishes reason from experience: "As much experience is *prudence,* so is much science, *sapience*" (*L. V*, 21). But it is misleading to say that prudence is simply experience, and generally Hobbes does not use "prudence" in this way. Prudence involves inductive reasoning, which is reasoning from experience, rather than deductive reasoning, which is reasoning with words. Although he says that prudence plus sapience is better than prudence alone, he also says: "But yet they that have no *science* are in better and nobler condition with their natural prudence then men that by mis-reasoning, or by trusting them that reason wrong, fall upon false and absurd general rules" (*L. V*, 19). He continues to extol science, but only when it is used to enhance our natural prudence, not when it replaces natural prudence. Further, it is not even possible to reason using words if one does not have the experience to determine that one is using words aptly. Contrasting reason with prudence provides one sense in which Hobbes uses the term "reason," but it is not the most important sense of the term.

The most important sense of the term "reason" is that in which it is contrasted with emotion:

> Emotions or *perturbations* of the mind are species of appetite and aversion, their differences having been taken from the diversity and circumstances of the object that we desire or shun. They are called *perturbations* because they frequently obstruct right reasoning. They obstruct right reasoning in this, that they militate against the real good, and in favor of the apparent and most immediate good, which turns out frequently to be evil when everything associated with it hath been considered. (*D.H.* XII, 1)

Hobbes goes on to say it is the job of reason to determine the real long-term good, but that "appetite seizeth upon a present good without foreseeing the greater evils that necessarily attach to it" (ibid.). In this sense of reason, reason is not the

artificial reasoning with words that is contrasted with experience
or prudence: it is natural. It is this sense of reason that he is talking
about when he says that one of the two maxims of human nature
is the "rational, which teaches every man to fly a contra-natural
dissolution, as the greatest mischief that can arrive to nature" (*D.C.*
Ded., p. 93).

Hobbes is clear and consistent that the primary goal of reason is
the avoidance of avoidable death. It is only by understanding
"reason" in this sense that we can understand why Hobbes intro-
duces the right of nature, by saying that it is not "against the dictates of true reason, for a man to use all his endeavours to preserve
and defend his body, and the members thereof from death and
sorrows" (*D.C.* I, 7). He explicitly derives both the laws of nature
and the right of nature from "a precept, or general rule, of reason
that every man ought to endeavour peace, as far as he has hopes of
obtaining it, and when he cannot obtain it, that he may seek and
use all helps and advantages of war" (*L.* XIV, 4). When Hobbes calls
the laws of nature the dictates of reason, it is clear this is the sense
of "reason" that he is using.

The primary goal of reason is self-preservation, but reason also
has the goal of avoiding pain and disability. In addition to these
negative goals, reason has the positive goal of obtaining felicity.
However unlike the negative goals, this positive goal has no specific
content, for he defines felicity as "*Continual success* in obtaining
those things which a man from time to time desireth, that is to say,
continual prospering" (*L.* VI, 58). Hobbes also regards it as rational
to seek power, but this desire also has no specific content; it does
not mean power over others, but only the ability to satisfy one's
desires. "The power of a man (to take it universally) is his present
means to obtain some future apparent good" (*L.* X, 1). It should be
clear from the above that the only specific goals of reason are negative ones, to avoid death, pain, and disability. The seemingly positive goals of felicity and power are not specific goals at all, but
rather the nonspecific long-term goals of satisfying the desires one
has and having the ability to satisfy one's future desires. However,
for Hobbes, a rational person does not have desires that are incompatible with the specific negative goals of reason, avoiding death,
pain, and disability. Further, all of these goals, the positive desires
for felicity and power as well as the negative goals of avoiding
death, pain, and disability, are long-term goals and demand consideration of the long-term consequences of one's actions. I agree
with Hobbes that someone who acts on his emotions without

considering their negative effect on achieving these long-term goals is acting irrationally.

Some have taken Hobbes's account of felicity as identical to the currently popular view of rationality as involving maximizing the satisfaction of all of one's desires. However, it is quite clear that the desires that Hobbes envisions one satisfying when obtaining felicity rule out the crazy desires that are allowed by the current maximizing views. The negative goals of reason put limits on the contents of the desires to be satisfied when obtaining felicity. Hobbes, quite rightly, would not consider a person to be continually prospering if he has continual success in satisfying his desires to cut off his fingers one at a time in a food processor. Felicity also differs from the maximizing view in that it does not require maximizing the satisfaction of one's desires. For Hobbes, felicity is simply being able to get what you want when you want it, and what you want are the things people normally want: good company, good food, a good job, etc. Unlike John Rawls's concept of rationality, Hobbes's concept of felicity does not require that all of one's desires form a coherent system. Hobbes does not require anyone having a life plan sufficiently well thought out that it makes sense to talk of maximizing the satisfaction of one's desires in anything more than a loose and general way.

It is clear from the previous paragraph that Hobbes's account of rationality is significantly different from the currently most popular account of rationality, which claims that the sole goal of reason is maximizing the satisfaction of one's desires, with no limitations on the content of one's desires. Hobbes's account of rationality rules out certain desires as irrational, viz., desires for death, pain, or disability. The maximizing view of rationality does not rule out any desire as intrinsically irrational; a desire becomes irrational only when its satisfaction conflicts with maximizing the satisfaction of all of one's desires. This view is plausible only because of the neglect of those persons with mentally disorders who have, as their dominant desires, desires for death, pain, or disability. Hobbes is one of the few philosophers who discusses mental disorders and takes them into account when formulating his account of rationality.

The maximizing view of rationality does explain how acting on one's emotions may lead to irrational action by satisfying one desire at the expense of maximizing the satisfaction of more of one's other desires. But Hobbes's view of rationality not only explains this; it also explains how emotions may lead to irrational action by jeopardizing the goals of reason. Hobbes correctly regards emotions as reactions to present stimuli, either one's actual environment or one's present thoughts. He says: "emotions consist in various motions of the blood and animal spirits as they variously expand and contract; the causes of these motions are phantasms concerning good and evil excited in the mind by objects" (*D.H.* XII, 1). Acting on one's emotions sometimes results in one acting irrationally, i.e., acting in a way that conflicts with attaining the goals of reason because emotion "seizeth upon a present good without foreseeing the greater evils that necessarily attach to it" (ibid.). They may conflict in a fundamental way by conflicting with one's preservation, or with the avoidance of pain and disability, or they may conflict by conflicting with one's chances of obtaining felicity or coming as close to it as one might otherwise come.

In this conflict between reason and the emotions or passions, Hobbes's view is diametrically opposed to that of Hume. Hume, as is well known, holds that reason is, and ought to be, the slave of the passions. Hobbes, on the contrary, holds that the passions ought to be subservient to reason. He explicitly says: "for the natural state hath the same proportion to the civil (I mean liberty to subjection), which passion hath to reason, or a beast to man" (*D.C.* VII, 18). However, although Hobbes holds that passion ought to be subservient to reason, he is aware that the passions are generally so strong that they often lead persons to seek the apparent and most immediate good even when doing so is contrary to reason. "Men cannot put off this same irrational appetite, whereby they greedily prefer the present good (to which, by strict consequence, many unforeseen evils do adhere) before the future" (*D.C.* III, 32). But Hobbes is also aware that some passions are rational, i.e., those passions that support the goals of reason. These are, as mentioned before, "[t]he passions that incline men to peace are fear of death, desire of such things as are necessary to commodious living, and a hope by their industry to obtain them" (*L.* XIII, 14).

Throughout all of his works Hobbes is completely consistent on the point that the laws of nature are dictates of reason, and that as such they are concerned with self-preservation. In *Leviathan* he provides the following definition: "A law of nature, (*lex naturalis*) is a precept or general rule, found out by reason, by which a man is forbidden to do that, which is destructive of his life, or taketh away the means of preserving the same; and to omit that, by which he thinketh it may be best preserved" (*L.* XIV, 3). In *De Cive*, after rejecting alternative definitions of the law of nature, he concludes that "true reason is a certain law; which, since it is no less a part of human nature than any other faculty or affection of the mind, is also termed natural." He then says "Therefore the *law of nature*, that I may define it, is the dictate of right reason conversant about those things which are either to be done or omitted for the constant preservation of life and members, as much as in us lies" (*D.C.* II, 1).

Although Hobbes is primarily interested in those laws of nature that "appertain to the preservation of ourselves against those dangers which arise from discord" (*D.C.* III, 32), he recognizes that "there are other precepts of rational nature" (ibid.). Temperance "is a precept of reason, because intemperance tends to sickness and death. And so fortitude too, that is, that same faculty of resisting stoutly in present dangers, and which are more hardly declined than overcome; because it is a means tending to the preservation of him that resists" (ibid.) Hobbes is so clear and consistent in holding that reason has self-preservation as its goal that it is difficult to see why this point is not universally acknowledged by commentators who write about him. One explanation seems to be the contemporary acceptance of Hume's mistaken view of reason as only instrumental, i.e., having no goals of its own. But Hobbes's view that, except in special circumstances, it is irrational not to avoid death, pain, or disability is much more in accord with the ordinary view of what counts as rational.

In *De Homine*, after distinguishing between real and apparent good, Hobbes talks about those things that are real goods. "Moreover, the greatest of goods for each is his own preservation. For nature is so arranged that all desire good for themselves. Insofar as it is within their capacities, it is necessary to desire life, health, and further, insofar as it can be done, security of future time" (*D.H.* XI, 6) In this discussion it is quite clear that a real good is not merely that which one desires but that which is rationally desired. This explains why Hobbes's list of the goods is so strikingly close to the previously listed goals of reason. And when he talks about the evils, it is also quite clear that he is talking about rational aversions. In this discussion, Hobbes makes it clear that he does not hold that death must be avoided in all circumstances. Right after the sentence quoted above, he says, "On the other hand, though death is the greatest of all evils (especially when accompanied by torture), the pains of life can be so great that, unless their quick end is foreseen, they may lead men to number death among the goods." Applying Hobbes to a topic he never really considered, he would not consider it irrational for a person to choose to die when suffering from a chronic painful illness.

Sense and Imagination

Many of Hobbes's philosophical views about sense perception appear quite up to date. Many contemporary philosophers put forward views very similar to Hobbes's, though often in a slightly more sophisticated form. In what follows I shall discuss only Hobbes's philosophical views concerning psychological topics, not his empirical speculations. With regard to matters of sense, this is explicitly in accordance with his view of philosophy, for he says, in talking of phantasms involved in sense, we can only know "some ways and means by which they may be, I do not say they are, generated" (*De Corp.* XXV, 1). Hobbes was quite inventive to say that "phantasms seem to be without, by reaction of the endeavour outwards, so pleasure and pain, by reason of the endeavour of the organ inwards, seem to be within" (*De Corp.* CXXV, 12; see also *L.* I, 4 and *D.H.* XI, 1). He knows that this is merely speculation, and it should not be included in what would now be classified as his philosophical views concerning sense.

Hobbes's philosophical position is clearly and explicitly a materialist one. The mind consists of motions in the body. He did not know what these motions are like, and neither do we, though we now think that the part of the body involved is the brain and know somewhat more about these matters than Hobbes knew. Different aspects of the mind involve different motions, e.g., "Sense, therefore, in the sentient, can be nothing else but motion in some of the internal parts of the sentient; and the parts so moved are parts of the organs of sense" (*De Corp.* XXV, 2). Hobbes defines imagination as "sense decaying, or weakened, by the absence of the object" (*De Corp.* XXV, 5; see also *L.* II, 2). This definition is sometimes condescendingly quoted, but all that is of philosophical significance is that Hobbes regards imagination as a motion which is related to the motions of sense, an eminently sensible view.

Sense is important to Hobbes, for he holds an empiricist view that "there is no conception in a man's mind, which hath not at first, totally, or by part, been begotten upon the organs of sense. The rest are derived from that original" (*L.* I, 1). He differs from standard empiricism in that he appreciates that language is included in that which is at first begotten upon the organs of sense, and he explicitly says of understanding that it is "nothing else but conception caused by speech" (*L.* IV, 22; see also *L.* II, 10). Thus, to view Hobbes as holding that thought consists of a succession of phantasms, i.e., pictures, is to mistakenly impose on him the more limited view of what counts as "begotten on the organs of sense" held by later empiricists. Hobbes, much more than other empiricists, recognizes the extraordinary impact of language on thought, remarking that "A natural fool that could never learn by heart the order of the numeral words, as *one, two,* and *three,* may observe every stroke of the clock, and nod to it, or say *one, one, one,* but can never know what hour it strikes" (*L.* IV, 10).

Hobbes claims that his philosophical view of sense is a direct consequence of his materialist view. This is brought out most clearly when he uses the basic principle "that when a thing is in motion, it will eternally be in motion, unless something else stay it" (*L.* II, 1) to explain imagination. This explanation consists primarily in making an analogy between what is presently being sensed obscuring imagination in the way that the sun obscures the stars. This analogy may, however, lead to Hobbes's most interesting philosophical discovery concerning sense, namely, that sense, or what we would call perception, requires variety. "Sense, therefore, properly so called, must necessarily have in it a perpetual variety of phantasms, that they may be discerned one from another" (*De Corp.* XXV, 5). Hobbes points out that to see one thing continually and not to see at all come to the same thing. But, like all other materialist philosophers both before and after him, he never provides a satisfactory account of phantasms or appearances, that is, an account of the fact that we are aware of something related to the motions of sense.

Hobbes does attempt to explain how the motions of sense are involved in voluntary motion. According to him:

> There be in animals, two sorts of *motions* peculiar to them: one called *vital;* begun in generation, and continued without interruption through their whole life; such as are the *course* of the *blood,* the *pulse,* the *breathing,* the *concoction, nutrition, excretion,* &c., to which motions there need no help of imagination; the other is *animal motion,* otherwise called *voluntary motion;* so as to *go,* to *speak,* to *move* any of our limbs, in such manner as first fancied in our minds. . . . And because *going, speaking,* and the like voluntary motions, depend always upon a precedent thought of *whither, which way,* and *what;* it is evident, that the imagination is the first internal beginning of all voluntary motion. (*L.* VI, 1)

Here again Hobbes puts forward a rather crude picture of the interaction of the various motions in the body, but he knows that this picture is speculative. His philosophical purpose is to explain how the motions of sense provide the basis for a distinction between two kinds of observable motion in the body. The first, which he calls vital motion, e.g., the circulation of the blood, has no need of sense; these are the kinds of motions that go on even during sleep. Were these motions to stop, the organism would be dead, which is why Hobbes calls them the vital motions. Hobbes has no great interest in these motions. They are relevant to his concerns only because they provide a plausible explanation of appetite and aversion, pleasure and pain. They allow him to show that a materialist account is compatible with an accurate explanation of human behavior, but it is not important to his projects to provide that accurate explanation.

Appetite, Aversion, Pleasure, Pain and the Passions

Hobbes wants to show that there is a plausible explanation of all of the features of human psychology, e.g., sense, imagination, dreams, appetites, and aversions, in terms of the motions in the body (*L.* VI, 9). Thus, he speculates that the motions of sense and imagination can interact with the vital motion in order to provide a plausible explanation of voluntary motion. The motions of sense interact with the vital motion in such a way that they produce voluntary motion by means of a purely theoretically derived motion which Hobbes calls endeavor. Endeavor is the key concept in Hobbes's attempt to show the compatibility of his philosophy of motion with the explanation of voluntary behavior. Having shown the plausibility, perhaps even the necessity, of invisible and insensible motions, Hobbes continues: "These small beginnings of motion, within the body of man, before they appear in walking, speaking, striking, and other visible actions, are commonly called ENDEAVOUR" (*L.* VI, 1). Hobbes then goes on to use endeavor to define the more common psychological terms that he will use in his analyses of particular passions: "This endeavour, when it is toward something that causes it, is called APPETITE or DESIRE . . . And when the endeavour is fromward something, it is generally called AVERSION" (*L.* VI, 2; see also *D.H.* XI, 1).

Hobbes attempts to relate appetite and aversion to pleasure and pain in two somewhat different ways. In *Leviathan* he says: "This motion which is called appetite, and for the appearance of it *delight*, and *pleasure*, seemeth to be a corroboration of vital motion" (*L.* VI,

10). Here, pleasure is an appearance of the motion of appetite, just as sense is really "only motion, caused by the action of external objects, but in appearance; to the eye, light and colour, to the ear sound, to the nostril odour, &c" (*L.* VI, 9). Here in a single sentence, Hobbes seems to be holding both reductive materialism and epiphenomenalism. However, in *De Homine*, he relates delight to appetite in a different way: "Appetite and aversion do not differ from delight and annoyance otherwise than desire from satisfaction of desire, that is, than the future differs from the present" (*D.H.* XI, 1). Appearances have disappeared, and delight simply becomes having an appetite for what you now have: annoyance, having an aversion to the situation one is now in. This latter account seems to be a more thoroughgoing materialism than the epiphenomenalism of the former account. Nevertheless, this extremely sophisticated account of pleasure does not depend upon holding any kind of materialist view.

However, in both works, (*L.* VI and *D.H.* XIII) once Hobbes has the concepts of appetite and aversion, pleasure and pain, his account of the individual passions completely ignores the relation between human behavior and his materialist philosophy. He simply proceeds by way of introspection and experience, along with liberal borrowings from Aristotle's account of the passions in the *Rhetoric*.[3] In the Introduction to *Leviathan*, Hobbes admits that he does not use his materialist philosophy to explain either the individual passions or human behavior in general. He is quite clear that introspection and experience, not a materialist philosophy, provide the key to understanding human behavior. This is made explicit in the final sentences of the Introduction, "when I shall have set down my own reading orderly, and perspicuously, the pains left another, will be only to consider, if he also find not the same in himself. For this kind of doctrine admitteth no other demonstration" (*L.* Intro., 8).

Hobbes's definitions of the particular passions are noteworthy primarily for their conciseness. For example, "For appetite, with an opinion of obtaining, is called HOPE. The same without such opinion, DESPAIR" (*L.* VI, 15, 16). These definitions seem reasonable, but obviously they are not to be taken as serious attempts at analyses of the concepts of hope and despair. Thus when Hobbes defines DIFFIDENCE as "*constant* despair" (*L.* VI, 21), it is clear that this definition will not be very useful in explaining his famous remark in Chapter XIII of *Leviathan*: "So that in the nature of man,

[3] See Strauss *The Political Philosophy of Hobbes*, ch. III, esp. pp. 36–41.

we find three principle causes of quarrel. First competition; secondly, diffidence; thirdly, glory" (*L*. XIII, 6). Recognizing this, Hobbes explains what he means in the next paragraph: "The first maketh men to invade for gain; the second for safety; and the third, for reputation." Hobbes should have used fear, instead of diffidence, for not only does fear actually fit better with what he says in this latter paragraph, it also fits better with his own definition of FEAR as, "*Aversion*, with opinion of HURT from the object" (*L*. VI. 16). It may simply be that it is because Hobbes wanted to use the passion of fear as one of "the passions that incline men to peace" (*L*. XIII, 14) that he decided to use a different word when he wanted a passion that led to war.

Hobbes's definition of GLORYING as "Joy arising from imagination of a man's own power and ability" (*L*. VI, 39) does fit in somewhat better with his use of glory as one of the causes of quarrel. But on this definition, it is the desire for glory, not glory itself, that is a cause of quarrel. Here again, it would seem that Hobbes did not use the right term, even given his own definition. It probably would have been more correct to use pride, rather than glory, but, surprisingly, Hobbes does not even include pride in the list of passions that he defines in Chapter VI of *Leviathan*. This is all the more surprising, for he does define SHAME as "*Grief* for the discovery of some defect of ability" (*L*. XIII, 44). If pride is the opposite of shame, then it does not seem to be relevant to Hobbes's concerns. However, in Chapter XIV of *Leviathan* he defines "pride" as failing to acknowledge others as one's equal by nature (*L*. XIV, 21), and this kind of pride does seem to be a cause of quarrel. I think that this shows that Hobbes does not intend that the definitions that he put forward in Chapter VI of *Leviathan* to be taken literally. Both he and his readers knew what was meant by these terms, and his definitions in that chapter were merely an attempt to show that all of the passions could be explained by relating them to some simpler passions.

Finally, it does not seem that "competition" is the right term for the first cause of quarrel. In Chapter VI he had already defined COVETOUSNESS as "Desire of riches" (*L*. VI, 23), which seems to be close to what he intended by "competition." However, in that definition he had noted that covetousness is "used always in signification of blame" and it may be that he does not want to use the kind of term that he himself had said was of inconstant signification. This examination of Hobbes's misuse of "competition," "diffidence," and "glory" as naming the three causes of quarrel does not create problems because, in the next paragraph, he provides an explanation of what he means by these terms. His point is as clear as if he had used the right terms. Also, it is important to note that of the three causes of war, only diffidence (or fear) is a passion that naturally leads to peace as well as war. The other two passions, competition (or covetousness), and glory (or pride), do not naturally lead to peace. Pride, in particular, may be the passion most responsible for Hobbes's view that the sovereign should have almost unlimited power, for in *Job* the Leviathan is created to rule over the kingdom of the proud.

Hobbes's definition of deliberation as "the whole sum of desires, aversions, hopes and fears, continued till the thing be done, or thought impossible" (*L.* VI, 50) is another example of an oversimple analysis of a concept. His folk etymological analysis that this process is "called *deliberation*; because it is putting an end to the *liberty* we had of doing, or omitting, according to our own appetite, or aversion" (*L.* VI, 51) may be partly responsible for the inadequacy of the definition. Although his definition does explain why we cannot deliberate about the past, and of things thought impossible (ibid.), it makes deliberation sound more like a succession of emotional states than a consideration of the consequences of the various alternative courses of actions.

Although Hobbes claims that definitions are the beginning of all science (*L.* IV, 12; V, 4, 8, 20), we have now seen that many of his own definitions, especially of the passions, are not carefully formulated. However, what is important for Hobbes is that he uses words in ways that everyone would agree that the terms refer to the same things. He does not want to use terms that are primarily expressions of the attitudes of the person using them (*L.* IV, 24). He anticipates many of the views of the philosophers of language of the twentieth century, e.g., he realizes that language is not used merely to describe the world but also to express our attitudes about it (*L.* IV, 24). He also recognizes the performative nature of promising (*L.* XIV, 7–16). He denies that there is a natural relationship between words and the world (*D.H.* X, 2), so he maintains that language is a human invention. However, he does not claim that some individual invented it.

Although Hobbes often equates emotions or passions with appetites and desires, when he is more careful, he is aware that the former are only a subclass of the latter (see *D.H.* XII, 1). In addition to our emotional desires, we also have rational desires. These rationally required desires are long-term desires for real goods. Hobbes is referring to these rationally required desires when he says:

"[T]he greatest of goods for each is his own preservation. For nature is so arranged that all desire good for themselves. Insofar as it is within their capacities, it is necessary to desire life, health, and further, insofar as it can be done, security of future time" (*D.H.* II, 6). Hobbes is not claiming that, in fact, everyone desires self-preservation more than anything else; he explicitly notes: "[M]ost men would rather lose their lives (that I say not, their peace) then suffer slander" (*D.C.* III, 12; see also *L.* XV, 20). Hobbes explicitly refers to the distinction between the rational desires and the emotional ones in the Dedication to *De Cive*:

> Having therefore thus arrived at two maxims of human nature; the one arising from the *concupiscible* part, which desires to appropriate to itself the use of those things in which all others have a joint interest; the other proceeding from the *rational*, which teaches every man to fly a contra-natural dissolution, as the greatest mischief that can arrive to nature. (p. 93)

The objects of the rational desires are the same in all persons, but Hobbes is aware that the objects of the emotional desires, or the passions, differ from person to person. In the Introduction to *Leviathan*, right after claiming that introspection tells us that the passions "are the same in all men," he points out that this is not true of "the *objects* of the passions, which are the things desired, feared, hoped &c.: for these the constitution individual, and particular education, do so vary, and they are so easy to be kept from our knowledge" (*L.* Intro., 3). It is the universality of the objects of the rational desires that allows Hobbes to use reason as the basis for his arguments concerning morality and the proper ordering of the state. When Hobbes makes claims about human nature that are true of all persons, these are statements about the rationally required desires, and not, as most commentators have taken them, statements about the passions. When he talks about any other desires, he is only talking about those that are widespread enough to have an effect on the organization of the state.

Only the rationally required desires are universal. Hobbes is one of the few philosophers to realize that to talk of that part of human nature that involves the passions is to talk about human populations. He says in the Preface to *De Cive*: "Though the wicked were fewer than the righteous, yet because we cannot distinguish them, there is a necessity of suspecting, heeding, anticipating, subjugating, self-defending, every incident to the most honest and fairest conditioned" (p. 100). This kind of passage shows that Hobbes is aware that premises about the passions do not need to apply to each and every person in order to play the role that he wants them to play in his moral and political philosophy. When arguing for the necessity of an unlimited sovereign, he does not have to claim that all people need to be kept in awe but only that some people would behave badly if there were not such a sovereign. It also shows that he is aware that people are quite different in their psychological characteristics, including the degree to which their behavior is governed by the passions rather than "good education and experience" (ibid; see also *D.C.* III, 26, 27).

Mental Disorders

At the present time there is a debate among psychiatrists about whether deviant behavior is a sufficient condition for a mental disorder, or whether the person also needs to be suffering an evil. Surprisingly, Hobbes seems to support both sides in the current debate. He says: "[T]o have stronger and more vehement passions for any thing, than is ordinarily seen in others, is that which men call Madness" (*L.* VIII, 16). But later he says: "[I]f the excesses be madness, there is no doubt but the passions themselves, when they tend to evil, are degrees of the same" (*L.* VIII, 20). I suspect that just as those current psychiatrists who seem to regard deviance as a sufficient condition for having a mental disorder think that deviance leads to suffering, Hobbes also seems to regard the more vehement passions as tending to evil.

Hobbes also anticipates modern psychiatry's view that mental disorders can have either mental or physical causes:

> Sometimes the extraordinary and extravagant passion, proceedeth from the evil constitution of the organs of the body, or harm done them; and sometimes the hurt, and indisposition of the organs, is caused by the vehemence, or long continuance of the passion. But in both cases the madness is of one and the same nature. (*L.* VIII, 17)

This view shows how little Hobbes's materialism restricts his views about human nature even though it is not inconsistent with that materialism either. Hobbes's materialism does not limit his views on mental disorders at all. He seems to hold that sometimes a defective bodily organ causes one to have passions that are too vehement, and sometimes these vehement passions cause a defect in a bodily organ.

Hobbes's discussion of madness also makes clear that he did not hold the simple view that everyone is most strongly motivated by the desire to avoid death. It is only insofar as one is rational that the desire to avoid death is supreme. He tells the story about the fit of madness

> [in a] Grecian city which seized only the young maidens; and caused them to hang themselves. . . . But one that suspected, that contempt of life in them, might proceed from some passion of the mind, and supposing they did not contemn also their honour, gave counsel to the magistrates, to strip such as so hanged themselves, and let them hang out naked. This the story says, cured that madness. (*L.* VIII, 25)

Hobbes is aware that the natural rational desire to avoid death is often much weaker than the learned social desire to avoid shame.

Human Nature and Psychological Egoism

Hobbes's view about human nature is rather ordinary. He claims that infants are born with neither a moral sense nor concern for anyone other than themselves. However, he thinks that they have the capacity to develop these traits, for he holds that education and training can make people act in a wide variety of ways and from a wide variety of motives, from very good to very bad, from selfish to unselfish (see *D.C.* Pref., p. 100). Hobbes is also aware that the constitution of the body affects people's behavior, and even discusses such mental disorders as depression (see *L.* VIII, 20). Once one realizes that Hobbes is aware of the wide variety of human behavior, it becomes quite clear that his remarks about human nature are remarks about some widespread features of the human population. Especially when he talks about human nature in the state of nature, he should not be taken as talking about actual persons in the real world, but only about how people would act if they were not trained and educated by their families. Interpreting Hobbes in this way does not take away any premise about human nature that he needs for building his political theory and allows one to account for many apparent inconsistencies.

It is important to realize that when Hobbes talks about human nature, unless he is talking about what is rational, he does not mean to be saying something that he thinks true of each and every human being. He is only saying something that holds for a large enough portion of the human population that it must be taken into account when constructing a workable political theory. Failure to recognize this is one explanation of the standard practice of claiming that Hobbes subscribed to psychological egoism, the view that all motives for action can be classified as motives of self-interest. In fact, like all keen observers of the human scene, Hobbes was aware that real people behave as they do, not primarily because of the way they are born, but because of the way that they have been trained. This point is made in many places, e.g., where he says that children "have no other rule of good and evil manners, but the correction they receive from their parents and masters," and then adds, "that children are constant to their rule" (*L.* XI, 21; see also *D.C.* Pref., p. 100, and I, 2, n.).

Hobbes does not even hold that psychological egoism is true of infants; rather, he says that children simply act on their natural passions without considering either the consequences of their actions or whether they are morally acceptable. He says in the Preface to *De Cive*: "Unless you give children all they ask for, they are peevish and cry, aye, and strike their parents sometimes; and all this they have from nature" (p. 100). Since people in the state of nature are assumed to be like infants, without any kind of education or training, they behave like children, so they would not be psychological egoists either (see ibid. and *D.C.* I, 2, n.). But Hobbes's claim that in the state of nature we are considering people "as if but even now sprung out of the earth, and suddenly, like mushrooms, come to full maturity, without all kind of engagement to one another" (*D.C.* VIII, 1), shows that he knew that no person was ever actually in the state of nature. Hobbes never claims that the fictitious persons in the state of nature, let alone the actual persons that are raised up in families, are psychological egoists; rather, he holds that unless they are properly brought up, they act on their passions rather than their reason.

Attributing to Hobbes the view that no one is ever motivated by concern for others is not only inconsistent with Hobbes's definition of benevolence; it is also inconsistent with his remarks about charity, where he characterizes a lack of charity as "a mind insensible to another's evils" (*D.H.* XIII, 9). Numerous passages concerning friends and family members also show that Hobbes did not deny people were ever motivated by love and concern for others (see *D.C.* II, 19, and VI, 5). What he does deny is that people naturally love all other human beings (see *D.C.* I, 2). All that he needs in order to support his claim that there is a need for unlimited sovereign power is that altruism is limited. Indeed, given that in *Leviathan* Hobbes is concerned with the danger posed by popular men, e.g., Julius Caesar, who "won to himself the affections of his army" (*L.* XIX, 18), it would be absurd for him to hold that people are never motivated by their concern for others. Although he knows that particular individuals might act primarily on their self-interest, he is quite aware that the danger to the state does not arise from people acting on their own self-interest. Rather, he views false moral beliefs, including those beliefs derived from religion as well as those derived from studying ancient philosophy, as the primary source of civil unrest.

One reason why Hobbes is often regarded as having such a distorted account of human nature is traceable to his political rhetoric, e.g., his use of the term "power." When he says, "So that in the first place, I put for a general inclination of all mankind, a perpetual and restless desire of power after power, that ceaseth only in death" (*L.* XI, 2), this sounds as if he is claiming that all people are like Saddam Hussein or other power hungry dictators. However, when we look at his definition of power, "The power *of a man*, (to take it universally), is his present means to obtain some future apparent good" (*L.* X, 1), we see that this is quite misleading. What he is really claiming is, "the voluntary actions, and inclination of all men, tend, not only to the procuring, but also to the assuring of a contented life; and differ only in the way" (*L.* XI, 1). Hobbes's disturbing statement about power is only a claim that all people tend to be concerned about their future; it explains pension funds and medical checkups more than it does anti-social power grabs. Indeed, for Hobbes, the former are not only more common than the latter; they are also more rational.

Rationality and the Good

Although Hobbes did not hold that all natural desires were rational (*L.* XI, 21; see also *D.C.* Pref., p. 100, and I, 2, n.), he did hold that the rationally required desires were natural (*D.C.* Ded., p. 93). He holds the latter because if these desires were the result of training and education, they could not be taken as universal. Hobbes held that the only rationally required desires are those that concern people's own long-term benefit, primarily their preservation. The emotions or emotional desires are not in themselves irrational; they only become irrational when they conflict with reason, i.e., they conflict with satisfying the rationally required desires (*D.H.* XII, 1). Hobbes does not regard all sacrifice for others as irrational; on the contrary, he lists charity together with justice as encompassing all of the virtues (*D.H.* XIII, 9). He holds the plausible view that it is irrational to sacrifice one's life unless one has some extremely strong reason for doing so. He explicitly says that risking one's life for the proper cause is not irrational, making it a law of nature, i.e., a dictate of reason, "that every man is bound by nature, as much as in him lieth, to protect in war the authority, by which he is himself protected in time of peace" (*L.* Rev. and Con., 6).

Hobbes denies that people always act rationally; indeed, he constantly laments the power of the irrational appetites (see *D.C.* III, 32 and *L.* XV, 34). He explicitly states: "The definition of the will, given by the Schools, that it is a *rational appetite*, is not good. For if it were, then there could be no voluntary act against reason" (*L.* VI, 54). Hobbes is aware that people are naturally motivated as much, if not more, by their emotions than they are by reason. He is not discouraged by this because he holds that it is possible for people to be trained and educated to act rationally by the precepts, and even more the examples, of "fathers, teachers, and tutors of youth" (*D.H.* XIII, 7). He holds that "man is made fit for society not by nature, but by education" (*D.C.* I, 2, n.). He also stresses the need of the sovereign to educate the citizenry, holding that it is more important than "any civil law or terror of legal punishment" (*L.* XXX, 4).

Many philosophers do not like Hobbes's view of human nature because, unlike Aristotle, Mill and many other philosophers, he not only does not put forward the life of the philosopher as the best life, he does not put forward any view of the best life. His observation of the way we use language leads him to agree with Aristotle in defining "*good* as that which all men desire" (*D.H.* XI, 4). However, his knowledge of language also enables to him to realize that this definition of "good" does not require that there be a universally agreed upon objective good. In fact, he explicitly states: "[T]here is no such *finis ultimus*, utmost end, nor *summum bonum*, greatest good, as is spoken of in the books of the old moral philosophers" (*L.* XI, 1). Hobbes is aware that although there is agreement on the rationally required negative goals, people have a wide variety of positive goals. Although he may have his personal preferences, he denies that there is any objective ranking of these positive goals. So while he does not stress tolerance as a moral or political virtue, intellectually he is probably more liberal and tolerant than most other moral and political philosophers, including Mill. On the other hand, he is not a relativist: he realizes that it is compatible with complete tolerance toward different positive goals to regard desires for death, pain, and disability as irrational. He holds, contrary to Mill, that there are many rational positive goals, but that none of these is rationally required and that there is no objective ranking of these goals. Although not a generally accepted philosophical view, it is not only a very sophisticated view, it seems to me to be a correct one.

Hobbes holds that "good is said to be relative to person, place, and time" (*D.H.* XI, 4), but he realizes that this is not incompatible with holding that some things are good for everyone. In one sentence he makes both of these points: "At times one can also talk of a good for everyone, like health: but this way of speaking is relative; therefore one cannot speak of something as being *simply* good; since whatsoever is good, is good for someone or other" (ibid.). Hobbes also realizes that people often desire what is not good for them, and this leads him to note that "good (like evil) is divided into *real* and *apparent*" (*D.H.* XI, 5). He is aware that people desire many different things, but unlike Hume, he does not regard reason simply to be the slave of the passions. In talking about human nature, Hobbes views reason as having the long-term goals of "life, health, and insofar as it can be done, security of future time" (*D.H.* XI, 6). He also holds that reason in the widest sense, including both prudence and sapience, helps people to determine how to achieve these goals. It is these common goals of reason that allow Hobbes to make a list of those things that are real goods, as opposed to those things that are only apparent goods (see *D.H.* XI). And it is these common goals of reason that supply the foundation of both the right of nature and the laws of nature (see *D.C.* I, 7 and II, 1; see also *L.* XIV, 1, 3).

Rationality and Human Nature

Hobbes regards it as a conceptual truth that everyone ought to follow reason, that is, that no one ever ought to act irrationally. He does not argue for this claim, nor does he argue for the claim that unless one has very strong reasons to the contrary, it is irrational to act in ways that significantly increase one's chances of death. These two claims, which he expected to be universally accepted and which seem to me to be correct, are the foundation of his moral and political theories. He does, however, argue for his claim that reason requires acting morally (*D.C.* III, 32). A major element in his justification of morality is his attempt to point out some indisputable facts about human nature that prove that reason requires acting morally (*L.* XIII 1–10; *D.C.* I, 12). The two most important facts are that all persons are vulnerable, i.e., any person can be killed by other people, and that all persons have limited knowledge and are fallible, i.e., all people make mistakes. Also important is that most, if not all, people sometimes act on their emotions even when this leads them to act irrationally.

Other important facts are not truths about every human being but truths about populations (*D.C.* Pref., p. 100). He holds that in any large population, (1) some people hold false views about what is morally acceptable behavior, and (2) some people do not care about acting morally, but are only concerned with benefiting themselves, their family, and their friends. As we shall see in the next chapter, Hobbes's moral theory is an attempt to provide a description, explanation, and justification of morality that would persuade those people holding false moral views to change their views. Hobbes's political theory includes his moral theory together with an attempt to provide a guide for constructing a government that can protect its citizens from both those who hold false moral views and those who do not care about morality.

3

Hobbes's Moral Theory

Moral Theories

A moral theory is an attempt to describe, explain, and justify morality. If the description of morality that a philosopher provides does not match what is commonly thought of as morality, then there may not be much interest in his explanation or justification of what he describes. Hobbes, like Aristotle, Kant, and Mill, took himself to be explaining and justifying what he thought of as common morality. Many contemporary philosophers also take themselves to be explaining and justifying what they think of as common morality. Those who describe morality by describing the traits of character that they take to be traditional moral virtues are called virtue theorists. Aristotle provides the model for this kind of moral theory. These virtue theorists regard virtues as those traits of character that are essential for flourishing or living a successful life. Those who describe morality by describing the duties that they take to be the essential features of morality are called deontologists. Kant provides the model for this kind of moral theory. Deontologists who follow Kant explain and justify these duties by referring to the nature of reason or of rational persons. Those who describe morality by describing the rules that they take as the essential element of morality used to be called rule utilitarians, but are now generally called rule consequentialists. Mill provides the model for this kind of moral theory. Rule consequentialists differ from deontologists by using the consequences of everyone acting on or internalizing these rules in order to explain and justify them. Hobbes combines elements of all three of these moral theories, and attempts to put him solely in one of these categories result in distortions of his moral theory

Hobbes uses the concept of laws of nature to present his moral theory. He follows Aristotle by describing morality in terms of what he takes to be traditional moral virtues. He says: "Now the science of virtue and vice is moral philosophy; and therefore the true doctrine of the laws of nature is the true moral philosophy" (*L. XV*, 40). But he also anticipates Kant in describing the laws of nature that prescribe these virtues as the dictates of reason (*L. XV*, 41; *D.C.* II, 1). He regards these laws as following from the nature of rational persons. Hobbes also anticipates Mill by explaining and justifying these laws by citing the consequences of rejecting or accepting these laws: "The laws of nature are immutable and eternal, for injustice, ingratitude, arrogance, pride, iniquity, acception of persons and the rest can never be made lawful. For it can never be that war shall preserve life and peace destroy it" (*L. XV*, 38). He also makes clear that the virtues dictated by these laws "come to be praised as the means of peaceable, sociable, and comfortable living" (*L. XV*, 40; see also *D.C.* III, 31).

Some contemporary moral philosophers put forward a view that is called act consequentialism. This moral theory, which holds that we should always do that act that has the best consequences for all affected by the action, involves trying to explain why common morality is an inadequate guide for behavior. Act consequentialists argue that common morality is confused and that the guide they propose should replace common morality. For example, act consequentialism claims that a student ought to cheat on a pass–fail exam that is not graded on a curve (so others would not be harmed by his cheating) if the following conditions are met: he would not be caught; his cheating on this exam would not lead him to cheat when others would be harmed; the course is a required course that will not be relevant to anything he plans to do after college, e.g., it is a course in metaphysics; and the consequences of his cheating are better for all affected, e.g., his parents will feel bad if he flunks, than his not cheating. Hobbes's moral theory does not include elements of this moral theory.

Hobbes holds that the moral virtues are based on the intended consequences of an action, not its actual consequences. For Hobbes, it is intentions that are relevant in determining whether a person is acting in the way that morality requires, so he clearly does not hold that the actual consequences are the primary, let alone the sole, factor in determining whether a person is acting in the way that morality requires. He says: "[T]he laws which oblige conscience may be broken by an act not only contrary to them, but also agreeable with them; if so be that he who does it, be of another opinion. For though the act itself be answerable to the laws, yet his conscience is against them" (*D.C.* III. 28; see also *L.* XV, 37). For Hobbes, the laws of nature dictate what character traits a person should have, and so are primarily about his desires, emotions, and intentions, and only secondarily about his actions:

> The same laws [the laws of nature] because they oblige only to a desire and endeavour (I mean an unfeigned and constant endeavour) are easy to be observed. For in that they require nothing but endeavour, he that endeavoureth their performance fulfilleth them; and he that fulfilleth the law is just. (*L.* XV, 39; see also *D.C.* III. 30)

Hobbes's moral theory is still so commonly misunderstood not only because it is sometimes taken as a version of one of the standard moral theories, but also because it is sometimes taken as a version of act consequentialism.

Natural Law Theory

The least misleading description of Hobbes's moral theory is that it is a form of natural law theory, i.e., the theory that every rational person knows the duties, rules, and virtues that morality requires. Hobbes explicitly presents his theory in this way. However, unlike most natural law theories, which claim that the authority and force of the moral law depends on God having implanted this moral knowledge in everyone, God plays no philosophical role in Hobbes's moral theory. Rather, Hobbes shows that natural reason, which is limited to knowledge of the natural world, is sufficient not only to yield to the laws of nature, but also to provide an incentive to follow them (*D.C.* II, 1). Hobbes does say that the laws of nature, in addition to being the dictates of reason and the moral law, can be considered as the commands of God. He may believe this, but it is also the case that he realizes that his account of morality will not gain general acceptance unless he shows it to be compatible with Christianity.

As pointed out in the previous chapter, until recently the standard interpretations of Hobbes's account of human nature made it difficult to understand why his moral and political theories were taken seriously at all. Interpreting Hobbes as arguing for psychological egoism, the theory that every action of every person is motivated by self-interest, makes it impossible to understand how he could be offering a description and justification of common morality. On any plausible account, morality sometimes requires us to act in ways that are contrary to our self-interest. One result of misinterpreting Hobbes as arguing for psychological egoism is that some commentators deny that he puts forward an account of morality at all; they claim that he simply describes prudence using moral terminology. Other commentators, accepting the mistaken egoistic interpretation of Hobbes's account of human nature but realizing that he is attempting to describe and justify our common morality, claim that he puts forward a moral theory that is completely independent of his account of human nature.

Hobbes's rhetorical style is partly responsible for some of the mistaken interpretations of his account of human nature and the criticisms of his moral theory, but many of the criticisms stem from the fact that he was considered an atheist. In Hobbes's time, most people held, and many still do hold, that God or belief in God is a necessary feature of morality. Many hold this view because they believe that only the threat of punishment in hell, supplemented by promise of reward in heaven, by a being from whom nothing that you think or do can be hidden, provides sufficient incentive for people to act morally. They, not Hobbes, hold that self-interest is the only sure motivation for acting morally. Thus, when Hobbes presents an account of morality that does not depend upon God, they immediately take him to be providing some other way of having self-interest provide the motivation for acting morally. Self-interest does play a significant role in Hobbes's moral theory, although not as completely and directly as it does in the account of morality that depends upon belief in the traditional Christian God. Further, punishment plays no part in his moral theory, although it plays a large role in his political theory.

Despite Hobbes's effort to gain support for his account of morality by citing scripture, it is generally recognized that he provides an account of morality that does not depend upon the traditional Christian God or even belief in such a God. Hobbes is not an atheist; he clearly believes that there is a God (*D.C.* XIV, 19, n.), that is, a creator of the universe, but he does not hold that morality depends on God or religion (*D.C.* XV, 3; *L.* XXXI, 2). He regards atheists and deists as subject to both the civil law and the laws of nature, even though they do not believe in God or that God intervenes in this world. Indeed, it is quite likely that Hobbes is one of those chiefly responsible for the fact that almost all non-religiously affiliated English-speaking philosophers hold that morality is independent of religion and does not depend on God or belief in God.

Hobbes's Concept of Reason

As stated in the previous chapter, Hobbes holds both that everyone ought to follow reason and that it is contrary to reason to act in ways that significantly increase one's chances of death. By "contrary to reason," Hobbes does not mean being mentally ill, but rather acting irrationally in the sense that one's emotions or desires for present goods overwhelm one's rational preferences for long-term goods. Hobbes follows Aristotle in holding that reason has its own goals, and is not merely an instrument for aiding the passions in gaining their goals. The failure to appreciate that Hobbes holds that reason has its own goal is partly due to the fact that, unlike Aristotle, Hobbes denies that there is a *summum bonum*, or greatest good (*L.* XI, 1). But he does not deny that there is a *summum malum*, or greatest evil. For Hobbes, the primary goal of reason is a negative one, avoiding an avoidable death (*D.C.* Ded., p. 93). He acknowledges that reason also has other goals, but he uses the rationality of avoiding death to stand for all that is rationally required when he develops his moral and political theories. This does not result in a significant distortion of his views, because what reason requires us to do to avoid death results in our avoiding the other harms as well as helping us achieve the positive goals of reason. Thus, for Hobbes, acting in accordance with those dictates of reason, i.e., the laws of nature, which significantly decrease one's risks of dying earlier than "nature ordinarily alloweth men to live" (*L.* XIV, 4; see also *D.C.* I, 13), is all that is necessary to be acting rationally.

For Hobbes, morality is justified by showing that the moral virtues are dictated by reason, not reason in some metaphysical sense of the kind put forward by Kant, but reason in a more ordinary sense. In his moral and political theory, Hobbes's primary use of the word "reason" is to refer to natural reason, that is, to that reason which dictates self-preservation. However, he also includes as part of reason those mental faculties that are necessary for natural reason to achieve its goal. Thus, he considers prudence or reasoning from experience to be a part of reason. He also includes as part of reason the faculty of reasoning with words, which is not natural, but attained by industry. Hobbes's view of reason is therefore complex: it not only dictates an end, self-preservation, it also includes both prudence and sapience, that is, reasoning from experience and reasoning with words, because both are necessary for achieving this end. Prudence and sapience are included as part of reason only because they help natural reason perform its primary function, which is to dictate "about those things which are either to be done or omitted for the constant preservation of life and members, as much as in us lies" (*D.C.* II, 1; see also *L.* XIV, 3).

Although natural reason must be aided by prudence and sapience in order to dictate the laws of nature, it is natural reason that is fundamental in Hobbes's moral theory. Hobbes allows that there are several ways of acting irrationally, viz., pursuing the wrong ends, using the wrong means, and reasoning incorrectly, but it is only the first that he consistently labels as irrational. Hobbes claims that every rational adult who thinks about what is necessary to avoid death has sufficient experience and sufficient ability to reason to realize that peace is essential for long-term preservation. Realizing this, reason dictates the necessary means to peace:

> Reason, declaring peace to be good, it follows by the same reason, that all the necessary means to peace be good also; and therefore that modesty, equity, trust, humanity, mercy (which we have demonstrated to be necessary to peace) are good manners or virtues. The law therefore, in the means to peace, commands also good manners, or the practice of virtue: and therefore it is called moral. (*D.C.* III, 31; see also *L.* XV, 40)

The Laws of Nature and Morality

As should be evident from the previous paragraph, it is in his discussion of the laws of nature that Hobbes presents his account of morality. Thus, much of this chapter will concentrate on what he says about those laws of nature that command the practice of moral virtue. These include only the first ten (*De Cive*) or eleven (*Leviathan*) laws of nature;[1] the remaining eight or nine laws are primarily

---

[1] The reason for this difference in number is that in *Leviathan* the command to seek peace is counted as one of the laws and derived from the more general rule of reason, which says to seek peace or be prepared for war (*L.* XIV, 4), whereas in *De Cive* (*D.C.* II, 2) Hobbes goes directly from this more general rule of reason to the law requiring a person to give up his right of nature, which he calls the first special law of nature.

concerned with problems of distribution and with rules concerning the behavior of judges. Hobbes also presents as a law of nature "that all men that mediate peace be allowed safe conduct" (*L*. XV, 27; see also *D.C*. III, 19). Thus the laws of nature that dictate the means to peace dictate more than the practice of moral virtue. Although Hobbes seems to present the negative version of the Golden Rule, *"Do not that to another, which thou woudst not have done to thyself"* (*L*. XV, 35; see also *D.C*. III, 26), as a summary of the laws of nature, some of the laws of nature dictating peace are about political procedures not moral virtues. Further, it is not even the case that all of the laws of nature are dictates concerning the means to achieving and maintaining peace.

For Hobbes, nothing is a virtue unless it is a trait of character that decreases a person's risks of dying an unnatural death, that is, a death caused by a human being, oneself, or someone else, rather than nature. Although every such trait of character is a virtue, not all of these virtues are moral virtues. The laws of nature dictate all of the virtues, but Hobbes explicitly acknowledges that not all of the laws of nature are concerned with dictating peace, and those that are not concerned with achieving peace are not moral virtues. "There be other things tending to the destruction of particular men (as drunkenness and all other parts of intemperance), which may therefore also be reckoned amongst those things which the law of nature hath forbidden; but are not necessary to be mentioned, nor are pertinent enough to this place" (*L*. XV, 34; see also *D.C*. III, 32). Hobbes acknowledges that the dictates of reason that command virtues that are useful for preserving the lives of individual persons are laws of nature, but he does not regard them as moral virtues, only as personal virtues. So he does not consider them relevant to civil and moral philosophy. He is most explicit about the distinction between moral virtues and personal virtues in *De Homine* when, after saying that all the moral virtues are contained in justice and charity, he says: "However, the other three virtues (except for justice) that are called cardinal – courage, prudence, and temperance – are not virtues of citizens as citizens, but as men, for these virtues are useful not so much to the state as they are to the individual men who have them" (*D.H*. XIII, 9).

Hobbes is attempting to prove that reason requires developing and acting on the moral virtues. Therefore it is essential that he put forward a traditional list of moral virtues and of moral vices (*L*. XV, 38, 40). It is also essential that he provide a generally accepted account of these virtues and vices, for he is trying to provide an explanation and justification of traditional morality. In fact, Hobbes's list of moral virtues and vices is remarkably close to what, even now, are generally regarded as moral virtues and vices. His modification of the traditional list of moral virtues and vices is an improvement on this traditional list, i.e., he does not include fortitude, prudence, and temperance as moral virtues (*D.C.* III, 32; *L.* XV, 34). He does regard them as virtues, but as personal virtues rather than as moral ones. This is an important point, for it shows that Hobbes does not regard moral virtues merely as those traits of character that lead to an individual's preservation. The laws of nature dictate courage, prudence, and temperance because they tend to the preservation of the person who has them. However, other people need not praise the person who has these virtues, for a person who has these virtues need not act in ways that benefit them (*D.H.* XIII, 9). Only those traits of character that all rational persons praise are moral virtues.

For Hobbes, no trait of character is a virtue unless it is dictated by reason, and so tends to the preservation of the person who has it. A virtue is a trait of character that all persons insofar as they are rational want to have, but being dictated by reason is not sufficient for a trait of character to be classified as a moral virtue. Moral virtues do not merely lead to one's own preservation: they lead to peace, and by leading to peace they lead to everyone's preservation. Hobbes calls the virtues that lead to peace moral virtues, because they are the traits of character that all people praise; what he means by a moral virtue is a trait of character that all people call "good." All people praise the moral virtues because they benefit everyone, not only the person who has them. They do this because they are the traits necessary for people living together in a peaceful and harmonious society (*L.* XV, 40). This is a remarkably clear and coherent justification of the moral virtues that does not distort the sense of what is meant by "moral virtue."

It is important to realize that although in the section relating the natural law to the moral law Hobbes starts by saying, "the natural law is the same with the moral" (*D.C.* III, 31), he does not mean that the natural law is equivalent to the moral law. He expresses himself more carefully in the last sentence of this same section: "The law therefore, in the means to peace, commands also good manners, or the practice of virtue; and therefore is called *moral*." Hobbes is aware that the natural law, although it contains the moral law, also commands both some political procedures and the personal virtues. Although Hobbes is primarily interested in those laws of nature that command the practice of the moral virtues and sometimes writes as if all of the laws of nature do this, he is clear that there is more to the laws of nature than the moral laws. Equating the natural law with the moral law gives rise to interpretations of the laws of nature that are clearly inadequate.

Philosopher or Polemicist

Unlike most contemporary philosophers, Hobbes is not writing for other philosophers; he wants to have a significant impact in the public arena. He is more concerned about being persuasive than in writing with the precision that contemporary philosophers regard as crucial. Hobbes lived during a civil war and he was intimately involved in the political controversies of his time. He sought to persuade the reading public and those in power to adopt the policies that he thought most likely to lead to a lasting peace. No contemporary philosopher writing on moral and political philosophy would devote half of his book to interpretation of the Scriptures, even if he thought that most people were more likely to act on their religious beliefs than on philosophical arguments. Hobbes did have an impact, although not quite the impact he intended. The Catholic Church put his books on the index and people were dismissed from teaching at Oxford for being Hobbists. His books were burned and Hobbes himself was accused of being a heretic and threatened accordingly. However, his long-term impact, especially his view that religion should not be allowed to threaten the stability of the state, and that morality is independent of religion, is probably still not adequately appreciated.

Hobbes's interest in being persuasive presents some problems in interpreting his views, for in attempting to persuade, he often supports his arguments by engaging in rhetorical exaggeration, making statements that he does not intend to be taken literally, e.g., "all things obey money" (*D.C.* XIII, 13). This statement is made when Hobbes is trying to persuade the sovereign to be wary of factions caused by people with excessive wealth. The statement, "of the voluntary acts of every man, the object is some good to himself" (*L.* XIV, 8, 29; see also *D.C.* II, 18), which is a passage often used to support the claim that Hobbes holds psychological egoism, is made in the context of trying to show that there are some inalienable rights. Nonetheless, it is usually clear when Hobbes is engaged in rhetorical exaggerations, and, for the most part, he is remarkably consistent in stating his moral and political positions: *Leviathan* and *De Cive*, e.g., put forward essentially the same moral and political theory. A careful and sympathetic reading of his texts reveals an extremely powerful description, explanation, and justification of morality.

Interpretations of the Laws of Nature

The proper interpretation of the laws of nature has been a topic of much discussion among Hobbes scholars. The views include regarding them as prudential maxims, as the moral law, or as the commands of God. Although there are individual passages in both *De Cive* and *Leviathan* that support these different interpretations, it is quite surprising, given the overall clarity of Hobbes's moral theory, that there are such diverse interpretations. Especially since the laws of nature are so central to Hobbes's moral theory, it would seem as if there ought to be more congruence concerning what he took them to be. Everyone agrees that the laws of nature are dictates of reason, for Hobbes is completely consistent in defining the laws of nature as such dictates: "Therefore the law of nature, that I may define it, is the dictate of right reason, conversant about those things which are either to be done or omitted for the constant preservation of life and members, as much as in us lies" (*D.C.* II, 1; see also *L.* XIV, 3).

The disagreement about the interpretation of the laws of nature is thus a disagreement about what it means to be a dictate of reason. If Hobbes is viewed as holding a purely instrumental view of reason, i.e., that acting rationally is simply acting in the most efficient manner to achieve one's goals, whatever they are, then the laws of nature would have no content unless everyone had the same goals. Although some commentators do claim that Hobbes held that all persons have as their primary goal preserving themselves, Hobbes explicitly points out that it is not true. In his discussion of the law of nature against contumely, that is, disrespecting others, he even cites as an argument for obeying this law that "most men would rather lose their lives . . . than suffer slander" (*D.C.* III, 12, 7th law; see also *L.* XV, 20, 8th law). Hobbes does hold that all persons, insofar as they are rational, have as one of their primary goals preserving themselves, but he laments, "men cannot put off this same irrational appetite, whereby they greedily prefer the present good . . . before the future" (*D.C.* III, 32; see also *D.H.* XII, 1). Hobbes does not hold that no persons act in ways that are contrary to their preservation, but he does hold that it is irrational to act in these ways. He denies the Humean view that reason is purely instrumental; rather, he holds that reason has a goal of its own, namely, self-preservation.

There can be no doubt, therefore, that the laws of nature resemble prudential maxims in some fairly important ways, for they dictate that a person act in those ways that are most likely to result in avoiding death, pain, and disability. However, even if the laws of nature are taken as prudential maxims, they have considerably more force than prudential maxims are normally taken to have. For Hobbes, it is a basic premise that no one ever ought to act contrary to the dictates of reason, and failing to follow the laws of nature is acting contrary to the dictates of reason. Hobbes explicitly defines the laws of nature as the dictates of reason and says that they command the practice of virtue. Thus, calling the laws of nature prudential maxims is somewhat misleading. Nonetheless, on Hobbes's complex account of reason, which includes both a goal and the special abilities of prudence and sapience necessary to attain this goal, there is no doubt that the laws of nature have the same kind of content as the prudential maxims of a wise and thoughtful person. Reason has self-preservation as a goal and, when combined with the other elements of reason, i.e., reasoning from experience and with words, reason dictates all of the laws of nature

However, interpreting the laws of nature as very strong prudential maxims does not conflict with regarding some of these natural laws as moral laws. Hobbes correctly regards the following as obviously true: "It can never be that war shall preserve life, and peace destroy it" (*L.* XV, 38; see also *D.C.* III, 29). Therefore, because reason dictates that we act so as to preserve ourselves, it also dictates that we seek peace. Hobbes then continues: "Reason declaring peace to be good, it follows by the same reason, that all the necessary means to peace be good also; and therefore that modesty, equity, trust, humanity, mercy (which we have demonstrated to be necessary to peace), are good manners or habits, that is, virtues" (*D.C.* III, 31; see also *L.* XV, 38). Of course, not all of the laws of nature that dictate peace also dictate the moral virtues; some of them dictate procedural policies. But that some of the laws of nature do dictate the practice of moral virtue is sufficient to allow the law of nature to be called the moral law. "The law therefore, in the means to peace, commands also good manners, or the practice of virtue, and therefore it is called moral" (*D.C.* III, 31; see also *L.* XV, 40). Hobbes is trying to show that the same reason that dictates self-preservation, thereby yielding what can be considered as prudential maxims, also dictates the moral virtues, and so these dictates of reason can be considered the moral law.

Finally, it is clear that Hobbes claims that these dictates or theorems of reason "as delivered in the word of God" (*L.* XV, 40; see also *D.C*, III, 35) can be considered the commands of God. Hobbes starts Chapter IV of *De Cive*, which has the title "That the Law of Nature is a Divine Law," by saying: "The same law which is natural and moral, is also wont to be called divine, nor undeservedly." He continues:

> [A]s well because reason, which is the law of nature, is given by God to every man for the rule of his actions; as because the precepts of living which are thence derived, are the same with those which have been delivered from the divine Majesty for the laws of his heavenly kingdom, by our Lord Jesus Christ, and his holy prophets and apostles.

Thus, by accepting the commonly held view that reason is given to man by God, Hobbes can claim that the dictates of reason are the commands of God. If, as Aquinas and others believe, there is no conflict between reason and Scripture, then the laws of nature will also be found in the Holy Scriptures properly interpreted. Since Hobbes hopes to persuade people to accept his account of morality, he needs to show that not only is there no incompatibility between his account of morality and that presented in Scripture, but also that Scripture puts forward the very same account of how people should behave.

We have already seen that by definition all the laws of nature are dictates of reason related to our preservation and that it is not true that all the laws of nature command the practice of moral virtue. The moral law is a subclass of the laws of nature; it is even a subclass of the laws of nature that dictate the means to peace. Although only some laws of nature are moral laws, these are the laws with which Hobbes is most concerned, sometimes even misleadingly summarizing the laws of nature by means of the negative Golden Rule. However, although Hobbes is primarily interested in that subclass of the laws of nature that dictate the moral virtues as means to peace, he is clear that there are laws of nature that are related to peace but do not dictate the moral virtues. He is also aware that there are laws of nature that are not related to peace at all, but to the preservation of individual persons, and these laws command the personal virtues: prudence, temperance, and courage (*D.C.* III, 32; see also *L.* XV, 34).

In order to show that the laws of nature dictate the moral virtues, Hobbes must have some independent way of determining what the moral virtues are. He does have such a way: the moral virtues are those traits of character that all persons praise, that is, that all men call "good" (see *L.* XV, 40; see also *D.C.* III, 31, and *D.H.* XIII, 9). Hobbes accepts that universally praised traits of character are moral virtues, but he thinks that most people do not understand why these traits of character are universally praised. His explanation and justification of the universal praise for the commonly accepted moral virtues are his explanation and justification of morality.

Hobbes's explanation and justification use two obviously correct facts about human nature. The first is that all persons are vulnerable and can be killed by others. This enables him to conclude that it is never the case that war preserves life and peace destroys it. The second is that because people are fallible, the commonly accepted moral virtues are necessary means to peace. Neither of these facts is controversial, so it can easily be overlooked that Hobbes's argument that the laws of nature dictate the moral law depends on these facts about human nature. Neither of these facts is about what motivates people; the first is about their vulnerability and the second is that the fallibility of people makes the commonly accepted moral virtues necessary as "the means of peaceable, sociable, and comfortable living" (*L.* XV, 40; see also *D.C.* III, 31). Hobbes is using the laws of nature, or the dictates of reason concerning preservation, to explain and justify common morality, that is, the commonly accepted moral virtues.

We have already seen that, although Hobbes does not define the laws of nature as the moral law, he argues for interpreting them in this way. This argument, which is basically the same in both *Leviathan* and *De Cive*, starts by claiming that to live without a sovereign is to live in a state of war of all against all. He calls this state of war the state of nature and points out all of the disadvantages of living in such a state: "[There is] no culture of the earth, no navigation . . . no knowledge of the face of the earth, no account of time, no arts, no letters, no society, and which is worst of all, continual fear and danger of violent death, and the life of man is solitary, poor, nasty, brutish, and short" (*L.* XIII, 9; see also *D.C.* I, 12–13). From this description of the state of nature, Hobbes infers that in this state, "there can be no security to any man (how strong or wise soever he be) of living out the time which nature ordinarily alloweth men to live" (*L.* XIV, 4; see also *D.C.* I, 13). In the very next sentence, he concludes: "And consequently it is precept, or general rule, of reason that every man ought to endeavour peace as far as has hope of obtaining it, and when he cannot obtain it, that he may seek and use all helps and advantages of war" (*L.* XIV, 4; see also *D.C.* I, 15). He then simply states: "The first branch of which rule containeth the first and fundamental law of nature, which is to seek peace and follow it" (*L.* XIV, 4; see also *D.C.* II, 2).

Although Hobbes says that to seek peace and follow it is the first and fundamental law of nature, it is quite clear that this law is derived from his definition of a law of nature as "a precept or general rule, found out by reason, by which a man is forbidden to do that which is destructive of his life or taketh away the means of preserving the same, and to omit that by which he thinketh it may be best preserved" (*L.* XIV, 3; see also *D.C.* II, 1). Hobbes is clearly aware of this relationship because, in *Leviathan*, after he has provided all 19 particular laws of nature, he says:

> These are the laws of nature dictating peace for a means of the con-
> servation of men in multitudes: and which only concern the doctrine
> of civil society. There be other things tending to the destruction of
> particular men (as drunkenness and all other parts of intemperance),
> which may therefore also be reckoned amongst those things which
> the law of nature hath forbidden; but are not necessary to be men-
> tioned, nor are pertinent to this place. (*L.* XV, 34; see also *D.C.* III, 32)

Hobbes is primarily interested in the laws of nature that dictate the virtues that lead to peace, not those laws of nature that are concerned only with the preservation of individual persons. That is why he says that the laws of nature are the moral law, even though he knows that the laws of nature contain more than the moral law.

Hobbes expresses himself more precisely when he says: "The law therefore, in the means to peace, commands also good manners, or the practice of virtue; and therefore it is called moral" (*D.C.* III, 31; see also *L.* XV, 40). This emphasis on the laws of nature as commanding the virtues that are the means to peace is also evident in the following passage: "The laws of nature are immutable and eternal; for injustice, ingratitude, arrogance, pride, iniquity, acception of persons, and the rest can never be made lawful. For it can never be that war shall preserve life and peace destroy it" (*L.* XV, 38; see also *D.C.* III, 29). That the laws of nature command the practice of moral virtue is central to Hobbes's moral theory because the

laws of nature are the dictates of reason concerning our preservation. Showing that acting in accordance with the laws of nature
dictating one's preservation requires acquiring and acting on the
moral virtues provides one of the most powerful justifications of
morality in the philosophical literature.

Morality for Hobbes needs to be justified, and it is justified by
natural reason, not by the commands of God. This bothered many
of Hobbes's contemporaries, and still bothers many today. Many
hold that if morality can be justified, it must be justified by the commands of God, not by a natural reason that dictates that we preserve
ourselves. Hobbes does say that natural reason comes to us from
God, and that the Scriptures also put forward the same account of
how to behave. However, everyone recognized that Hobbes's view
about natural reason dictating the laws of nature is so powerful in
itself that there is no need to bring in God. But the power of Hobbes's argument depends upon his viewing morality as being concerned with traits of character, not with particular acts; e.g., Hobbes's
arguments defending his views against the fool depends upon
viewing the laws of nature as dictating the moral virtues.

God and the Laws of Nature

When we look at what Hobbes actually says about the laws of
nature, it is clear that there need be no conflict between the different interpretations. To the question of whether Hobbes regards
the laws of nature as prudential maxims, as moral laws, or as commands of God, the unsurprising answer is: he regards them as all
three. There is no need to choose among these three interpretations,
for all of them are correct. However, that does not mean that
Hobbes regards all three interpretations as serving the same function. The standard interpretation of Hobbes's contemporaries,
which is also my view, is that regarding the laws of nature as commands of God plays no theoretical or philosophical role in Hobbes's
moral or political theory. Rather, Hobbes thinks it important that
the laws of nature can be regarded as commands of God for practical reasons. Because religion was so important in Hobbes's time, as
evidenced by the religious wars in both England and continent, he
could not hope to persuade people to accept his view unless he
showed that it was endorsed by Scripture. Hobbes is interested in
influencing political behavior, not merely in providing a philosophical argument.

Hobbes is not being deceptive in claiming that the laws of nature can be viewed as the commands of God. He spends much time and effort to show that what he presents as the laws of nature can be found in Scripture. All of Chapter IV of *De Cive* is devoted to trying to show that this is the case. Even though there is no comparable chapter in *Leviathan*, Hobbes spends a much larger proportion of *Leviathan* discussing Scripture than he does in *De Cive*. It is quite likely that Hobbes does believe that the Scriptures put forward a guide to behavior that supports his account of the moral law. However, it is also quite clear that he thinks that the philosophical power of his arguments about the laws of nature does not depend upon their being considered as the commands of God. He starts Part III of *Leviathan*, "Of A Christian Commonwealth," with the following sentence:

> I have derived the rights of sovereign power, and the duty of sub-jects, hitherto from the principles of nature only; such as experience has found true or consent (concerning the use of words) has made so; that is to say, from the nature of men, known to us by experience, and from definitions (of such words as are essential to all political reasoning). universally agreed on. (*L*. XXXII, 1)

Then, when talking of Christian commonwealth, he continues by saying that he must make use of "supernatural revelations of the will of God."

Throughout his discussion of the laws of nature, Hobbes con-tinually warns against taking them to be anything more than the dictates of natural reason. In his reply to the fool who asserts that there is no such thing as justice, or that being just is not rational, Hobbes argues that the fool's reasoning is false, even "taking away the fear of God" (*L*. XV, 4). That is, Hobbes argues that even if there is no God, "[j]ustice, therefore, that is to say, keeping of covenant is a rule of reason by which we are forbidden to do anything destructive to our life, and consequently a law of nature" (*L*. XV, 7). If this were not clear enough, immediately after saying this, Hobbes says:

> There be some that proceed further, and will not have the law of nature to be those rules which conduce to the preservation of man's life on earth, but to the attaining of eternal felicity after death. . . . But because there is no natural knowledge of man's estate after death . . . breach of faith cannot be called a precept of reason or nature. (*L*. XV, 8)

Nowhere does Hobbes ever say that the force or power of the laws of nature depend upon their being taken as the commands of God.

Hobbes does say, in accordance with his official definition of "law" as "command . . . addressed to one formerly obliged to obey him" (*L.* XXV1, 2; see also *D.C.* XIV, 1), that the laws of nature can only be properly called laws when we consider these theorems or dictates of reason as "delivered in the name of God" (*L.* XV, 41; see also *D.C.* III, 33). However, it is not clear why anyone should take this verbal point about the proper use of the term "law" to be philosophically significant with regard to the force of the laws of nature in the state of nature. The following quote shows that Hobbes himself does not regard it as important that the laws of nature are not properly called laws in the state of nature:

> [T]he laws of nature, which consisteth in equity, justice, gratitude, and other moral virtues on these depending, in the condition of mere nature (as I have said before in the end of the 15th chapter) are not properly laws, but qualities that dispose men to peace and to obedience. When the commonwealth is once settled, then are they actually laws, and not before, as being then the commands of the commonwealth; and therefore also civil laws; for it is the sovereign power that obliges men to obey them. (*L.* XXVI, 8: see also *D.C.* XIV, 14)

It does not make any difference to Hobbes's moral theory whether the laws of nature are properly called laws because Hobbes believes that every person should follow the laws of nature simply because they are the dictates of reason. The laws of nature would gain force by being properly called "laws" only if the moral obligation to obey a law were a basic obligation, but it is not. Hobbes is clear that the obligation to obey a law depends upon the obligation to keep one's covenant, which is not only a dictate of reason and a law of nature, but also a moral law. In "Of the Liberty of Subjects" Hobbes says that there is "no obligation on any man which ariseth not from some act of his own; for all men equally are by nature free" (*L.* XXI, 10). Hobbes is so clear about this point that, even though he knew it would be used against him, he maintains that, although atheists and deists may be imprudent, they are not unjust because they never submitted their wills to God (*D.C.* XIV, 19). Further, Hobbes never says that the laws of nature do not apply to atheists and deists; on the contrary, he says, "only children and madmen are excused from offences against the law natural" (*L.* XXVII, 23). Nor are atheists and deists exempt from the civil laws when they have submitted to the sovereign. None of his arguments for the laws of nature applying to people and having the content that they do depends in any way upon there being a God or people believing in such a God. He also clearly holds that the laws of nature apply to non-Christians, for he explicitly talks about non-Christian commonwealths and never claims that they differ in any significant way from Christian commonwealths.

Distinguishing between Justice and Morality

Currently, the most common interpretation of Hobbes's moral theory is that it is a form of social contract theory, that is, morality is regarded as the result of an agreement among people about the kind of moral code that they want to govern their behavior. On this account, different societies can have different moralities, so Hobbes is sometimes interpreted as an ethical relativist, that is, as holding that different societies do indeed have different moralities. This is an improvement over earlier interpretations of Hobbes as holding that might makes right, that is, that the sovereign determines what is moral and immoral and that there is no universal standard of morality independent of the sovereign. Both of these kinds of interpretations are the result of failing to distinguish between justice and morality.

Hobbes says, "the definition of INJUSTICE is no other than *the not performance of covenant* (*L.* XV, 2). Here Hobbes is using "covenant" in an extended sense that includes making a free gift of one's right to decide about the best way to act. This is made clear by Hobbes's more careful account of how laying down a right in any way results in injustice (see *L.* XIV, 7). Hobbes also does occasionally misuse the word "just" when he should use the term "moral" to refer to a person who obeys all the laws of nature (*L.* XV, 39; *D.C.* III, 30). His occasional loose use of the terminology may be partly responsible for his being interpreted as a social contract theorist and for the confusion between justice and morality. However, Hobbes is usually quite clear that the sovereign has made no contract or covenant with (or laid down any right to) the citizens, so that he cannot be unjust, but that he can be immoral by violating the other laws of nature. Justice is only one of the moral virtues (*L.* XV, 38; *D.C.* III, 29).

I shall discuss justice in more detail in the following chapter on Hobbes's political theory, but in order to provide a clear account of his moral theory, it is necessary to distinguish between justice and the rest of morality. The law of nature dictating the practice of justice, that is, the keeping of one's covenants (in an extended sense) is central to his political theory, but justice is only one of the moral virtues that are dictated by the laws of nature. It is plausible, even though slightly misleading, to regard Hobbes as a political social contract theorist. For justice, which is the primary political virtue, or virtue of citizens, depends upon a prior giving up of one's right to decide how to act (*L*. XV, 2; see also *D.C.* III, 4).

This right can be given up by a contract between equals who agree to make a free gift of their obedience to whomever they choose to make the laws that will govern them (*L*. XIX, 1). Or, because of hope or fear, they can make a free gift of that right to someone who has sufficient power to kill them if they do not accept the laws that this person or group puts forward (*L*. XIV, 7). The former way of giving up a right results in what Hobbes calls sovereignty by institution; the latter way he calls sovereignty by acquisition (*L*. XX, 1–2). If sovereignty by institution were concerned with morality rather than with justice, it would provide some support for the interpretation of Hobbes as a moral social contract theorist. If sovereignty by acquisition were about morality rather than justice, it would provide some support for interpreting Hobbes as holding that might makes right. But Hobbes distinguishes between justice and the rest of morality; justice is the only moral virtue that depends upon one's giving up one's right to decide how to act.

Hobbes does say that in the state of nature there is no place for justice (*L*. XIII, 14), but he never says that in the state of nature there is no place for morality. On the contrary, he insists that the moral virtues, which the laws of nature dictate, is eternal: "For *pride, ingratitude, breach of contract, (or injury), inhumanity, contumely* will never be lawful, nor the contrary virtues to these ever unlawful, as we take them for dispositions of the mind, that is, as they are considered in the court of conscience, where only they oblige and are laws" (*D.C.* III, 29; see also *L*. XV, 38). Hobbes claims that even in the state of nature we should always want to act morally and should always act morally when we can do so safely (*L*. XV, 36; *D.C.* III, 27). He is explicit that "there are certain natural laws, whose exercise ceaseth not even in the time of war itself. For I cannot understand what drunkenness or cruelty, that is, revenge which respects not the future good, can advance toward peace, or the preservation of any man" (*D.C.* III, 27, n.). Although he admits, "that by nature, that is, by reason, men are [not] obliged to the exercise of all these laws in that state of men wherein they are not practiced by others", he continues: "We are obliged yet, in the interim, to a readiness of mind to observe them, whensoever their observation shall seem to conduce to the end for which they were ordained" (*D.C.* III, 27; see also *L.* XV, 36).

Because Hobbes devotes so much space to discussing the law of nature dictating justice, many have taken his discussion of justice to be central to his discussion of morality. His arguments for obeying the civil law are so powerful that it is easy to think that he regards morality as consisting simply in obedience to the civil law. Hobbes does regard obeying the law, which is required by justice, as the primary moral virtue of citizens. But the very next law of nature that he discusses is the one that dictates the virtue of gratitude. Gratitude is the primary moral virtue of those in government. Morality requires them to act in such a way that the citizens will not repent that they have given up their right to decide how to act to the government. Gratitude is a moral virtue for the same reason that justice is; it is a trait of character that everyone calls good because it is conducive to the preservation of all. Every moral virtue that Hobbes says is dictated by the laws of nature, e.g., justice, gratitude, modesty, equity, and mercy, has the same justification; all people call them good because by leading to peace they are conducive to the preservation of all. My examination of each of the laws of nature that dictates a moral virtue will show how Hobbes can go from the rationality of preserving oneself to genuine moral virtues.

Examination of each of the Laws of Nature that Dictates a Moral Virtue

Peace-loving

The fundamental law of nature in both *De Cive* and *Leviathan* is "to seek peace and follow it" (*L.* XIV, 4). But in *De Cive* this law is stated as part of a more general dictate of reason to seek peace or to defend oneself, whereas in *Leviathan* it is derived from that more general dictate. This may be the reason that "seek peace" is not listed as one of the special laws of nature in *De Cive*. An understanding of this law, and the virtue that it dictates, makes it easier to understand all of the other laws of nature that dictate moral virtues. For Hobbes, a peace-loving person is not a pacifist, one who refuses to fight no matter what. Rather, a peace-loving person does whatever he can do to bring about and maintain peace, but when peace cannot be achieved, he is prepared to "use all helps and advantages of war" (*L.* XIV, 4; see also *D.C.* II, 2). All persons should be trained to be peace-loving, because this fundamental moral virtue is never in conflict with the natural and rational desire to preserve one's life.

"Dispositions, when they are so strengthened by habit that they beget their actions with ease and with reason unresisting, are called *manners*. Moreover, manners, if they be good, are called *virtues*, if evil, *vices*" (*D.H.* XIII, 8). Although Hobbes does not name the virtue dictated by this first law of nature, it seems appropriate to call it the virtue of being peace-loving. Having this virtue involves endeavoring to seek peace at all times that one can do so safely. In Chapter XIII of *De Homine*, Hobbes points out the various sources of the dispositions, that is, the ways in which dispositions are formed. One of the most important sources is education:

> Whence it must be understood, not only how much fathers, teachers, and tutors of youth must imbue the minds of youths with precepts which are good and true, but also how much they must bear themselves justly and in a righteous manner in their presence, for the dispositions of youths are not less, but much more disposed to bad habits by example than they are to good ones by precept. (*D.H.* XIII, 8)

Hobbes is pointing out that the virtues can be inculcated. But, being Hobbes, he also points out that bad dispositions can be inculcated: "Therefore among all peoples' religion and doctrine, which everyone has been taught from their early years, so shackle them forever that they hate and revile dissenters: . . . The dispositions of these men is not suited to peace and society" (*D.H.* XIII, 3). Hobbes's moral theory depends on the fact that not only can people be trained to act in a wide variety of ways, but also that they can be trained to feel like acting in these ways, that is, their attitude, emotions, and desires can be trained. People can be trained to have certain dispositions, that is, to have either virtues or vices.

Interpreting Hobbes as holding psychological egoism makes it impossible to come up with even a plausible account of his moral theory. As we have shown, even though Hobbes holds that avoiding death is a rational goal, and acting contrary to it is irrational, he acknowledges that not everyone actually takes avoiding death as their primary goal. Hobbes is trying to persuade people to seek peace. Training people to be peace-loving is inculcating a moral virtue; it is a virtue because it is a disposition or manner that tends to a person's preservation; it is a moral virtue because it is praised by all people because it leads to the preservation of all. It is, in fact, the fundamental moral virtue, one that, as Hobbes describes it, is always rational to want to act on. Seeking peace, as Hobbes understands it, is not in conflict with the primary goal of reason, self-preservation; on the contrary seeking peace is a dictate of reason because it is necessary for long-term preservation.

Humility

Hobbes then says:

> From this fundamental law of nature, by which men are commanded to endeavour peace, is derived this second law of nature: that a man be willing when others are so too, as far-forth as for peace and defence of himself he shall think necessary, to lay down this right to all things, and be contented with so much liberty against other men, as he would allow other men against himself. (*L*. XIV, 5; see also *D.C.* II, 3)

This virtue involves acknowledging that without peace, "there can be no security to any man (how strong or wise soever he be) of living out the time which nature ordinarily alloweth men to live" (*L*. XIV, 4). Hobbes does not name the virtue dictated by this law, so I call it "humility." As I understand humility, it does not involve thinking of oneself as inferior to others; rather, it requires recognizing that one has the same limitations as all other persons. It involves acknowledging that, like everyone else, one is vulnerable and can be killed by other men, so it involves the realization that one is dependent upon peace in the same way as everyone else. Because being vulnerable is so important, I regard humility as ruling out thinking of oneself as superior to others in any fundamental way.

Hobbes's statement of this law of nature in *Leviathan* is better than his statement in *De Cive*, for in *Leviathan* he adds to his statement that a person must give up his right to all things, that "he be contented with so much liberty against other men, as he would allow other men against himself" (*L*. XIV, 5). This requirement that one be impartial is not explicitly incorporated into a statement of the law in *De Cive*. With the explicit inclusion requiring equality or impartiality, this law of nature seems to make the laws of nature condemning pride and arrogance redundant. And perhaps it does. But Hobbes is not overly concerned with avoiding redundancy; he is far more concerned with stressing the points that he regards as most important. His explicit inclusion in *Leviathan* that all persons must be willing to give up all the rights they want others to give up, even though he already has laws of nature condemning pride and arrogance, shows how important he takes equality or impartiality to be to his moral theory. His lack of concern about redundancy is also shown by his support of this particular law, by quoting, "the law of the Gospel, 'whatsoever you require that others should do to you, that do ye to them,'" and the negative version in Latin (*L.* XIV, 5), and then summarizing all of the laws of nature concerning the moral virtues in terms of the negative version of the Golden Rule: "Do not that to another, which thou wouldst not have done to thyself" (*L.* XV, 35; see also *D.C.* III, 26).

Although Hobbes is not original in recognizing that impartiality is an essential feature of morality, he may be original in providing an argument to show why this is so. His argument for claiming that humility or impartiality is a moral virtue starts with his claim that no person, no matter "how strong or wise soever he be," can expect to survive for long in the state of nature. Thus, humility (or impartiality) is a character trait that, by tending to peace, tends to the preservation of the person who has it. Because long-term survival is the primary goal of all rational persons, they all have a reason of equal weight to give up whatever rights they expect anyone else to give up. No rational person is prepared to allow any particular person to retain some right that this person would not allow all others to retain. Once this is recognized, each person must be prepared to give up his right to all things and "be contented with so much liberty against other men, as he would allow other men against himself." Failure to be impartial or to acknowledge the fundamental equality of persons makes it impossible to form a society, and so it is against the fundamental law of nature that requires that one seek peace. Thus the character trait of humility is a virtue because it tends to the preservation of the person with the trait by leading to peace. It is a moral virtue because, by leading to peace, it tends to the preservation of everyone and so is praised by everyone.

Hobbes's dramatic description of life in the state of nature has more than rhetorical force. It is not only designed to deter people from civil war, which will lead back to the state of nature, but also serves to support his claim that reason dictates that everyone give up as much of his right of nature as he wants every- one else to give up. Every human being is vulnerable and fallible, and no one can expect to live very long in a state of nature. So in order to attain peace, everyone must be prepared to give up as much of his right of nature as he wants others to give up. Once this essential equality of human beings is established, Hobbes uses it in arguing for all of the laws of nature. Thus equality (or humility or impartiality) becomes central to Hobbes's concept of morality. All of the moral virtues are character traits that lead to peace and hence to the preservation of everyone, including the person who has the trait. There is nothing objectionably egoistic about this argument; it simply shows that being moral, that is, having the moral virtues, benefits the person who has those virtues. Hobbes uses this argument to justify and support morality. What he is attempting to do with regard to this particular law of nature is to show how humility (or impartiality) is a character trait that, by being necessary for peace, has the characteristic that all moral virtues have.

Justice

The next of law of nature dictates "that men perform their cove- nants made" (*L.* XV, 1; see also *D.C.* III, 1). but it is important to keep in mind that Hobbes is using "covenant" here in an extended sense to include all giving up or transferring of a right. Hobbes says, "in this law of nature consisteth the fountain and original of JUSTICE" (*L.* XV, 2). Justice is the primary virtue of citizens, for it is the virtue that requires obeying the law. Hobbes says many differ- ent things about justice, but there is no doubt that the fundamental sense of justice is that which is related to the keeping of covenants, "the definition of INJUSTICE, is no other than *the not performance of covenant.* And whatsoever is not unjust is *just*" (*L.* XV, 2; see also *D.C.* III, 5).

This definition, which defines what is just in terms of what is not unjust, allows for an ambiguity in the term "just," which Hobbes sometimes exploits. Although the paradigm case of a just person is one who performs his covenants, his definition allows that any action of a person who has not made a covenant is a just action. It is only in this non-paradigm sense that all of the actions of God and the sovereign are just. For citizens, however, it is the paradigm sense of justice, keeping one's covenants, that applies:

> But when the words are applied to persons, *to be just* signifies as
> much as to be delighted in just dealing, to study how to do righteous-
> ness, or to endeavour in all things to do that which is just; and *to be
> unjust* is to neglect righteous dealing, or to think it is to be measured
> not according to my contract, but some present benefit. (*D.C.* III, 5;
> see also *L.* XV, 10)

Although one might call the virtue that Hobbes calls justice, fidelity or trustworthiness (Hobbes describes this law of nature as
"keeping trust" in *De Cive*, III, 1), there is no doubt that it is a traditional moral virtue. Further, there is no question that Hobbes
describes it absolutely correctly. In his argument with the fool that
justice is not contrary to reason, Hobbes does not change or modify
his account of justice at all. Rather, he tries to show that, given the
nature of human beings, the disposition to keep one's covenants is
more likely to lead to one's survival than the disposition to act for
one's personal benefit without regard to one's covenants. He offers
two arguments against the fool's claim that justice is not a virtue.
The first argument depends not only on human beings' vulnerability, but also on their fallibility: "[F]irst that when a man doth a thing
which, notwithstanding anything can be foreseen and reckoned on,
tendeth to his own destruction (howsoever some accident he could
not expect, arriving, may turn it to his benefit), yet such events do
not make it reasonably or wisely done" (*L.* XV, 5). Hobbes is arguing
that breaking of covenants generally has bad consequences, so that
even if, in a particular case, breaking a covenant turns out to have
a beneficial result, this cannot be counted on. Since Hobbes is
arguing for the rationality of having a character trait, that is, a disposition to keep one's covenants, this is a strong argument.

Hobbes's second argument against the fool's view starts by
pointing out that "no man can hope by his own strength or wit to
defend himself from destruction without the help of confederates"
(*L.* XV, 5). He then points out that a person who breaks his covenants "cannot be received into any society that unite themselves for
peace and defence but by the error of them that receive him; nor
when he is received, be retained in it without seeing the dangers of
their error; which errors a man cannot reasonably reckon on as the
means of his security." He then concludes that the unjust man has
acted "against the reason of his preservation, and so as all men that
contribute not to his destruction forbear him only out of ignorance
of what is good for themselves." Here Hobbes is making the specific
point that an unjust man can get away with being unjust only if

others don't realize their error in allowing him to live among them; and the unjust person cannot reasonably expect that all people will make this kind of error. When talking about the disposition to keep covenants, or to obey the law, this argument has far more force than an argument against a one-time act of breaking a covenant.

When talking about the virtue of justice, Hobbes is talking about a genuine moral virtue and not some prudential substitute for it. The following passage makes this clear:

> That which gives to human action the relish of justice, is a certain nobleness or gallantness of courage, rarely found, by which a man scorns to be beholden for the contentment of his life, to fraud, or breach of promise. This justice of the manners, is that which is meant, where justice is called a virtue; and injustice a vice. (*L*. XV, 10)

Far from holding that fear of punishment is a proper motive for justice, Hobbes explicitly says: "But that man is to be accounted just, who doth just things because the law commands it, unjust things only by reason of his infirmity; and he is properly said to be unjust, who doth righteousness for fear of the punishment annexed unto the law" (*D.C.* III, 5). In this passage, Hobbes seems to be regarding a just man as one who has a disposition to obey the law because it is the law. But when he is more careful, he is clear that the just man obeys the law because he has obliged oneself to obey the law by laying down his right of nature to decide how to act (see *D.C.* XIV, 2, n.).

Hobbes regards justice, that is, the keeping of one's covenants, as the most important moral virtue of citizens because this virtue requires people to obey the law. That citizens have the disposition to obey the laws is necessary for there to be a stable state, and a stable state is necessary for long-term peace. As noted at the beginning of the discussion of justice, when Hobbes talks about justice as the disposition to keep one's covenants, he does not mean by "covenant" only a mutual transfer of right, but an extended sense of "covenant" that includes any way of laying down one's right. Hobbes holds that the obligation to obey the law is based on the obligation not to do what one has given away the right to do, either as the result of a mutual transfer of right, or as a result of a free-gift of one's right. Hobbes says:

> And when a man hath in either manner abandoned or granted away his right, then he is said to be OBLIGED or BOUND not to hinder those to whom such right is granted or abandoned from the benefit of it;

and [it is said] that he *ought*, and it is his Duty, not to make void that voluntary act of his own, and that such hindrance is Injustice, and Injury, as being *sine jure* [without right], the right being before renounced or transferred. (*L*. XIV, 7)

Failure to realize that Hobbes is using "covenant" in this extended sense partly explains why he is interpreted as holding a social contract theory of justice.

As will become evident in the discussion of the next law of nature, that dictating gratitude, Hobbes denies that the sovereign enters into a contract or covenant with the citizens. This is not a minor matter, because for Hobbes it is important that the sovereign has not made any contract or covenant with the citizens, for otherwise the sovereign might be guilty of injustice and thus subject to punishment. Rather, in both sovereignty by institution and sovereignty by acquisition, the sovereign has the same authority, for in both the citizen makes a free gift of his obedience to the sovereign: "And in this kind of dominion or sovereignty [sovereignty by acquisition] differeth from sovereignty by institution only in this, that men who choose their sovereign do it for fear of one another, and not of him whom they institute; but in this case they subject themselves to him they are afraid of" (*L*. XX, 2; see also *D.C*. VIII, 1). In both cases, the sovereign is a recipient of a free-gift of obedience, and this free-gift is what creates their obligation to obey the law. It is therefore misleading to describe Hobbes's theory of justice as based on a contract or covenant in his standard definitions of these terms. Doing so creates unnecessary problems for his political theory. It is also interesting, although seldom commented upon, that the virtue of justice is the only moral virtue that applies only to citizens and not at all to the sovereign.

Gratitude

Hobbes's formulation of the law of nature dictating gratitude is, "that a man which receiveth benefit from another of mere grace, endeavour that he which giveth it, have no reasonable cause to repent him of his good will" (*L*. XV, 16; see also *D.C*. III, 8). Hobbes's account of gratitude is extremely good, for it avoids talk about a debt of gratitude that must be repaid (I am grateful to Claudia Card to calling this to my attention). One of the nice features of this definition is that it counts having a friendly attitude to one's benefactor, or sharing with the benefactor the joy one has received from the gift, as showing gratitude. It also makes a proper amount of thanks an expression of gratitude, but not an excessive thanking that would be repugnant to most benefactors.

Like his account of justice, Hobbes's account of gratitude keeps it as a genuine virtue, not some prudential substitute. Gratitude is not endeavoring to act so as to receive future gifts; it is endeavoring to act so that one's benefactor will "have no reasonable cause to repent him of his good will." He argues for this law of nature by pointing that, without gratitude, "there will be no beginning of benevolence or trust; nor, consequently, of mutual help, nor of reconciliation of one man to another" (*L.* XV, 16; see also *D.C.* III, 8). Although gratitude is a genuine virtue, it is not clear why Hobbes lists it right after justice and before the laws condemning pride and arrogance. If Hobbes held that citizens should obey the law out of gratitude for the benefits of citizenship, this might explain why he gives the law of nature dictating gratitude such a prominent place. However, Hobbes holds that it is justice that obliges citizens to obey the law; he never claims that gratitude is a virtue related to obeying the law.

It does not seem now, nor is there any reason to think it was true in Hobbes's time, that gratitude is one of the major virtues, thus some effort must be made to explain why Hobbes gives gratitude such prominence. A clue to what makes gratitude important to Hobbes comes from his statement that ingratitude "hath the same relationship to grace, that injustice hath to obligation by covenant" (*L.* XV, 16). Hobbes explains what he means by "grace" in the following passage: "When the transferring of right is not mutual, but one of the parties transferreth in hope to gain thereby friendship or service from another . . . this is not contract, but GIFT, FREE-GIFT, GRACE, which words signify one and the same thing" (*L.* XIV, 12). The question that needs to be answered, therefore, is what role do free-gift or grace have in Hobbes's political theory, for Hobbes is more concerned with political theory than with moral theory, as can be seen by the amount of space that he devotes to each.

It is interesting, although I am not sure how important, that Hobbes's account of free-gift or grace has some unusual consequences when considering the relationship between human beings and God. In Hobbes's account of grace, one of the reasons he offers for transferring one's right is "hope of reward in heaven" (*L.* XIV, 12). However, he denies that we can oblige ourselves by free-gift to God, except under very special circumstances that no longer obtain, because he wants to eliminate any pretext for disobeying the civil or natural law (see *L.* XIV, 23, and *D.C.* II, 12–13). Were it to be granted that a person can transfer his right to God by free-gift, then we would have human beings giving grace to God – a reversal of what is regarded as the standard relationship. It is not surprising that, although Hobbes did believe in God, he did not have a traditional view and his writings did not please those holding standard religious views.

The importance of free-gift will be discussed in detail in the next chapter on Hobbes's political theory, but, as mentioned in the discussion of justice, Hobbes regards the formation of a state as depending not on a covenant between the future citizens and their sovereign, but on a free-gift of their right of nature to the sovereign. So the law of nature concerning gratitude applies primarily to the sovereign. Reason dictates that the sovereign endeavor that the citizens have no reasonable cause to repent them of their free-gift of obedience to his commands. Concentration on the virtue of justice leads to the view that Hobbes's moral theory is concerned with showing that reason dictates those moral virtues that are primarily virtues of ordinary citizens. However, apart from the moral virtues of justice, usefulness, or complaisance, and that virtue which corresponds to the vice of contumely, most of the moral virtues dictated by the laws of nature seem to be primarily addressed to the sovereign, or to members of the government, or to the privileged members of the state. This should not be surprising, for moral suasion is the only tool that Hobbes has for persuading the sovereign to be moral.

Complaisance or considerateness

Hobbes's statement of this law of nature is not completely clear. In *Leviathan* the law requires *"that every man strive to accommodate himself to the rest"* (*L.* XV, 17), whereas in *De Cive* it requires *"that every man render himself useful unto others"* (*D.C.* III, 9). This lack of clarity is also shown by the many different words he uses to describe the associated virtue and its contrary vice. In *Leviathan*, he says: "The observers of this law, may be called Sociable, the Latins call them *commodi*; the contrary, *stubborn, insociable, froward, intractable*" (*L.* XV, 17). In *De Cive*, he calls the virtue usefulness, and says, "[b]ut he that breaks this law may be called *useless* and troublesome. Yet Cicero opposeth *inhumanity* to this *usefulness*, as having regard to this very law" (*D.C.* III, 9). However, his discussion of the law is remarkably similar in both *De Cive* and *Leviathan*, and a very familiar but different virtue and vice seem to suggest themselves.

He begins by using the analogy of a stone that is "not fit for use" because "in regard of its sharp and angular form [it] takes up more room from other stones than it fills up itself, neither because of the hardness of its matter cannot well be pressed together, or easily cut" (*D.C.* III, 9; see also *L.* XV, 17). Then he compares this stone with "a man, for the harshness of his disposition in retaining superfluities for himself, and detaining the necessaries from others" (*D.C.* III, 9; see also *L.* XV, 17). These comments make it clear that not distinguishing acting in self-interest from acting for self-preservation results in a distortion of Hobbes's moral philosophy. By his comments on this law of nature, Hobbes makes clear that it dictates to the wealthy that they consider the plight of the poor and act accordingly. A common name for a rich person who does not consider the plight of the poor is "inconsiderate" and a common name for the corresponding virtue would be "considerateness."

It is certainly a moral virtue for those with what Hobbes calls "superfluities" to use them to help those who do not have enough to maintain an adequate standard of living. Hobbes would probably claim that those wealthy persons who oppose higher taxes on themselves to provide welfare for the poor are *insociable* or, as I say, inconsiderate. Claiming that reason dictates being more concerned with aiding those who need help than with maintaining a luxurious lifestyle is a strong argument for such concern. If self-interest is taken to include amassing great wealth at the expense of the poor, then Hobbes claims that self-interest is not rational. His claim is that being disposed to help those who need help when one can do so is a moral virtue, and failing to be disposed to do so is a moral vice. This shows that, for Hobbes, what is a moral virtue depends directly on its tendency to promote peace and only indirectly on its tendency to promote the preservation of the person with the virtue. The moral virtue of considerateness, if it is widespread, increases the cohesiveness of the society, and thus benefits all of the citizens. Whatever the best name for the virtue, it is clear that a person who has the disposition to follow this law has what Hobbes and we agree is a moral virtue.

Facility to pardon or mercy

Hobbes states the next law of nature as, "that upon caution of the future time, a man ought to pardon the offences past of them that repenting, desire it" (*L.* XV, 18; see also *D.C.* III, 10). This virtue, which Hobbes calls having the facility to pardon, one can also call being forgiving, as long as one remembers that it is only a virtue to forgive those who truly repent. The contrary vice can be called being unforgiving or vindictive. Although Hobbes does not use the word "mercy" in his discussion of this law, in his brief summary of the contents of each of the sections of Chapter III in *De Cive*, he says that this law is about mercy. Even though there is no law in *Leviathan* explicitly said to be about mercy, in his list of the moral virtues in both *De Cive* and *Leviathan*, mercy is included (see *L.* XV, 40; see also *D.C.* III, 31). Hobbes's account of mercy is what is meant when we talk about showing mercy to an enemy or a sinner. It is according to this sense of mercy that God is sometimes said to show mercy to those who have truly repented. In this sense it is inappropriate to talk of mercy being shown except to those who have sinned, or who have been an enemy. Also, mercy can only be shown by someone who has it in his power to inflict some evil on the sinner or enemy and does not do so. Given that Hobbes provides an accurate account of mercy in this sense, it is interesting that it is a virtue that can only be had by those with power. It does not mean the same as compassion. Mercy does not involve relieving an evil; it means not inflicting an evil when one has the power or authority to do so.

On Hobbes's account of mercy, it is a disposition to forgive all those who genuinely repent. Saying that justice should be tempered with mercy means that those in power should not inflict evil when they have the power or authority to inflict it, but rather show mercy to those who repent. A conqueror also should show mercy to an enemy when the enemy submits and promises to obey him. As suggested by the previous sentences, mercy is properly characterized as refraining from inflicting evil by those who have the power or authority to inflict it – those in government, not ordinary citizens. Hobbes claims that a law of nature requires the practice of mercy, and failing to show mercy is to be vindictive, which is a moral vice. This law of nature is not directed primarily to ordinary citizens, but to sovereigns. Of course, sovereigns have the right to decide whether the repentance is sincere, so they are required to show mercy only when there is no danger in doing so. However, it is clear that this virtue, though more limited in scope than one might have thought, is still a genuine moral virtue, not some prudential substitute.

Against cruelty

The next law of nature is, "that in revenges (that is retribution of evil for evil), men not look at the greatness of the evil past, but the greatness of the good to follow" (*L.* XV, 19). In *De Cive* he states the law as follows: "that in revenge and punishments we must have our eye not at the evil past, but the future good" *D.C.* III, 11). By formulating this law in this way, Hobbes seems to be acknowledging that it is not part of what we mean by punishment, that it serve some useful purpose. This contrasts with his definition of punishment given in a later chapter, where he includes in the definition that its end is "that the will of men thereby the better be disposed to obedience" (*L.* XXVII, 1). It may be that once Hobbes has shown that reason requires punishment to be practiced not with regard to "the greatness of the evil past, but the greatness of the good to follow," he incorporates this into his definition. This law of nature condemns those who practice a retributivist account of punishment. Basing punishments on the greatness of the evil past and not on the good to come is not only irrational, but also immoral.

This law of nature, like the previous one, is primarily directed to those with power; either those with the authority to punish or to victors in a war. With regard to civil wars, these two laws show that Hobbes is clearly in favor of amnesty for those who agree to accept the victor as their sovereign. These laws show how completely and consistently Hobbes has kept his attention on the end to be achieved: peace and civil harmony. No matter what a person has done, no matter how outraged one might be by it, if no good is to be achieved by inflicting harm on a person, it should not be done. Revenge, or punishment, "without respect to the example, and profit to come, is a triumph, or glorying in the hurt of another, tending to no end (for the end is always somewhat to come), and glorying to no end, is vain-glory, and contrary to reason" (*L.* XV, 19).

Hobbes is completely correct in regarding the disposition to hurt a person other than to prevent some future evil as cruelty. To favor such hurting of another on the basis of some philosophical argument, e.g., Kantian or Hegelian, is simply to disguise one's cruelty. Hobbes would clearly have favored the Truth and Reconciliation law enacted in South Africa, whereby the majority blacks who finally took over power did not exact punishment on the minority whites who had treated them so badly. Those in the Middle East, who, partly for religious reasons, take revenge by killing others, sometimes even engaging in suicide-bombing, are simply extreme examples of cruelty begetting further cruelty with no end in sight. Hobbes is right in regarding such cruelty as irrational as well as being a moral vice. Having a disposition to exact revenge regardless of the consequences is clearly contrary to peace and hence to one's preservation.

Against contumely or disrespect

This law of nature dictates, *"that no man, either by deeds or words, countenance or laughter, do declare himself to hate or scorn another"* (D.C. III, 12; see also *L*. XV, 20). This vice may have been more serious in times when people took codes of honor more seriously, when insults resulted in duels, etc., but the emergence of the concept of "disrespect," and the serious consequences that it can provoke, shows that what Hobbes says is still relevant. Hobbes maintains that, without as much exaggeration as one might think, "all signs of hatred, or contempt, provoke to fight; insomuch as most men choose rather to hazard their life, than not to be revenged" (*L*. XV, 20; see also *D.C*. III, 12). In *De Cive*, Hobbes offers as examples of violation of this law, "the scoff and jeers of the powerful against the weak, and namely, of judges against guilty persons, which neither relate to the offence of the guilty, nor the duty of judges" (*D.C*. III, 12). This comment shows that this law, like the previous two, is directed primarily to those in power, and not to ordinary citizens. Nonetheless, it has sufficient generality to apply to all, and so having a disposition to violate this law is to have a moral vice.

Being respectful of other persons, having the disposition to avoid declaring hatred or contempt of another by deed, word, countenance, or gesture, is a moral virtue, and having the disposition to declare hatred or contempt of another by deed, word, countenance, or gesture is clearly a moral vice. This virtue, which I would call "being respectful," involves treating everyone respectfully, refraining from insulting anyone, including those guilty of some crime. The vice associated with this virtue we would now call "disrespectful." This moral virtue, like all the moral virtues dictated by the laws of nature, is not designed to serve the interests of the virtuous person, except by making peace more likely and society more stable.

Hobbes realizes that their emotions will prevent most people from acquiring the moral virtues even if they know that it is rational to have them. This law of nature, like the three preceding it, requires controlling those emotions that many people feel towards their enemies. In *De Homine*, Hobbes says of the emotions: "They are called perturbations because they frequently obstruct right reasoning. They obstruct right reasoning in this, that they militate against the real good and in favor of the apparent and most immediate good, which turns out frequently to be evil when everything associated with it hath been considered" (*D.H.* XII, 1). Hobbes is aware "that hope, fear, anger, ambition, covetousness, vain glory, and other perturbations of the mind, do hinder a person to the knowledge of these laws whilst those passions prevail in him" (*D.C.* III, 26; see also *L.* XV, 35). The real good, which reason seeks, is long-term preservation, and this requires that the emotions that conflict with gaining this real good be controlled. This law of nature makes clear that both reason and morality dictate that one should control these emotions and act in a respectful way toward all, even toward criminals and enemies.

Against pride

The law, "*that every man acknowledge another for his equal by nature*" (*L.* XV, 21; see also *D.C.* III, 13), is the first of three laws primarily concerned with equality. They are also the last three laws that command the practice of a moral virtue, the remainder being concerned with procedures, especially the practice of judges and arbiters. This concern with equality or impartiality also manifests itself in Hobbes's summary of the laws of nature dictating the virtues by summarizing them by means of the negative version of the Golden Rule: "*Do not that to another, which thou wouldst not have done to thy self*" (*L.* XV, 35; see also *D.C.* III, 26). One might have thought that Hobbes would have given this law more prominence, for pride is the passion he explicitly cites when talking about the passions of man that "compelled him to submit himself to government, together with the great power of his governor, whom I compared to *Leviathan*, taking that comparison out the two last verses of the one and fortieth of Job, [Job 41: 33–4; Revised Standard Version], where God, having set forth the great power of the *Leviathan*, calleth him King of the Proud" (*L.* XXVIII, 27).

Picking *Leviathan* as the title for his work strongly suggests that Hobbes regards the vice of pride as the vice that is primarily responsible for the requirement that the sovereign have the almost absolute power that Hobbes assigns to him. Hobbes calls the virtue corresponding to the vice of pride "modesty." This law of nature, even more clearly than any of the preceding laws, is about a character trait or disposition to behave and not about particular acts. Modesty does not require us to perform any particular act or even a kind of act, nor does pride prohibit any specific kind of act. On the contrary, the kind of act this law prohibits is one that manifests the moral vice of pride.

Many commentators are bothered by Hobbes's argument that in the state of nature people are equal because "the weakest has strength enough to kill the strongest, either by secret machination, or by confederacy with others" (*L.* XIII, 1; see also *D.C.* I, 3). But Hobbes does not base this law solely on the equal vulnerability of people; rather, he also uses the fact that people believe that they are equal: "If nature therefore hath made men equal, that equality is to be acknowledged: or if nature hath made men unequal; yet because men that think themselves equal, will not enter into conditions of peace, but upon equal terms, such equality must be admitted" (ibid.). This is not an argument that requires all people to be equally vulnerable; it only requires that everyone be vulnerable enough that they cannot count on surviving in the state of nature. Understanding that Hobbes's argument for equality requires only that no one can count on surviving in the state of nature makes it much stronger. So his argument that everyone be considered equal does not really depend on factual equality. Once one has granted that no person can count on surviving in the state of nature, if people cannot get out of the state of nature except by acknowledging the equality of others, then rationality requires acknowledging equality.

Hobbes uses the law of nature prohibiting the vice of pride in order to attack Aristotle's view "that some men by nature are made worthy to command, others only to serve" (*D.C.* III, 13; see also *L.* XV, 21). He is aware that this argument has as a consequence that men have no natural superiority over women. He completely accepts this conclusion, claiming that by nature men and women must be considered equal, and explaining that men are usually given dominion "because for the most part commonwealths have been erected by the fathers, not the mothers of families" (*L.* XX, 4; see also *D.C.* IX, 3). Hobbes also realizes that it would not escape the defenders of the monarchy that his argument completely denies the divine right of kings. But with his characteristic honesty, he accepts this conclusion even though he knows that it is likely to antagonize those on whom he depends for support. Hobbes's definition of pride as a moral vice also makes racism and other attempts to found unequal treatment on natural grounds moral vices. Pride, taken as a moral vice, remains exactly what it always was: regarding oneself as better than others in a way that is not conducive to social harmony.

Some commentators are troubled that basing equality on vulnerability has the result that, if a being were invulnerable, reason would not require her to acknowledge anyone as her equal. However, all people are vulnerable, so Hobbes has not exempted any human being from the rational requirement to avoid the vice of pride. If there were a completely invulnerable being, on the other hand, she would not be irrational to be proud, for she would not need peace or a stable society. Indeed, for such a being, reason would not dictate that she follow any of the laws of nature. Hobbes is aware of this consequence, and far from it bothering him, he uses it as part of his argument to show that God, being invulnerable, is not subject to the laws of nature. Morality is rationally required only for beings who are vulnerable to being harmed by others. This is not a defect of Hobbes's justification of morality, for Hobbes correctly regards morality as applying only to vulnerable beings. He also correctly holds that it is irrational for any human being to believe that she is not vulnerable. But he also correctly holds that reason allows an invulnerable being either to obey or to not obey the laws of nature. Hobbes's argument provides a way for God not to be subject to the laws of nature and yet for God to choose freely to have the moral virtues.

Against arrogance

Hobbes states this law as follows: "[T]hat at the entrance unto the conditions of peace, no man require to reserve to himself any right which he is not content should be reserved to every one of the rest" (*L.* XV, 22; see also *D.C.* III, 14). This law is merely a restatement of the second law in *Leviathan* requiring that one give up the right to all things, which Hobbes had revised from *De Cive* by adding "and be contented with so much liberty against other men, as he would allow other men against himself (*L.* XIV, 5). As mentioned earlier, this revision shows Hobbes's increasing concern with equality or impartiality. Keeping this unmodified law condemning arrogance shows that Hobbes is not concerned about redundancy in his statement of the laws of nature. His point is to show that it is rational to avoid the traditional moral vices and to have the traditional moral virtues. Indeed, Hobbes sometimes uses the same term "modest" to refer to the moral virtue dictated by both this law and the previous one.

Hobbes is one of the first and most consistent advocates of the universal equality of all those who are capable of entering into covenants. Whereas the previous law requires that one not regard oneself as better than others, the present law requires that one not demand more rights for oneself than one grants to others. Because Hobbes says that those who have this vice have "a desire of more than their share" (*L.* XV, 22), he might call the corresponding virtue, "fairness." Indeed, this law seems to be a source for Rawls's first principle of justice in *A Theory of Justice*, that everyone have as much liberty as is compatible with a like liberty for all. Hobbes does not argue for maximizing liberty, although he does say, "Unnecessary laws are not good laws" (*L.* XXX, 21; see also *D.C.* XIII, 15).

This law of nature and the next one concerning equity are additional specifications of the requirements of impartiality. This law requires impartiality between oneself and all others; the next law requires impartiality between all those whom one is called upon to judge. The virtue of fairness, or lack of arrogance, is the disposition not to claim any right for oneself that one is not prepared to allow others to have, i.e., to regard oneself as subject to the same laws and constraints as others. It is therefore incredible that any commentator would ever accuse Hobbes of turning all the moral virtues into prudential ones. Hobbes's account of the vice of arrogance absolutely rules out making any special exceptions for oneself. Anyone who claims that the corresponding virtue is not a moral virtue, but only a prudential one, clearly misunderstands the nature of moral virtue. For Hobbes, the benefit of the moral virtue to the person with it is that it leads to peace, but this benefits him no more than it benefits everyone else. The prudential value of the moral virtues depends upon their moral value, that is, it is because they lead to peace that all men praise these virtues, and it is in their leading to peace that they have prudential value.

Hobbes claims that the law of nature condemning arrogance simply follows from the previous law; if everyone is acknowledged as equal, no one has grounds for reserving any rights not granted to all others. More directly, a disposition to claim special rights for oneself clearly leads to civil discord. The problems caused by the actions of arrogant people, whether this arrogance is based on one's religious beliefs or on some other ideology, moral or political, are too obvious to need detailed support. Arrogance, which includes the disposition to regard oneself as allowed to break the law in circumstances where one would not allow others to do so, is a dangerous vice. It is clearly seen as a moral vice by those on the political left when exhibited by those on the political right, and vice versa. That they do not see it as a moral vice when it is exhibited by those whose political views they share is an example of how one's emotions and ideology can overwhelm one's reason. Hobbes's account of arrogance shows it to be a genuine moral vice.

Equity

The law of nature requiring equity is the final law of nature that prescribes a moral virtue. It says: "[I]f *a man is trusted to judge between man and man*, it is a precept of the law of nature that *he deal equally between them*" (*L.* XV, 23; see also *D.C.* III, 15). This law, like several of the previous laws, applies only to people who are in a certain role, viz., judges, rather than to all people. Hobbes usually simply includes equity in his list of moral virtues without giving it any special place (see *L.* XV, 40, and *D.C.* III, 31). The corresponding vice, Hobbes calls "acception of persons" (*L.* XV, 24), but it could easily be called "unfairness." In *De Homine* Hobbes sometimes seems to equate equity with justice, but usually equity has no special role in his list of virtues (see *D.H.* XIII, 9). Moreover, this law seems to be a transition from talking about moral virtues to talking about political procedures. The next law of nature, which dictates a procedure concerning things that cannot be divided equally, does not have any virtue related to it.

The virtue of equity sometimes seems to be given a special status because it is taken to be equivalent to impartiality, which is involved in most of the laws of nature that dictate moral virtues. However, as indicated in the discussion of arrogance, impartiality is not limited to a judge deciding between others; impartiality also requires that one not make special exceptions for oneself or one's friends and family with regard to obeying any civil law or law of nature. How close equity and impartiality are comes out quite clearly when Hobbes contrasts someone who deals equally between those he is judging with someone "that is partial in judgment" (*L.* XV, 23). This suggests that when Hobbes talks about those laws of nature that require equality, he can be best understood as talking about impartiality. The importance of impartiality in the laws of nature is clear from the fact that in his summary of the laws of nature, he claims that "they have been contracted into one easy sum, intelligible to even the meanest capacity; and that is, Do not that to another, which thou wouldest not have done to thyself" (*L.* XV, 35; see also *D.C.* III, 26). This negative version of the Golden Rule, like its positive version, is best thought of as a method of achieving impartiality in one's actions and judgments, and Hobbes clearly uses it in this way.

Impartiality and Rationality Yield the Moral Virtues

Impartiality by itself is not sufficient to generate the moral virtues; it must be accompanied by rationality. Treating others as you want to be treated will yield the virtues of justice, gratitude, etc., only if one is a rational person, i.e., one who wants to preserve his life and members as much as in him lies. One of Hobbes's primary goals in his formulation of the laws of nature is to show that, given the vulnerability of human beings and their need for peace and hence for a civil society, rationality requires impartiality. His discussions of the laws of nature against pride and arrogance, and for equity (*L.* XV, 21, 22, 23; *D.C.* III, 13, 14, 15), are all attempts to show that failing to treat people impartially, or making special exceptions for oneself, leads to war and hence is an irrational way to behave.

In considering the changes in the formulations of the laws of nature from *De Cive* to *Leviathan*, the most significant change is that impartiality is now incorporated into the very first special law of nature requiring that one lay down one's right to all things. This, as mentioned earlier, is no significant change in his overall position, but it does show that he came to appreciate even more how central impartiality is to the laws of nature, especially those involving the moral virtues. Hobbes's justification of morality can be summarized as follows: given the human situation, rationality and impartiality yield all the moral virtues, and rationality itself requires impartiality.

Charity

Although Hobbes says, "a common standard for virtues and vices doth not appear except in civil life" (*D.H.* XIII, 9), this involves confusion between justice and morality. Hobbes's argument is "whatsoever the laws are, not to violate them is always and everywhere held to be a virtue in citizens, and to neglect them held to be a vice," and continues by pointing out that "[a]lthough it is true that certain actions may be just in one state, and unjust in another, nevertheless, justice (that is, not to violate the laws) is and shall be everywhere the same" (ibid.). This argument is about justice, not morality. Most of the moral virtues that are dictated by the laws of nature do not even apply to ordinary citizens, but are addressed to the sovereign and his representatives. It is quite clear that the fundamental law of nature dictating that we seek peace is not limited to those in a civil society. Further, in the same section of *De Homine*, Hobbes says while justice and equity are the moral virtues that are measured by the civil law, "that moral virtue which we measure purely by the natural law is only charity" (ibid.).

In both *De Cive* and *Leviathan*, charity is conspicuously absent from the list of virtues that the laws of nature dictate. In *Leviathan*, it is simply included in the list of the passions as a synonym for benevolence. "Desire of good to another, BENEVOLENCE, GOOD WILL, CHARITY. If to a man generally, GOOD NATURE" (*L.* VI, 23). However, in *De Homine*, Hobbes gives charity a very special status. He not only says, "that moral virtue which we measure purely by natural laws is only charity" (*D.H.* XIII, 9), but also claims that "all the virtues are contained in justice and charity" (ibid). Whereas in *Leviathan* charity was not distinguished from benevolence, in *De Homine* he relates it very closely to compassion, for he says: "[V]ices are all contained in injustice, and in a mind insensible to another's evils, that is, in a lack of charity" (*D.H.* XIII, 9). This strongly suggests that Hobbes held that if one were sensible to another's evil he would do something to relieve it. However, although his statement in *De Homine* shows that Hobbes began to appreciate the importance of charity as a virtue, he devotes very little attention to it. But that may be due to the fact that charity is not a moral virtue that plays a significant role in his political theory. Rather, in his political theory, the function of charity is taken over by the moral virtue of complaisance or humanity, which dictates that the rich help the poor.

Summary

Although Hobbes talks about the laws of nature as prescribing the moral virtues, it is easier to think of them as proscribing the moral vices. The nine moral vices that are proscribed by the laws of nature are injustice, ingratitude, greed or inhumanity, vindictiveness (Hobbes does not name the moral vice corresponding to mercy, this is my attempt to provide one), cruelty, disrespect or contumely, pride, arrogance, and unfairness. The corresponding moral virtues that are prescribed by the laws of nature are justice, gratitude, humanity or complaisance, mercy, respect, humility, modesty, and equity or fairness. (Hobbes does not name the moral virtue corresponding to what he regards as cruelty, and I cannot think of one either.) The difficulty of coming up with names for some of the moral virtues, and even for some of the moral vices, indicates that not all of them are among the most common moral virtues and vices. Nonetheless, as described by Hobbes, they are genuine moral virtues and vices, traits of character such that all impartial rational persons would favor everyone having these virtues and no one having these vices.

All of these moral virtues are such that they benefit everyone impartially by promoting peace, and do not benefit the person having them more than they benefit anyone else. This is what makes them moral virtues and distinguishes them from the personal virtues of courage, prudence, and temperance (see *D.H.* XIII, 9). Hobbes correctly sees both that peace benefits all persons impartially and that impartiality is essential to morality. His account of the moral virtues explains why they are traits of character that are praised by all rational persons. His argument for the rationality of these moral virtues is that having these virtues enhances one's chances for long-term preservation. Granted that increasing one's chances for long-term preservation is in one's self-interest, there is no incompatibility between acting morally and acting for one's self-interest when what is in one's own self-interest is equally in the interest of everyone else. Hobbes sees this point quite clearly and it is at the heart of his justification of the moral virtues.

The Laws of Nature
Dictates concerning the Practice of Moral Virtue

L.1, *D.C*.0	Seek peace	*L*. XIV, 4	*D.C*, II, 2
L.2, *D.C*.1	Lay down right	*L*. XIV, 5	*D.C*. II, 3
L.3, *D.C*.2	Justice	*L*. XV, 1	*D.C*. III, 1
L.4, *D.C*.3	Gratitude	*L*. XV, 16	*D.C*. III, 8
L.5, *D.C*.4	Complaisance	*L*. XV, 17	*D.C*. III, 9
L.6, *D.C*.5	Mercy	*L*. XV, 18	*D.C*. III, 10
L.7, *D.C*.6	Against cruelty	*L*. XV, 19	*D.C*. III, 11

L.8, D.C.7	Against contumely	*L.* XV, 20	*D.C.* III, 12
L.9, D.C.8	Against pride	*L.* XV, 21	*D.C.* III, 13
L.10, D.C.9	Against arrogance	*L.* XV, 22	*D.C.* III, 14
L.11, D.C.10	Equity	*L.* XV, 23	*D.C.* III, 15
L.12–19, D.C.11–19	No longer about virtues, but about policies and procedures		
D.C. 20	Additional law against drunkenness		*D.C.* III, 25

4

Hobbes's Political Theory

Political theories are different from moral theories. As pointed out in the last chapter, most moral theories involve an attempt to describe, explain, and justify morality. This is because, for many, including Hobbes, "morality" is taken to refer to a code of conduct, or set of virtues, that is not consciously constructed by individuals. Although many hold that a universal morality depends on human nature, none holds that some individual invented this universal morality at a particular time and place. Even those who do not accept a universal morality still do not think of the moral system as being created or invented by particular individuals. Hobbes, like most who accept a universal morality, regards morality as something that is discovered rather than invented. A political theory, insofar as it is an application of a moral theory, also involves an attempt to describe, explain, and justify morality as it applies to the rights and duties of citizens and sovereigns. However, a political theory, including that which Hobbes puts forward, also includes a guide for constructing a society that will achieve a peaceful, sociable, comfortable life for everyone living in that society. Hobbes's political theory is an attempt to provide a guide for constructing a government that can protect its citizens from both those who hold false moral beliefs and those who do not care about morality. Because religious beliefs are a major source of false moral beliefs, Hobbes devotes much time and effort to show that on the correct interpretation Christianity supports his account of morality and his political theory.

Hobbes and Social Contract Theories

Both moral and political theories are often concerned with the requirement to obey the law. Some moral theories claim that there is a moral requirement to obey the law that is at the same basic level as the moral requirement to keep one's promises. However, other moral theories do not regard the requirement to obey the law as a basic moral requirement, claiming, rather, that it is based on the moral requirement to keep one's promise. Hobbes's political theory is a version of this latter kind. People are morally required to obey the law because of a more basic moral requirement, which he mis-leadingly states as "that men perform their covenants made" (*L.* XV, 1). Hobbes is then taken to belong to the group of what are called "social contract" political theorists. As pointed out in the last chapter, Hobbes's moral theory is best classified as a natural law theory rather than a social contract theory. However, the distinction between these two kinds of moral theories has limited value when moral social contract theorists talk about what all rational persons would agree to in an appropriately described purely hypothetical situation. A moral social contract theory of this kind is not signifi-cantly different from a natural law theory. Insofar as a political social contract theory talks about what all rational persons would agree to in some purely hypothetical situation, it also seems to be quite similar to a natural law account of the rights and duties of sovereign and subject.

Hobbes's political theory is not a natural law theory, nor is it the corresponding kind of political social contract theory. Although it may seem that Hobbes's description of the state of nature is a description of a purely hypothetical situation in which rational persons choose to form a commonwealth, Hobbes does not conceive of the state of nature in this way. For him, the state of nature is the state that would result from a civil war that completely destroyed the commonwealth, or it is the state that must have existed prior to the formation of commonwealths large enough to have a reasonable chance of providing protection to their citizens against attacks from outside (see *L.* XVII, 3; *D.C.* V, 3). Hobbes does not deny that a small group of people might live together without a common power to keep them all in awe, but he does deny that this is possible for a group of people large enough to create the kind of commonwealth that he is concerned with. He says: "For if we could suppose a great multitude of men to consent in the observation of justice and other laws of nature without a common power to keep them all in awe, we might as well suppose all mankind to do the same" (*L.* XVII, 4). This argument has force because Hobbes is talking about "a great multitude of men," not merely a small group of people. He is making use of the common-sense view that, when dealing with "a great multitude of men" and no "common power to keep them all in awe," there will be some who will not follow the laws of nature. This does not even require a pessimistic view of human nature, "For though the wicked were fewer than the righteous, yet because we cannot distinguish them, there is a necessity of suspecting, heeding, anticipating, subjugating, self-defending, ever incident to the most honest and fairest conditioned" (*D.C.* Pref., p. 100).

Hobbes's most general characterization of the state of nature is the following, "during the time men live without a common power to keep them all in awe, they are in that condition which is called war, and such a war as is of every man against every man" (*L.* XIII, 8). Hobbes's strong rhetorical description, that each person is at war with every other person, should not be taken literally. Hobbes knows that family members have strong bonds of affection that bind them to each other. His description of the state of nature describes a world in which there are only small families or groups that view each other with fear and hostility, and this kind of world is not purely hypothetical. Those who accuse Hobbes of arguing for psychological egoism distort his account of the state of nature by making it a purely hypothetical situation. Psychological egoism does not enhance any of the points he wants to make about a world in which there are no large commonwealths. On the contrary, psychological egoism would distort Hobbes's account of such a world and make it completely implausible and hence transform it into a purely hypothetical situation. Except for isolated passages that are of no significance for his moral or political theory, whenever Hobbes talks as if he accepts psychological egoism, he can and should be interpreted as holding that people usually act to benefit themselves, or their family and friends.

Hobbes realizes that "the estate of man can never be without some incommodity or other," but, he continues, "the greatest [incommodity] that in any form of government can possibly happen to the people in general is scarce sensible, in respect of the miseries and horrible calamities that accompany a civil war" (*L.* XVIII, 20). It is because of his belief that civil war can return people to the state of nature, which he takes as the state of war of all against all, that he is so concerned about avoiding a civil war. In a memorable passage I have quoted before, he describes the state of nature as having the following consequences:

> [T]here is no place for industry, because the fruit thereof is uncertain, and consequently no culture of the earth, no navigation, nor use of the commodities that may be imported by sea, no commodious building, no instruments of moving and removing such things as require much force, no knowledge of the face of the earth, no account of time, no arts, no letters, no society, and which is worst of all, continual fear and danger of violent death, and the life of man is solitary, poor, nasty, brutish, and short. (*L*. XIII, 9)

As pointed out in the previous paragraph, these consequences do not depend on taking Hobbes to mean "solitary" literally, that is, to be claiming that each person is completely on his own. Rather, these terrible consequences result from a state where there are only small families or groups in perpetual conflict with each other "without a common power to keep them all in awe." Although Hobbes's primary theoretical use of the concept of the state of nature is as that state that preceded the formation of large commonwealths, it is important to recognize that he thought that a civil war could return people to the state of nature. The primary practical purpose of his moral and political theories is to persuade citizens and sovereigns to act in ways that will promote their living together in peace. Hobbes is writing for those who are already living in a commonwealth, trying to persuade them not to act in ways that might lead to a civil war and a return to the state of nature. He is not writing for those in a state of nature looking for a way to get out of it by forming a commonwealth.

Unlike most contemporary political social contract theorists, Hobbes does not place any limits on the beliefs and desires that rational persons have in the state of nature; they can have all of the beliefs and desires that rational persons naturally have. However, when he is using the state of nature as a theoretical concept, he sometimes presents the persons in the state of nature as if they were not related to other persons in any significant way: "Let us return to the state of nature, and consider men as if but even now sprung out of the earth, and suddenly, like mushrooms, come to full maturity, without all of kind of engagement to each other" (*D.C.* VIII, 1). But this way of presenting the state of nature is only a rhetorical device used to emphasize that the state of nature is one in which people have not engaged in any contracts or covenants with, or free-gifts to, anyone, so they retain all of their right of nature and are consequently under no obligation to anyone. When people are in this kind of state, Hobbes claims that there are only three ways that a commonwealth can be formed: by institution, by acquisition, and by generation (see ibid.).

Ways of Forming a Commonwealth

Hobbes calls a commonwealth created by generation a "paternal commonwealth," and says that it is not really due to generation, but to the children being dependent on their parents for their survival (see *D.C.* IX, 1–3 and *L.* XX, 4). However, commonwealths formed in this way are too small to provide security against external attacks, and so Hobbes does not say much about them (see *D.C.* V, 3). He claims that there are only two ways that large commonwealths can be formed in the state of nature. The first is by institution:

> [W]hen a *multitude* of men do agree and *covenant, every one with every one*, that to whatsoever *man* or *assembly of men* shall be given by the major part the *right* to *present* the person of them all (that is to say, be their *representative*) every one . . . shall *authorize* all the actions and judgments of that man or assembly of men, as if they were his own, to the end, to live peacefully amongst themselves and be protected against other men. (*L.* XVIII, 1)

The second is by acquisition, "where the sovereign power is acquired by force; and it is acquired by force when men singly (or many together by plurality of voices) for fear of death or bonds do authorize all the actions of that man of assembly that hath their lives and liberty in their power" (*L.* XX, 1; see also *D.C.* V, 7–9).

According to Hobbes, both kinds of commonwealths, those formed by institution and those formed by acquisition, emerge as a result of fear. In the former, "men who choose their sovereign do it for fear of one another, and not of him whom they institute; but in [the latter] case they subject themselves to him they are afraid of. In both cases they do it for fear" (*L.* XX, 2; see also *D.C.* V, 12). Given that fear is the motive for both ways of forming large commonwealths, it should not be surprising that Hobbes insists that, contrary to what might be thought, the result, in both cases, is that the sovereign and the citizens have exactly the same rights and duties

(*L.* XX, 3). Hobbes regards commonwealths by acquisition or conquest as the natural method of formation (see *D.C.* V, 12), but he
discusses formation by institution in order to show that even if a
commonwealth were formed in this way, it would not make any
difference to the rights and duties of sovereign and citizen.

The essential feature of both ways of forming commonwealths is
that future citizens either renounce their right of nature or make a
free-gift of their natural right to decide how to act to the sovereign.
Neither act is a covenant in the strict sense, for a covenant is a
two-way transfer of rights, and both renouncing their right and
making a free-gift of it are only one-way transfers (see *L.* XIV, 7–12;
D.C. II, 4–9). The sovereign does not transfer any rights to the citizens, but they, because of their fear, either renounce their right or
make a free-gift of their right of nature to the sovereign. Hobbes
says, "the definition of INJUSTICE is no other than *the not performance
of covenant*" (*L.* XV, 2). However, as pointed out in the previous
chapter, this extended use of the term "covenant" includes renouncing or making a free-gift of one's natural right to act according to
one's own judgment about the best way to preserve oneself. This is
made clear by the following statement:

> And when a man hath in either manner abandoned or granted away
> his right, then he is said to be OBLIGED or BOUND not to hinder those
> to whom such right is granted or abandoned from the benefit of
> it; . . . and that such hindrance is INJUSTICE, and INJURY, as being *sine
> jure* [without right], the right being before renounced or transferred.
> (*L.* XIV, 7)

It is an important feature of Hobbes's political theory that the
transfer of rights between the citizens and the sovereign is a one-way
transfer. Hobbes denies that there is any contract or covenant
between the sovereign and the citizens, because he wants to guarantee that the sovereign cannot be guilty of injustice (see, *L.* XVIII,
4). Because the sovereign never renounces or transfers any right, it
is impossible for him to commit an injustice. According to Hobbes,
injustice is the only kind of immoral action that subjects a person
to punishment. However, even though the sovereign cannot be
unjust, he can be immoral, for he can be guilty of ingratitude, that
is, that he can act in such a way that gives a citizen "reasonable
cause to repent him of his good will" (*L.* XV, 16; see also *D.C.* III,
8). Gratitude is the primary moral virtue of the sovereign, whereas
justice is the primary moral virtue of citizens; ingratitude is the

primary vice of the sovereign, whereas injustice is the primary vice of citizens. The parallelism explains why gratitude comes right after justice in Hobbes's list of the laws of nature. It is important to recognize the distinction between justice and the other moral virtues and to realize that, according to Hobbes, injustice is the only moral vice that is legitimately subject to punishment. Failure to appreciate these facts about justice results in the false view that, according to Hobbes, the sovereign cannot be immoral. But, he argues, the sovereign can be immoral, for he can violate many of the laws of nature, but he cannot be unjust, for the same reason that no one can be unjust in the state of nature; that is, the sovereign, like people in the state of nature, never transfers or renounces any of his right of nature.

As is clear from the preceding, understanding the right of nature is crucial to understanding Hobbes's political theory, for giving up of the right of nature is necessary in order to form a commonwealth. It is the consequences of giving up this right that is what Hobbes calls civil philosophy. In his table of the sciences, in Chapter IX of *Leviathan*, he says: "POLITICS and CIVIL PHILOSOPHY" includes "1. Of consequences from the institution of COMMONWEALTHS, to the *rights* and *duties* of the *body politic*, or *sovereign*" and "2. Of consequences from the same, to the *duties* and *rights* of the *subjects*." This table confirms that Hobbes holds that the rights and duties of sovereigns and subjects are the same whether a commonwealth is created by institution or by acquisition. Also, whether the sovereign is a single person, as in a monarchy, a small group of people, as in an aristocracy, or all the people, as in a democracy, the rights of sovereigns and the duties of the citizens are the same in all three (*L*. XIX, 1). In Chapter XIX of *Leviathan* Hobbes gives his reasons for preferring a monarchy to the other two forms, but he is aware that all three forms have problems and does not incorporate his prefer-ence for a monarchy into his political theory. Those who have not read or who do not remember what Hobbes says about sovereignty may mistakenly conclude that he favors a monarchy because they equate "sovereign" with "monarch," whereas Hobbes consistently states that the sovereign, whether in a democracy, an aristocracy, or a monarchy, has exactly the same rights.

It is not merely tolerance on Hobbes's part to regard all three forms of commonwealth as having the same sovereign authority and power. It is, in fact, an essential feature of Hobbes's political theory that a democracy has the same absolute sovereignty that a monarchy has, with all of the same rights and powers, and that the citizens of each have the same duties. When we recall that Hobbes's primary practical purpose in putting forward a political theory is to avoid civil war, it would be absurd for him to regard any of the three forms of sovereignty as illegitimate. To do so would provide an excuse or justification for those living under that form of sovereignty to start a civil war in order to establish a legitimate form of sovereignty. Hobbes always argues that citizens should obey the sovereign, no matter what the form of the sovereign or how that sovereign power had been obtained. Hobbes was completely consistent when he presented Cromwell with a copy of *Leviathan* on his return to England after the civil war. Both Cromwell and Charles II, who regained the throne after Cromwell, understood this.

The Right of Nature and the Laws of Nature

Hobbes claims that previous writers did not clearly distinguish between the right of nature and a law of nature, but he thinks that it is crucial to make clear that they are completely different from each other. He says:

> For though they that speak of this subject use to confound *jus* and *lex* (*right* and *law*), yet they ought to be distinguished. RIGHT consisteth in liberty to do or to forbear, whereas LAW determineth and bindeth to one of them, so that law and right differ as much as obligation and liberty, which in one and the same matter are inconsistent. (*L.* XIV, 3)

As the discussion of the previous chapter showed, the laws of nature are the foundation of Hobbes's moral theory; Hobbes explicitly claims that "the true doctrine of the laws of nature is the true moral philosophy" (*L.* XV, 40). He then continues: the laws of nature "come to be praised as the means of peaceable, sociable, and comfortable living" (ibid.). The goal of morality is peace, but, according to Hobbes, this goal can only be achieved by creating the right kind of commonwealth. His political theory claims that people can only create this kind of commonwealth if all of them lay down their right of nature. The dependence of his political theory on his moral theory is shown by the fact that he holds that the first law of nature necessary to achieve peace is that one lay down one's right of nature (see *L.* XIV, 5 and *D.C.* II, 3).

Since both the right of nature and the law of nature are based on the rationality of self-preservation, it is puzzling how Hobbes can claim that they "differ as much as obligation and liberty, which in one and the same matter are inconsistent." As quoted previously, Hobbes defines a law of nature as a "precept or general rule, found out by reason, by which a man is forbidden to do that which is destructive of his life or taketh away the means of preserving the same, and to omit that by which he thinketh it may be best preserved" (*L.* XIV, 3; see also *D.C.* II, 1). The laws of nature are the dictates of reason; they require the kinds of acts that are necessary for our preservation. Given this, it seems that Hobbes is inconsistent when he defines the right of nature as "the liberty each man hath to use his own power, as he will himself, for the preservation of his own nature, that is to say, of his own life, and consequently doing anything which, in his own judgment and reason, he shall conceive to be the aptest means thereunto" (*L.* XIV, 1). How can people have the liberty to do whatever they believe to be necessary for their preservation and at the same time be required to perform the kinds of acts that Hobbes claims are is necessary for their preservation?

Hobbes solution to this problem is to point out that every rational person agrees that self-preservation requires seeking or preserving peace, for all rational persons agree that without peace no one is likely to live very long (*L.* XIV, 4). The dictate of reason requiring us to seek peace is the basis for all of the other laws of nature; for Hobbes, every law of nature dictates a kind of act that is necessary for obtaining or maintaining peace. It is only when peace cannot be achieved that people have the liberty to do whatever they believe is best for their preservation. So the right of nature applies only when the laws of nature do not, that is, when following the laws of nature will not achieve peace. This way of explaining the relationship between the right of nature and the law of nature is exactly the way that Hobbes puts it when he puts forward, "as a precept, or rule of reason *that every man ought to endeavour peace, as far as he has hope of obtaining it, and when he cannot obtain it, that he may seek and use all helps and advantages of war*" (*L.* XIV, 4). Hobbes continues: "[T]he first branch of which rule containeth the first and fundamental law of nature, which is *to seek peace, and follow it*. The second, the sum of the right of nature, which is *by all means we can, to defend ourselves*" (ibid.).

The relationship between peace and preservation also explains why Hobbes says that "[t]he laws of nature oblige *in foro interno*, that is to say, they bind to a desire that they should take place, but *in foro externo*, that is, to putting them in act, not always" (*L. XV*, 36). People are only obliged to follow the laws of nature, or practice the virtues, when following them will lead to peace and hence to preservation, for the ground of all of the laws of nature is the rationality of self-preservation. Hobbes says that the virtues "come to be praised as the means of peaceable, sociable, and comfortable living" (*L. XV*, 40), and so he holds that a person should not "be modest and tractable, and perform all he promises, in such time and place where no man else should do so," for such a person "should but make himself a prey to others, and procure his own certain ruin, contrary to the ground of all laws of nature, which tend to nature's preservation" (*L. XV*, 36). Every rational person agrees they ought to follow these laws of nature, or practice these moral virtues, whenever there is any hope of obtaining peace and following these laws does not create a risk to their lives.

It is only when following the laws of nature will not lead to peace that people have the right of nature to do whatever they think will best lead to their preservation. So, for Hobbes, citizens' rights do not derive from the civil law, but actually precede the civil law. That is why Hobbes says: "Now *natural liberty* is a right, not constituted, but allowed by the laws" (*D.C. XIV*, 3). He then misleadingly adds: "For the laws being removed, our *liberty* is absolute" (ibid.). Although it is understandable why Hobbes says this, the sentence is misleading, for it suggests that it is possible not only for civil laws to be removed, but also for the laws of nature to be removed. It is possible for the laws of nature not to apply *in foro externo*, that is, when following them will not lead to peace, but they always apply *in foro interno*. The next sentence, "This is first restrained by the natural and divine laws" (ibid.), is misleading in a similar way, for it suggests that the right of nature precedes the laws of nature, whereas, as is made clear in the previous paragraph, the general rule of reason yields the laws of nature and the right of nature simultaneously.

The right of nature, or rather, giving up the right of nature, is the foundation of Hobbes's political theory. For Hobbes, the law of nature requiring people to give up their right of nature follows directly from the dictate of reason requiring them to seek peace. This confirms that Hobbes regards his political theory as dependent on his moral theory. He holds that in order to achieve lasting peace it is necessary to form the kind of large commonwealth that can provide sufficient protection and security for all. In order to form such a commonwealth all must give up their right of nature

– the right to do anything one rationally believes is necessary for one's preservation. In the state of nature, which is prior to people having taken on any obligations, every person has this right to do whatever he thinks best serves his preservation. But even in the state of nature, the right of nature is limited by the basic law of nature to seek peace; for no rational person believes that his preservation is better protected by a state of war than by peace. Giving up the right of nature involves divesting oneself of the liberty to decide what is the best way to preserve oneself, and obliging oneself to act as the person or group to whom one gave the right decides is the best way to act. However, just as the laws of nature do not oblige *in foro externo* when they cannot be obeyed safely, so giving up the right of nature does not create an obligation to act as the sovereign commands when one is facing an immediate threat to one's life. To give up one's right of nature is to divest oneself the liberty to decide what is the best way to achieve long-term preservation.

The moral virtues dictated by the laws of nature are necessary for creating and maintaining a civil society; a civil society is necessary for achieving peace, and peace is necessary for the long-term preservation that is the primary goal of reason. The false attribution to Hobbes of Hume's account of reason as purely instrumental not only seems to involve backward causation but also involves failing to realize that, for Hobbes, reason does have its own goal, avoiding an unnatural death (see *D.C.* Ded., p. 93). Combined with the failure to realize the primacy of morality to politics, these mistaken interpretations of Hobbes may explain why some philosophers have claimed that he has no way for people to get out the state of nature. If, as they claim, seeking peace is not a fundamental dictate of reason, and morality starts only after one has given up one's natural right in order to achieve a civil state, then neither reason nor morality applies in the state of nature. However, on the correct account of Hobbes's view, seeking peace is a fundamental dictate of reason and morality, and both morality and reason require giving up one's right of nature in order to achieve peace. Further, both reason and morality require people to keep their covenants, that is, to refrain from doing what they have given up their natural right to do. For Hobbes, morality is eternal and applies even in the state of nature. Morality not only requires refraining from doing what one has given up one's natural right to do, but also requires giving up one's natural right. Only by giving up one's natural right to all things that everyone in the state of nature has is it possible to create a lasting

civil society. All of this is based on the moral and rational requirement to seek peace.

Moreover, Hobbes is not writing for people who are in a state of
nature, but for people who are already in a civil society. Thus it is
a mistake to interpret him as offering advice about how to get out
of the state of nature. Rather, he is providing arguments to members
of his society about why they should not act in ways that might
lead to civil war, for civil war leads to a state of nature. Because the
state of nature is that state in which everyone has the right to decide
about the best way to preserve himself, emerging from the state of
nature must involve everyone giving up their right of nature in
some way, either by free-gift or renouncing, or by a combination of
covenant and free-gift (*L*. XVII, 13–15). This means that all citizens
must have transferred to the sovereign their right to decide how to
act for their long-term preservation. This acquired right does not
allow the sovereign to do anything that he did not have the right
to do before, for the sovereign already had the natural right to do
whatever he thought would best preserve his life. However, it
imposes an obligation on citizens not to interfere with the sovereign's decision about how everyone in the commonwealth should
behave.

Natural rights have no corresponding duties, e.g., the right to
self-defense does not impose a duty on anyone else not to kill you.
However, an acquired right, e.g., a right that the sovereign has
acquired from the citizens by their free-gift, does involve a corresponding duty. This acquired right allows the sovereign to put
forward his view about how citizens should behave by means of
laws. Because the citizens have given up their right to decide how
to behave to the sovereign, the citizen is obliged to obey the laws
that the sovereign has put forward. Failure to obey the law is to be
guilty of injustice, and the sovereign's infliction of harm on citizens
who commit injustices is no longer merely the exercise of his right
of nature, but is appropriately called punishment.

Inalienable Rights

Hobbes's explanation of why self-defense is an inalienable right is
more complex than it seems at first sight. He says, "No man is
obliged by any contracts whatsoever not to resist him who shall
offer to kill, wound, or any way hurt his body" (*D.C*. II, 18). The
basis for this position is a claim about the limitations on the content

of covenants: "A covenant not to defend myself from force by force is always void" (*L.* XIV, 29). In his argument for this latter claim, Hobbes makes a statement that is commonly cited to show that he argues for psychological egoism: "For it [giving up a right] is a voluntary act, and of the voluntary acts of every man the object is some *good to himself*" (*L.* XIV, 8). This statement is taken to show that Hobbes holds that the object of all voluntary acts is the self-interest of the agent. Hobbes's argument is interpreted to be the following: no one is obliged by any contract not to defend himself because such contracts are always void; they are always void because a contract (giving up a right), being a voluntary act, must be for the good of the person making the contract (giving up a right), and no rational person would regard it as good for him not to defend himself.

But this interpretation has a number of problems. First, given that Hobbes's account of the meaning of the term "good" makes it fit with his tautological egoism, "some good to himself" means the same as "something that the person considers good." So that saying, "the voluntary acts of every man the object is some *good to himself*" need not mean that the object of voluntary acts of every man is his own self-interest. It is quite plausible to interpret Hobbes as holding that not defending oneself conflicts with satisfying all of a person's rational desires, that is, it conflicts with obtaining anything that she calls "good." Not defending oneself not only conflicts with rational self-interested desires, especially the desire for self-preservation, but also conflicts with satisfying any rational desire, including rational desires to preserve the lives of those one loves. Hobbes need not, and does not consider all voluntary acts to be acts of self-interest. However, he could be interpreted as holding that rational persons are egocentric, caring only for their own small group of friends or families. He could hold that such persons could not make covenants not to defend themselves because that would conflict with their rational desire to protect their friends and families. Although philosophers can construct cases where failing to defend oneself does not conflict with satisfying any of a person's rational desires, Hobbes rightly does not concern himself with these philosophical inventions.

But even this less egoistic interpretation has a serious problem. It seems to presuppose that all voluntary acts are rational, and Hobbes explicitly denies this: "The definition of the *will* given commonly by the Schools, that it is a *rational appetite*, is not good. For if it were, then could there be no voluntary act against reason. For a *voluntary* act is that which proceedeth from the *will*, and no other" (*L.* VI, 53). Hobbes admits that people often act irrationally, some people even preferring death to suffering slander, so he should not be saying that it is psychologically impossible for a person to make an irrational covenant. However, he does say: "For though a man may covenant thus *unless I do so, or so, kill me*, he cannot covenant, thus, *unless I do so, or so, I will not resist you, when you come to kill me*. For man by nature chooseth the lesser evil, which is the danger of death in resisting, rather than the greater, which is certain and present death in not resisting" (*L.* XIV, 29). Note the phrase "man by nature." Hobbes is not saying that actual civilized persons cannot choose the greater evil, but only that man by nature cannot. However, it is not clear why it is relevant that man by nature cannot choose the greater evil, unless it is important that "man by nature" does not act irrationally. Some clue is given by the fact that in this discussion Hobbes refers back to his previous discussion in this chapter (*L.* XIV, 8) of why the right to self-defense is an inalienable right.

This earlier discussion is where Hobbes says, "the voluntary acts of every man the object is some *good to himself*." In this discussion Hobbes talks about the point of giving up one's natural right to decide how to act, which is to escape from the state of nature and to gain the security of life in a commonwealth. Hobbes uses this explanation of why a person gives up his right of nature to explain why he cannot give up his right to defend himself: "[T]he motive and end for which this renouncing and transferring right is introduced, is nothing else but the security of a man's person, in his life and in the means of so preserving life as not to be weary of it" (*L.* XIV, 8). Given that this is the point of giving up one's right, no matter what a person says, his words should never be interpreted as giving up the right to defend himself. "And therefore if a man by words or other signs seem to despoil himself of the end for which those signs were intended, he is not to be understood as if he meant it, or that it was his will, but that he was ignorant of how such words and actions were to be interpreted" (ibid.). It is impossible to give up the right to defend oneself because nothing that one says or does can be interpreted as giving up that right. Thus the right to defend oneself is literally inalienable: nothing counts as giving it up.

Hobbes regards his moral and political theory to be *a priori*, that is, he regards himself as simply making explicit the consequences of the definitions of words referring to the actions that must have been taken to form a commonwealth. Commonwealths can only be created by people giving up their natural right to decide what is in their long-term self-interest to that person, or persons, who thereby becomes their sovereign. The limit of the obligations of these people, the citizens, is determined by what rights they give up to the sovereign. Because there are limits to what rights can be given up, there are corresponding limits to the obligations that citizens have. People give up their right to act on their own decisions and judgment about the best way to achieve their long-term preservation in order to escape from a state of nature where it is irrational for person to expect to live as long as nature normally allows people to live. But it would be absurd to give up the right to defend oneself against an immediate threat to one's life in order to gain a better chance at long-term preservation. So a rational person cannot be understood to have given up the right to defend himself from an immediate threat to his life. If the right to defend oneself is an inalienable right, it must be because it is impossible to give up that right. And it can only be impossible to give up a right if nothing one says or does can be interpreted as giving up that right.

Hobbes's primary argument in favor of the inalienable right to self-defense is that given in the previous paragraph. However, as discussed earlier, Hobbes has been interpreted as claiming that people have an inalienable right to self-defense because it is psychologically impossible not to resist being attacked. I have already shown that this argument does not have much force, because some people prefer death to suffering slander. A more positive argument against the view that it is psychologically impossible not to defend oneself is Hobbes's statement that some people, have "a certain nobleness or gallantness of courage (rarely found), by which a man scorns to be beholden for the contentment of his life to fraud or breach of promise" (*L.* XV, 10). Hobbes's arguments for various inalienable rights should not be taken as based on claims about what people are not psychologically able to do. That someone is psychologically unable to avoid doing what he gave away his right to do may provide an excuse for his doing it, but it does not show that he did not give away that right. That one cannot help but break a covenant does not show that one did not voluntarily make that covenant. For a right to be inalienable, it must be that it is impossible to give up that right, and it is only impossible to give up a right if it is never plausible to interpret what a person says or does as giving up that right. Hobbes's statements about the point of the transfer of natural right that citizens made when forming a commonwealth serves as the basis for his argument that nothing a person says can be interpreted as giving up the right to self-defense.

Looking at the arguments that Hobbes offers in defense of inalienable rights beyond that of self-defense makes it clear that he bases his claims about inalienable rights on why people gave up their right of nature in order to form a commonwealth. He argues that no one can be understood to give up the right to self-defense because the primary reason that people gave up their right of nature was to preserve themselves (L. XIV, 29). He gives a similar argument to show that no one is obliged to accuse himself because no person can be understood to have covenanted to "accuse oneself without assurance of pardon" (L. XIV, 30). He gives a different but related argument for saying that no one is obliged to accuse someone close to him:

> The same is also true of the accusation of those by whose condemnation a man falls into misery (as, of a father, wife, or benefactor). For the testimony of such an accuser, if it be not willingly given, is presumed to be corrupted by nature, and therefore not to be received; and where a man's testimony is not to be credited, he is not bound to give it. (Ibid.)

His claim, "Also accusations upon torture are not to be reputed as testimonies" (ibid.), is based upon a person's right to say anything to preserve himself. Hobbes is trying to provide arguments against torture or any kind of coerced testimony by showing that one cannot depend on what is said under such circumstances.

Hobbes is not claiming that neither coercion nor torture is ever successful in providing true testimony, only that such testimony should not be used because there is such a strong reason to believe that it is not credible. He then goes on to argue that because such testimony is not credible, no one is obliged to provide it. Even if one does not regard Hobbes's arguments as completely successful, it is clear that he is trying to provide arguments against torture or any kind of coerced testimony. These are not the kinds of arguments that one would expect from a person who defends absolute sovereignty. Because Hobbes's primary practical goal is to prevent civil war, he is against putting any legal limits on the power of the sovereign. However, it should be clear that he is providing arguments that are intended to persuade the sovereign not to engage in those practices that are regarded as immoral. These arguments, like those that are intended to persuade citizens to obey the law, include

both moral as well as rational or prudential arguments. Contrary
to the standard interpretation of Hobbes as claiming that once one
assumes the duties of citizenship, a citizen has no rights left, he
argues that citizens have more inalienable rights than simply the
right to defend themselves. His arguments may not be completely
successful, but it is clear that by pointing out that citizens retain
some rights he is trying to persuade the sovereign that to violate
these rights puts the citizens back into the state of nature where
they are no longer obliged to obey the sovereign.

Power of the Sovereign

One of the most common criticisms of Hobbes's political theory is
his claim that sovereignty is absolute, that is, that the sovereign has
the authority to do whatever he decides is best for maintaining
peace and defending his citizens, and his decisions cannot be legitimately challenged (*L.* XVIII, 8). When Hobbes discusses sovereignty
by institution in *Leviathan*, he seems to base the authority of the
sovereign on the fact that each of the citizens has authorized the
sovereign to act on his behalf. However, in *De Cive* he holds that
the sovereign has absolute authority, although he had not yet developed the concept of authorization. So although Hobbes uses the
concept of authorization to reinforce his views about the sovereign
not being subject to punishment, authorization is not necessary
to support his views about the absolute authority of the sovereign
(*L.* XVIII, 7). Moreover, he is completely clear and consistent in
holding that the power and authority of the sovereign is exactly the
same whether a commonwealth comes into existence naturally by
conquest or artificially by institution. Because sovereignty based on
conquest does not involve authorization, authorization cannot be
essential to his argument that the sovereign's decisions can never
be unjust or legitimately challenged. Hobbes's argument that all
forms of sovereignty are based on the free-gift of the future citizens
to the future sovereign, rather than on any covenant between subject
and sovereign, is sufficient to support his conclusion that the
sovereign can never act unjustly and so can never be legitimately
punished.

That the term "sovereign" is often mistakenly equated with the
term "monarch" may be partially responsible for the strong criticism of Hobbes's claim that the sovereign has absolute power and
authority. Hobbes does hold that monarchy is the best form of
sovereignty, but he is clear that this is not part of his political theory,

but simply a conclusion that he comes to on the basis of his observation of the different forms of government. None of his arguments
concerning the power of the sovereign is related more closely to
monarchy than to aristocracy or democracy. Hobbes explicitly says:
"The difference between these three kinds of commonwealths consisteth not in a difference of power, but in the difference in conven-
ience, or aptitude to produce the peace and security of the people,
for which end they were instituted" (*L.* XIX, 4). He not only consistently denies the doctrine of the divine right of kings but also claims
that sovereign power derives from the free-gift of their rights by
the citizens. Indeed, when talking about sovereignty by institution,
he seems to claim that the original commonwealth was a democracy
(see *L.* XVIII, 1, 5). So his defense of absolute sovereignty has no
connection at all with his preference for a monarchy over an aristocracy or a democracy.

Hobbes denies Aristotle's view of human beings as natural political creatures, that is, as living in large commonwealths in the same
way that large numbers of ants and bees "live sociably one with
one another" (*L.* XVII, 6). He points out that human beings differ
from other animals in ways that show Aristotle to be wrong. He
talks of the competition for honor and the resulting clashing emotions, but he thinks that the most important difference is that human
beings have language, and this results in problems that animals do
not have. Among these is that people make moral judgments even
when they are not personally affected. Their different moral and
religious beliefs lead them to come into conflict with each other.
Hobbes agrees that the clash of people's natural emotions are a
problem, but a more important reason why people need an absolute
sovereign is due to language giving some people the ability to persuade others of their moral and religious views. This linguistically
generated disagreement is the primary reason that Hobbes denies
that people naturally can live together peacefully in a commonwealth large enough to protect them without a sovereign with sufficient power to keep them all in awe (see *D.C.* V, 5; *L.* XVII, 7–12).
It is the clash of moral and religious views that requires an absolute
sovereign.

The view that an absolute sovereign is necessary because all
people are self-interested makes no sense; everyone acting on their
own self-interest would never lead to a civil war. Since the primary
practical task of Hobbes's political theory is to design a commonwealth that will not succumb to civil war, it would be pointless for
him to hold the view that all people are completely selfish. It would

be almost as pointless for him to hold the view that all people act only in order to benefit themselves and their family and friends. An absolute sovereign is needed in order to provide a peaceful way of settling disputes – not only practical disputes about what is the best way to achieve peace and defense, but also the moral and religious disputes that pose such a threat to civil amity. Hobbes holds that the sovereign needs the power to settle any disputes that might lead to civil war. The only kinds of disputes that lead to civil war are those based on moral, political, and religious beliefs, where large numbers of people hold differing views so strongly that they are prepared to fight for them.

When one realizes that the point of an absolute sovereign is to settle disputes that might lead to civil war, it should become clear that, except for anarchists, everyone believes that the sovereign is absolute, that is, that the decision of the sovereign is final and cannot be challenged. In the United States, the decisions of the Supreme Court are final and cannot be challenged. Every stable country is similar in that there is a final decision-maker whose decision is final and cannot be challenged. Every stable country has a limited number of procedures that are regarded as legitimate ways to make fundamental changes in the way the country is governed. Attempts to make fundamental changes in ways that are not legitimate are regarded as treason and can be severely punished. The absolute power of all sovereigns may not be widely recognized because in most modern countries sovereignty is so dispersed that it is difficult to identify. Indeed, it seems that the concept of sovereignty with which Hobbes was concerned has little relevance to modern commonwealths. Nonetheless, in every stable state the overwhelming majority accepts the authorized procedures for resolving disagreements, including who is authorized to make the final decision. This is true even though these procedures may not designate the same authority as the final decision-maker for all of the different kinds of disagreements.

In the United States the sovereign power can be thought of as divided among the three branches of government, with the power to make laws vested in a complicated arrangement between the executive and legislative branches, and the power to interpret the law and to determine whether it is consistent with the constitution vested in the judicial branch. Hobbes might claim that the sovereign is actually the people, because at stated times they have elections that enable them to change the members of the executive and legislative branches. However, the system is arranged so that they cannot change them all at the same time. Further, the people cannot change the members of the judicial branch, so that there is some limit to their sovereign power. It might even be claimed that in the United States the real sovereign in Hobbes's sense is an aristocracy consisting of state legislators, for, if three-quarters of the state legislatures agree, they can modify the constitution in any way they want and there is no check or limitation on what they can do. However, as a practical matter, this aristocracy with unlimited sovereign power rarely acts, and when it does, as when amendments to the constitution are approved, it makes only relatively minor changes. And unless these state legislatures act with a speed that they have never yet shown, elections will be held in which the people can change the members of the state legislature and the new legislature can rescind the vote for constitutional changes for which the previous state legislature voted.

Nonetheless, all stable modern states have a government that does what Hobbes claims that the sovereign should do: namely, provide an agreed-upon way to settle all disagreements. Stable modern states do not need a sovereign in Hobbes's sense because there is such widespread agreement about how any particular disagreement should be resolved. In the United States, even those who vehemently disagree with a particular decision of the Supreme Court do not deny that the Court has the final authority to make that decision. There are some accepted ways that those who disagree with the decision of the Supreme Court can act to achieve the result denied them by that decision. If the decision involves the interpretation of a law, the legislature and the President may pass a different law that will not be subject to an interpretation to which they object. If the decision involves interpreting the constitution, it is more difficult to reverse the result, but a constitutional amendment is always a possibility. Also, if one is prepared to take the necessary amount of time, then one can wait until some justices retire and try to have them replaced by judges who will reverse the decision. All of these are acceptable ways to try to reverse a Supreme Court decision, but none of them involves challenging the authority of the Court. Everyone now takes Hobbes's view that settling a disagreement in a way that preserves the stability of the commonwealth is far more important than acting in a way that threatens the stability of the commonwealth, no matter how important the issue on which people disagree.

If there is widespread disagreement about who has the final authority to settle a particular dispute, and if both sides view the dispute as important, this creates a significant risk of civil war. The religious disputes in the time of Hobbes coincided with disagreements between those who claimed sovereignty for the king and those who claimed sovereignty for Parliament. Hobbes championed the claim of sovereignty for the king, but on the basis of his own theory about how sovereignty is achieved, not on grounds of the divine right of kings that others who championed the claim of sovereignty for the king accepted. About 150 years ago in the United States of America, there was disagreement about whether final authority lay with the federal government or with the individual state governments. Although this disagreement existed for some time before a fighting war developed, Hobbes would have said that a civil war was almost inevitable once an important issue on which these opposing claimants to sovereignty disagreed had arisen. Slavery was an issue about which there was significant dispute between those who claimed sovereignty for the federal government and those in some southern states who claimed sovereignty for the individual states.

The disagreement about where sovereign power lay is evident in the different names that were given to the war by those supporting the sovereignty of federal government and by those supporting the sovereignty of the individual states. The former referred to it as "the civil war" and the latter referred to it as "the war between the states." But once the war was over and those on the side of the federal government had won, there was no longer any question about sovereignty. On Hobbes's theory, regardless of who held sovereign power before the war, the federal government clearly held it after the war. In the same way, when Cromwell's forces won the English civil war, there was no longer any doubt about who had the sovereign power. It may be that it is this aspect of Hobbes's political theory that gives rise to the mistaken view that he held that might makes right. Hobbes does hold that might makes authority, or rather that submission to might results in authority for that person or group to whom one has submitted. But he consistently holds that this political authority should be exercised for the benefit of those who have submitted, and that the laws of nature, or the moral law, is eternal and not subject to the command of the sovereign.

In both *De Cive* and *Leviathan*, Hobbes argues: "Now the duties of rulers are contained in this one sentence, *the safety of the people is the supreme law*" (*D.C.* XIII, 2: see also *L.* XXX, 1). In both works he is clear: "But by safety here is not meant a bare preservation, but also all other contentments of life, which every man by lawful industry, without danger or hurt to the commonwealth, shall acquire to himself" (*L.* XXX, 1; see also *D.C.* XIII, 4). Hobbes lists the four kinds of benefits that the sovereign should provide to the subjects. "1. That they be defended against foreign enemies. 2. That peace be preserved at home. 3. That they be enriched, as much as may be consistent with public security. 4. That they enjoy a harmless liberty" (*D.C.* XIII, 6). He even talks about people who, due to some accident, "become unable to maintain themselves by their labour," and says, "they ought not to be left to the charity of private persons, but to be provided for (as far forth as the necessities of nature require) by the laws of the commonwealth." (*L.* XXX, 18). Hobbes's support for at least a minimal welfare state comes as a surprise to those that take the traditional view of his political theory.

Although Hobbes says that no law can be unjust, his view of a good law supports the view that I have been putting forward: "A good law is that which is *needful* for the *good of the people*, and withal *perspicuous*" (*L.* XXX, 20). He denies that a law that "is for the benefit of the sovereign, though it be not necessary for the people," is good, because he holds that "the good of the sovereign and the good of the people cannot be separated" (ibid.). When he goes on to say that "[u]nnecessary laws are not good laws" (ibid.), it is clear that he means unnecessary for the good of the people. Hobbes holds that the sovereign, by enacting good laws, can initiate a virtuous cycle. Good laws make the citizens of the commonwealth more likely to obey the law and less likely to engage in the kind of behavior that might lead to civil war. The more satisfied the citizens are with the sovereign, the more freedom the sovereign can allow the citizens, including the freedom to criticize the sovereign. The more freedom the citizens have to criticize the sovereign, the less likely they are to engage in the kind of behavior that might lead to civil war. By enacting bad laws the sovereign may initiate a vicious cycle, one that makes it more likely that there will be a civil war. Were Hobbes alive today, he would change many of the details of his views about sovereignty, and his preference for a monarchy would be replaced by a preference for the stable western democracies.

In *De Cive* Hobbes talks about the duties of the sovereign, but he is clear that these duties are not duties in the sense that citizens have duties, the neglecting of which counts as injustice and which can be enforced by punishment. Rather, with regard to the sovereign, Hobbes holds, "it is their duty in all things, as much as they possibly can, to yield obedience unto right reason, which is the natural, moral, and divine law" (*D.C.* XIII, 2). In *Leviathan*, he avoids a possible ambiguity by substituting the word "office" for the word "duty," but this does not indicate any change in his view about what the sovereign should do (*L.* XXX, 1). All of his statements about how the sovereign ought to behave, or what the laws ought to be, constitute advice or counsel to the sovereign, who is, as Hobbes knows, free to accept or reject them. However, if the sovereign is rational, that is, concerned with his own safety and the safety of the people, he will accept them. Although Hobbes claims that citizens have no right to revolt, he is aware they will do so if they become sufficiently dissatisfied with the behavior of the sovereign. He does stress that the duty or office of the sovereign requires teaching the citizens why they should obey the law. Part of what Hobbes does to commend his advice to the sovereign is to provide arguments that the sovereign can use to try to persuade the citizen to obey the law. However, Hobbes knows that, just as with children, citizens are influenced more by bad examples than by good precepts, so his advice to the sovereign is to set a good example by following the laws of nature, e.g., the laws concerning gratitude and equity.

Arguments for Obeying the Law

Hobbes's initial moral argument for obeying the law might be called a deontological argument. It claims that all citizens gave to the sovereign the right to decide how they should act, and that citizens therefore have no right to act contrary to the decisions of the sovereign, that is, to the law. We have quoted the relevant passage before (see above):

> And when a man hath in either manner abandoned or granted away his right, then is he said to be OBLIGED or BOUND not to hinder those to whom such right is granted or abandoned from the benefit of it; and that he *ought*, and it is his DUTY not to make void that voluntary act of his own, and that hindrance is INJUSTICE, and INJURY, as being *sine jure*, the right being before renounced or transferred. (*L.* XIV, 7)

Because being unjust is violating a law of nature, it is immoral not to obey the civil law. This argument depends upon Hobbes's claim that every citizen, explicitly or implicitly, transfers his natural right to act as he thinks best to the sovereign. Citizens do this because they know that not making this free-gift will result in their living in a state of nature, or state of war, with everyone else. The rational fear of living in the state of nature, and the hope to avoid or escape that state, is what leads every rational person to give up his right of nature.

Hobbes's social contract theory of political obligation requires that the contract, covenant, free-gift, or renunciation not be a hypothetical contract, covenant, free-gift, or renunciation, because it is only by virtue of an actual granting away of one's right that one becomes obliged. Hobbes's state of nature is either a state that people want to avoid going into, or a state that they want to get out of. It is not the kind of hypothetical state that no one could possibly ever be in, such as Rawls's original position. It is a state in which there are no commonwealths with governments large enough to provide security for a reasonably satisfactory life. Hobbes holds that all citizens, or their ancestors, did actually renounce or grant away their natural right to the sovereign. Hobbes does not claim that everyone explicitly says the words that constitute the performative act of granting away one's right. He is prepared to accept that one's actions, e.g., in openly accepting the protection of the sovereign, can constitute granting of one's right to the sovereign (see *L.* XIV, 7, 14).

Because Hobbes argues that it is fear that leads people to enter into those covenants that are necessary for creating a commonwealth, he must hold that "[c]ovenants entered into by fear, in the condition of mere nature, are obligatory" (*L.* XIV, 27). He holds that the covenants necessary to form a commonwealth, or, more precisely, the making of a free-gift of one's right of nature, is always done from fear, either fear of the person to whom one made a free-gift of one's right or fear of others. Hobbes takes covenants so seriously that he holds that in the state of nature, "if I covenant to pay a ransom, or service, for my life, to an enemy, I am bound by it" (ibid.). Hobbes must therefore explain why covenants made from fear in a civil society do not oblige. Most covenants made from fear do oblige in a civil society, e.g., if my fear of an extreme rise in the price of oil leads me to sign a contract to buy 1,000 gallons of oil at the present price, that contract is valid. However, Hobbes claims that even coerced covenants oblige in the state of nature, so he has to explain why coerced covenants do not oblige in a civil society. His explanation is that the civil law can make coerced covenants not obligatory. "And even in commonwealth, if I be forced to redeem myself from a thief by promising him money, I am bound to pay it, till the civil law discharge me" (*L.* XIV, 27).

Hobbes takes the obligatory nature of covenants so seriously that he seems to be saying that even in a civil society coerced covenants do oblige, but that the civil law can then later remove that obligation. However, this does not seem correct. Rather, what seems to be the case is that the civil law prohibits coercing a person into making a covenant and says that covenants made under coercion are null and void *ab initio*, from the start. So that if in a commonwealth one is threatened and so says the words "If you let me go I promise to pay you $10.000," the civil law does not allow those words to count as the making of a promise. Regardless of what I intend, it is the civil law that determines whether stating "I promise," constitutes a promise. It is the sovereign – or the law or the judicial system – that determines when my stated intention to make a promise actually constitutes the making of a promise. The sovereign, or the law or the judicial system, and not the person himself, also determines whether someone who injures or kills another was acting in self-defense. Hobbes holds that everyone retains the right to defend himself from any immediate threat to his life. However, the claim that there was an immediate threat to one's life is subject to the judgment of the courts, and so a claim of self-defense is also subject to the judgment of the commonwealth. Hobbes takes away from the individual and grants to the commonwealth the right and duty to determine what that person has done, even when that person has no doubt about what he intended to do. The commonwealth has the authority to settle all disputes because the primary goal of Hobbes's political theory, overriding all other concerns, is the avoidance of civil war.

Hobbes is not content to show that it is unjust not to obey the civil law; he also wants to show that the best way to guarantee everyone's long-term survival is for all people to recognize that they have obliged themselves to accept the decision of the sovereign, i.e., the laws, as their guide. Hobbes's argument is that the uniformity of action that comes from everyone following the decision of the sovereign is more likely to lead to everyone's long-term preservation than each individual acting on his own diverse decisions. Avoiding civil war is almost always more important for everyone's preservation than any improvement in the administration of the commonwealth. Hobbes claims that anarchy and civil war are a greater threat to a person's preservation than almost anything that happens in a stable civil society. The only way to avoid anarchy and civil war and maintain a stable civil society is for everyone to understand that they have given to the sovereign their right to act on their own decisions. They have therefore obliged themselves to act on the decisions of the sovereign, i.e., according to the laws of the commonwealth. Not to obey the law is not only to be guilty of injustice but also to act in a way that threatens the stability of the commonwealth and hence increases the risk of civil war and a return to the state of nature.

This argument that it is morally and rationally required for people to act justly, that is, to obey the law, is uniquely a political argument. It involves an individual's relationship to his government; it is not about the relationship of one individual to another. It is an argument for accepting the laws of one's society as the guide to one's actions even when one believes that a particular law requires actions that are not in the best interest of its citizens. The argument has great force whether a person is concerned with her own preservation, or of her family's, or with the preservation of all. Hobbes's argument appeals to each person's self-interest, but because peace and a stable society are equally in the interest of everyone, it is not an egoistic argument. It has as much force to a rational person with an impartial concern for the preservation of everyone in the society as it does to a rational egoist.

It is a powerful argument against autonomy, if autonomy is taken as acting on one's own decisions rather than on the decisions of someone else. If one is impartially concerned with the welfare of everyone, then, except in extraordinary cases, one should obey the law rather than act on the dictates of one's own conscience. Because we know that people's consciences often tell them to act in different ways, the actual result of citizens following their own consciences will almost certainly be worse for everyone than if everyone obeys the law. This argument against autonomy is based on moral considerations, the welfare of all the citizens. However, there is a parallel argument against people acting autonomously even when concerned with only egoistic considerations, that is, being concerned only with one's own preservation. A surprising feature of Hobbes's arguments for obeying the law is that they do not depend at all on the present law being the best law. Even if one's conscience advises acting in some way that, if the sovereign had put it forward, that is, if it were the law, it would have a better result than obeying the present law, it is still better to obey the present law rather than follow one's own conscience.

The example of speed limits makes this point very clearly. Some highways have both maximum and minimum speed limits; suppose the maximum speed is 65 miles an hour and the minimum speed is 40 miles an hour. Now it might be the case that traffic would move more efficiently and there would be fewer accidents if the maximum speed limit were raised to 70 miles an hour or the minimum speed limit were slowed to 30 miles per hour. Nonetheless, people should obey the legal speed limits because these are the limits that everyone has agreed to follow. If some people went faster or others went slower than allowed by the present law, traffic would move less efficiently and there would be more accidents. People count on others to obey the law, and even if a proposed substitute law would be a better law, failure to obey the present law will make things worse. But since speed limits rarely evoke sufficient passion to result in a threat to the stability of the commonwealth, it is worthwhile to mention that the same point applies to the disputes about abortion and the acceptable treatment of animals. Both of these disputes arouse sufficient passion to lead people to disobey the law and even to resort to violence. The United States Supreme Court has provided a complex decision concerning the acceptability of abortion. Some disagree because they hold that all abortions should be legally prohibited; others disagree because they hold that no abortions should be legally prohibited. Hobbes correctly holds that no matter how strongly one disagrees with the Supreme Court decision, one is morally required not to disobey the law in order to follow one's conscience.

This is an extraordinarily powerful argument for accepting the sovereign's decisions or obeying the law even when it goes against one's conscience, especially in those cases where people's consciences differ. One reason that its force has not been appreciated is due to the rhetorical power of autonomy. Most philosophers and political scientists have become so entranced by autonomy that they find it hard even to consider, let alone to accept, an argument showing that complete autonomy is a bad thing. It may be that, because Hobbes has an argument against autonomy and for obeying the law, many have concluded that he does not put forward a genuine moral theory. However, Hobbes's argument is clearly a moral argument, one that should be accepted by completely impartial rational persons who are concerned with protecting the welfare of all persons. No doubt his emphasis on the fact that most persons are not impartially concerned with everyone plays some role in leading his readers to overlook the moral character of his argument against autonomy, but this cannot be the whole story. Many people take morality to require autonomy, but if autonomy means that morality requires each person always to act on her own decisions concerning what is best even when this is against the law, Hobbes is decidedly and correctly anti-autonomy.

Hobbes holds that we should obey the laws no matter who is sovereign, so it would be inconsistent for him to hold that we should obey the law because the sovereign's decisions are better than those of private citizens. His argument is that if individuals and groups believe that they are morally and rationally allowed to act on the decisions they personally regard as best, rather than accepting the commands of the sovereign, i.e., the laws, as the over-riding guide for their actions, then the result is anarchy and civil war. This argument has force even if each one of the diverse decisions of citizens, if accepted by the sovereign as its decision, would be more likely to lead to everyone's long-term preservation than the actual decision made by the sovereign. And it shows that justice – that is, keeping one's covenants, or, more generally, not doing what one had given up the right to do – is a law of nature. Since it is a law of nature dictating those virtues that are necessary for peace, it is a moral law in addition to being a dictate of reason concerning the best way to preserve one's life. These arguments for obeying the law are so powerful that it is easy to think that Hobbes regards morality as consisting simply in obedience to the law. He does regard justice, that is, obeying the law, as the primary moral virtue of citizens, but, as discussed in the previous chapter, justice is only one of the moral virtues, and many of the other moral virtues, e.g., gratitude, apply primarily to the sovereign.

Arguments for Entering into a Commonwealth

Since Hobbes is writing to those that are already citizens of a commonwealth, his primary concern is to provide rational, moral, and sometimes religious arguments for obeying the law. These arguments presuppose that all citizens have given to the sovereign their right of nature to decide for themselves how they should act, and so have obliged themselves to obey his commands, that is, obey the law. If one accepts Hobbes's presupposition that everyone has given up their right of nature to the sovereign, then it is the case that he has provided strong moral and rational arguments showing that it is unjust, and hence immoral, not to obey the law. However, because very few people give up their right of nature to the sovereign explicitly or expressly, many may doubt that they do actually give up this right. Hobbes's arguments showing that it is unjust to disobey the law will not have any force for them. He does try to show that these people implicitly or "by inference" have given up their right of nature to the sovereign (*L.* XIV, 13–15), but he is aware that many will not be persuaded by this claim. So what he does is try to show that, insofar as they are moral and rational, they must obey the law not only because they obliged themselves to do so, but also because it is moral and rational to oblige themselves, that is, to give up their right to decide for themselves how they should act. This also fits in with his theoretical framework of showing that all rational persons in a state of nature will do whatever they can to get out of that state, including giving up their right of nature.

Hobbes's strong statements about the horrors of the state of nature, e.g., that in it "the life of man is solitary, poor, nasty, brutish, and short" (*L.* XIII, 9), are used by him to support his claim that no one, no matter how clever or strong, can reasonably hope to survive for long in such a state. This is then used to support his conclusion that in entering into a civil state everyone must be "contented with as much liberty against other men, as he would allow other men against himself" (*L.* XIV, 5). His argument that one should not act in any way that might lead to civil war is that civil war makes it impossible to maintain the peaceful, sociable, and comfortable life that citizens of a commonwealth have. Even worse, it also has the result that "every man returneth into the condition and calamity of a war with every other man (which is the greatest evil that can happen in this life)" (*L.* XXX, 3). Hobbes's rhetoric about how miserable life is in the state of nature does not presuppose psychological egoism because it applies equally to a state in which small families or groups have no common power to keep them all in awe.

What is confusing about Hobbes's arguments about the state of nature is that when he is talking about the state of nature as a state that existed prior to any large commonwealths, the miserable character of that state is attributed to the characteristics of individual persons. It is not that everyone in this state of nature has moral vices, but enough people are greedy and ambitious that it makes life miserable for all. "For though the wicked be fewer than the righteous, yet because we cannot distinguish them, there is a necessity of suspecting, self-defending, ever incident to the most honest and fairest conditioned" (*D.C.* Pref., 3, p. 100). However, when he talks about the state of nature that will come about if there is a civil war, the causes of the civil war are not the moral vices of individual persons, but false moral beliefs:

How many kings, and those good men too, hath this one error, that a tyrant king might lawfully be put to death, been the slaughter of! How many throats hath this false position cut, that a prince for some causes may by certain men be deposed! And what bloodshed hath not this erroneous doctrine caused, that kings are not superiors to, but administrators for the multitude! Lastly, how many rebellions hath this opinion been the cause of, which teacheth that the knowledge whether the commands of kings be just or unjust, belongs to private men; and that before they yield obedience, they not only may, but ought to dispute them! (*D.C.* Pref., 2, pp. 96–7)

Hobbes's political theory, like every other plausible political theory, involves an account of human nature, that is, of the behavior of human beings that are the citizens and sovereigns of a commonwealth. However, it is a serious mistake to think that this account of human nature must claim that all human beings have identical motivation. Because of his account of rationality, Hobbes can claim, without making any universal claims about human nature, that all rational human beings desire to avoid death and to gain power and felicity. His remark that even if the wicked be fewer than the righteous, the life of all are affected, shows that Hobbes knows that a political theory must take into account widespread differences in human nature. That some people are immoral is enough to require any large commonwealth to have a police force large enough to protect the vast majority that is moral. That some people have such strong moral and religious beliefs that they are prepared to act in ways that can precipitate a civil war requires a sovereign power strong enough to keep them all in awe. It also requires that the sovereign has the power to prohibit the teaching of those rebellious doctrines. Hobbes's political theory is incompatible with the obviously false view of psychological egoism. Except insofar as people are rational, Hobbes does not even hold that all people are motivated in any of the same ways. Although he does have an account of rationality that is universal, he explicitly claims that the degree to which people act rationally differs greatly.

Summary

The primary practical purpose of Hobbes's political theory is to prevent civil war. His belief that a civil war will lead to a state of nature that is worse than almost any civil state explains why he claims that, no matter what kind of sovereign is involved, the primary duty of citizens is to obey the sovereign and the primary duty of the sovereign is to achieve a peaceful, sociable, and comfortable life for the citizens of the commonwealth. Hobbes, like most philosophers, had an unrealistic view of the force of his arguments to change the behavior of those who read them. Even more than most philosophers, however, he refused to distort or modify his arguments in order to make them more persuasive. He argued for an account of human nature that he knew would be controversial. Although he wanted to use religion to support his moral and political views, he did not change these views in order to make them more palatable to the religious views of most of his fellow citizens. Indeed, sometimes he seems to use language deliberately in a way that he must have known would cause great controversy. But one cannot help but be impressed by a close examination of the systematic way in which he used his account of human nature to develop his moral and political theories.

5

After Hobbes

Hobbes's most important influence is in the field of political theory, but he has also had a significant influence in moral philosophy. However, his English contemporaries did not accept his views and almost all those who wrote about Hobbes tried to refute his theory. Most of them were upset by his view that neither morality nor politics depends on religion in any significant way. Although Hobbes explicitly claims that God can be taken to support his moral and political theories, his contemporaries realized that God plays no essential role in either. Nonetheless, Hobbes developed his moral and political theories in such a systematic and forceful way that although his contemporaries did not accept his answers, they took over the way he framed the problems. For Hobbes, the problem that political theory has to solve is how, given the facts of human nature, to construct a commonwealth that will make it most likely that people will live together in peace and harmony. It is important to note the phrase "make it most likely that people will live together in peace and harmony," for Hobbes was aware that, "given the facts of human nature," it is not possible to construct a commonwealth that will guarantee that people will live together in peace and harmony.

Hobbes is aware that all three forms of commonwealths – democracy, aristocracy, or monarchy – have serious problems. He favors a monarchy because he thinks that it is likely to have fewer problems, or fewer serious problems, than either an aristocracy or a democracy. Despite this, Hobbes's political theory claims that the rights of the sovereign and the duties of the citizens are the same in all three forms of sovereignty. Criticisms of Hobbes that are based on his favoring a monarchy should not be taken as criticisms of his political theory, for he explicitly claims that it is not part of his political theory that a monarchy is the best form of sovereignty. It may be that his favoring of a monarchy indicates some flaw in his account of human nature, but I do not think that this is true. Rather, I think that Hobbes's favoring of a monarchy is the result of his not sufficiently appreciating that his account of human nature applies to sovereigns as well as to citizens. Were he to have appreciated that sovereigns are as likely as citizens to act on their emotions rather than their reason, he would most likely have favored a democracy. In a democracy, there will be conflicting emotions, and that makes it more likely that compromises will be made, thus providing an opportunity for reason to have more influence. Of course, it may be that Hobbes supported a monarchy because at the time when he was developing his political theory the sovereign was a monarch, and he did not want to provide any grounds for rejecting the sovereign. But the fact that he presented a copy of *Leviathan* to Cromwell when he returned to England shows that he realized that his political theory favored whatever kind of sovereign was in power.

On the continent, Hobbes was an acknowledged influence. Both Spinoza and Leibniz thought very highly of Hobbes's work and his influence on Spinoza's *Theological-Political Treatise* is universally acknowledged. Spinoza clearly accepted Hobbes's view that religion was a great danger to civil peace and, like Hobbes, tries to diminish its power and authority. Hobbes tries to diminish the power of religion by giving the sovereign power over religion, while Spinoza argues more for tolerance of different religious beliefs. This difference may be due to their situations: Hobbes living in a commonwealth where the sovereign was the head of the Church, and Spinoza being concerned with the followers of non-Christian religions. However, Spinoza, like Hobbes, thinks that the sovereign has the authority to control religion and Hobbes, like Spinoza, thinks that the sovereign should be tolerant of all religions that do not threaten the peace and stability of the commonwealth. Both men knew about the religious wars that had devastated Europe and sought to diminish the power of religion to cause civil and international strife. Perhaps Hobbes's most significant influence was in providing an account of morality and politics in which religion was divested of any significant public role. He does not underestimate the power of religion; on the contrary, he is acutely aware of the motivating force of religious beliefs. This is why, in addition to subordinating religion to the state, he tries to provide an interpretation of Christianity that supports the moral and political theories that he puts forward.

Most of Hobbes's contemporaries in England who accepted his views about the absolute authority of the sovereign were those who believed in the divine right of kings. Hobbes does not accept this theory; rather, he holds that sovereign authority comes from the submission of the citizens. That sovereign authority and power derives from the people was accepted by all those who denied the divine right of kings. Even though most denied the absolute authority of the sovereign that Hobbes put forward, they accepted his view that the limits on the authority and power of the sovereign depend on how much authority and power the people grant to the sovereign. Hobbes regards sovereign authority to be absolute because he thinks that the submission of the citizens or future citizens is complete. He holds that all rational persons would agree to obey all the commands of the sovereign because they realize that any civil society is preferable to the state of nature. They also recognize that in order to maintain a civil society they need a power that will keep all the citizens in awe.

Hobbes holds that the state of nature is so terrible because of his views about the nature of human populations. Given the large number of people necessary to create a stable commonwealth, enough of them will act on their emotions rather than their reason to make it necessary for there to be a sovereign to keep everyone in awe. This is necessary even for those in whom reason is dominant, for in the absence of such a sovereign power they are forced to protect themselves by whatever means seems best to them. The result of there being no sovereign power to keep everyone in awe is that the state of nature will be a state of war, even though most people, if they felt secure, would be prepared to live and let live.

Hobbes versus Locke

John Locke, like almost all political philosophers after Hobbes, accepts Hobbes's view that the source of sovereign authority and power comes from the people. Hobbes and Locke also agree that in the state of nature all people are free and equal. They also agree that the laws of nature apply even in the state of nature and so people in this state are not free to do whatever they feel like doing, but only free to behave in ways that they regard as rational. Both hold that the laws of nature are the dictates of reason and that it is a law of nature that every man is "bound to preserve himself," so they both hold that a person can do what he believes is necessary to preserve himself. But there are also some important differences between them. Locke holds that the law of nature also dictates that "when his own preservation comes not in competition, ought he, as much as he can, to preserve the rest of mankind" (2nd Treatise, Chap. II, par. 6). Locke's account of the right of nature is also more inclusive than Hobbes's. Whereas both Hobbes and Locke hold that everyone has the right to do whatever he believes is necessary for his preservation, including killing another person, Locke also holds that *"every Man hath a right to punish the Offender, and be an Executioner of the Law of Nature"* (ibid., par. 8). Hobbes does not hold that people in the state of nature have the right of punishing; he even denies that punishment, in the strict sense, is even possible in the state of nature.

The most important difference between Hobbes and Locke is about whether the state of nature is a state of war. According to Hobbes, the state of nature is a state of war. He says: "Hereby it is manifest that during the time men live without a common power to keep them all in awe, they are in that condition which is called war, and such a war is of every man against every man" (*L*. XIII, 8). Hobbes explains this view by comparing war to weather, saying: "For as the nature of foul weather lieth not in a shower or two of rain, but in an inclination thereto of many days together, so the nature of war consisteth not in actual fighting, but in the known disposition thereto during all the time there is no assurance to the contrary" (ibid.). Hobbes is claiming that when people "live without a common power to keep them all in awe," which is the state of nature, they are always prepared to fight. He does not say that they are always actually fighting; only that fighting is likely to break out at any moment.

Locke criticizes Hobbes's view about the relationship between the state of nature and the state of war:

> And here we have the plain *difference between the State of Nature, and the State of War*, which however, some Men have confounded, are as far distant, as a State of Peace, Good Will, Mutual Assistance, and Preservation, and a State of Enmity, Malice, Violence, and Mutual Destruction are from each other. Men living together according to reason, without a common Superior on Earth to judge between them, is *properly the State of Nature*. (2nd Treatise, Chap. II, par. 19)

Note that Locke includes in his account of the state of nature that people are "living together according to reason." Hobbes holds that there never was, nor ever will be, a state of nature in Locke's sense because if a large number of people are living together, not all will live according to reason. Even Locke seems to agree that without an agreed-upon authority that will serve as judge, the state of nature will become a state of war. That the state of nature is a state of war serves as the foundation for Hobbes's claim that rational people will agree to create a sovereign powerful enough keep them all in awe.

Locke, on the other hand, does not want to characterize the state of nature as the state of war because he does not want the state of nature to be such that people would be willing to give up as much of their right to decide how to act to the sovereign as Hobbes does. It is important to remember that in the *Two Treatises of Government*, first published in 1690, Locke was defending the Glorious Revolution of 1688 in which William of Orange replaced James II as king of England and agreed to share power with Parliament. At that time he did not think that revolutions were necessarily bad. In his *Two Tracts of Government*, written in 1660 but which Locke never had published,[1] he takes a much more authoritarian position. I do not claim that Locke changes his views in response to the changed circumstances in which he is writing, but Locke's *Two Treatises* were much more in tune with his times than Hobbes's *Leviathan* was in tune with his times. Although Hobbes and Locke share many views in common, not only do they differ in tone and style, they also have some substantive differences.

Locke, unlike Hobbes, is not concerned with describing a state that might have preceded commonwealths of sufficient size to provide protection to its citizens, or that might result from a protracted civil war. Locke, unlike Hobbes, is not primarily concerned with avoiding a return to a state of nature that would result from a civil war. Rather, he is concerned with avoiding what he calls a state of war, namely where someone exercises power immorally, whether in what Hobbes calls a state of nature or in a civil society. *"Want of a common Judge with Authority, puts all Men in a State of Nature: Force without Right, upon a Man's Person, makes a state of War,* both where there is, and is not, a Common Judge" (2nd Treatise, Chap. II, par. 19). Hobbes and Locke are not disagreeing about how

[1] *Two Tracts of Government*, ed. Philip Abrams. Cambridge: Cambridge University Press, 1967.

actual people will behave in the absence of government; rather, they are simply disagreeing in how they define a state of nature. Locke includes in his account that all people act according to reason. Hobbes would claim that, when talking about a large number of people, Locke's state of nature never did and never will exist, and it does not seem that Locke disagrees with this.

Although Hobbes and Locke agree that the dictates of reason that are the laws of nature apply in the state of nature, Hobbes means by this only that if someone violates a law of nature in the state of nature he is acting irrationally and immorally. However, Hobbes realizes that in the state of nature, defined as that state where there is no common power to keep them all in awe, not everyone will abide by the laws of nature. That is why he says that the state of nature is a state of war. Locke includes in his definition of a state of nature that everyone does follow the laws of nature. This is why he says that the state of nature is a state of peace. However, Locke does realize that a state without a common superior on Earth to judge between people is quite likely to turn into a state of war, and he suggests the same method for getting out of this state as Hobbes does:

> To avoid this State of War (where there is no appeal but to heaven, and wherein every the least difference is apt to end, where there is no Authority to decide between the contenders) is one great reason of Mens putting themselves into Society and quitting the State of Nature. For where there is an Authority, a Power on Earth, from which relief can be had by *appeal*, there the continuance of the State of War is excluded, and the Controversie is decided by that Power. (2nd Treatise, Chap. III, par. 21)

Locke should not be talking about "quitting the State of Nature" for this suggests that he agrees with Hobbes that the state of nature is the state of war. So it seems that Locke does not really disagree with Hobbes.

Locke defines political power in much the same way that Hobbes defines the power of the sovereign:

> Political Power then I take to be a Right of making Laws with Penalties of Death, and consequently all less Penalties, for the Regulating and Preserving of Property, and of employing the force of the community, in the Execution of such Laws, and in defence of the Common-wealth from Foreign Injury, and all this for the Publick Good. (2nd Treatise, Chap. I, par. 3)

Locke's talk about the point of creating political power differs primarily in style from the way that Hobbes talks about the point of creating a sovereign. Hobbes says the point of creating a sovereign is, *"the procuration of the safety of the people"* (L. XXX, 1). He then continues: "But by safety here is not meant a bare preservation, but all the other contentments of life, which every man by lawful industry, without danger or hurt to the commonwealth, shall acquire to himself" (ibid.). Locke's view is similar but he expresses it somewhat differently: "The great and chief end therefore, of Mens uniting into Commonwealths, and putting themselves under Government, is the Preservation of their Property" (2nd Treatise, Chap. IX, par. 124). Although Locke defines people's property as their "Lives, Liberties and Estates" (ibid., par. 123), the emphasis is different from that of Hobbes.

Although they both hold that it is the basic law of nature that every man is "bound to preserve himself," Locke holds that there is another basic law of nature, which dictates that "when his own preservation comes not in competition, ought he, as much as he can, to preserve the rest of mankind" (ibid., Chap. II, par. 6). Hobbes limits the right of nature to the right to do what one believes is necessary to preserve oneself, whereas Locke adds an additional right: "every man has a Right to punish the Offender, and be Executioner of the Law of Nature" (ibid., par. 8). Locke holds that what "we call *punishment*" is what "one Man may lawfully do harm to another" for the two reasons of *"Reparation* and *Restraint"* (ibid.). So Locke seems to hold that what we would now call vigilantism counts as punishment if done for the right reasons. Further, Hobbes distinguishes between inflicting harm, even inflicting harm that one has the right to inflict, and punishment. He holds that it is not appropriate to talk of punishment in the state of nature; he argues that only those who are authorized to do so can punish. Punishment occurs only when the person inflicting the harm has received the right of nature of another person who then does what he no longer has a right to do. If one were to take what Locke says literally, it would be impossible to maintain a stable civil society. Hobbes is very careful to avoid this kind of vigilantism.

Hobbes tries to derive all of the laws of nature and the right of nature from the basic dictate of reason that one should seek peace in order to preserve oneself and that if one cannot achieve peace one is rationally allowed to do whatever one believes is necessary to preserve oneself. Locke puts forward two basic dictates of reason: the first is identical to Hobbes, that one seek to preserve oneself, but the second is that, when there is no conflict with the first dictate, one is rationally required to preserve others as well. From the first dictate of reason Locke concludes, like Hobbes, that we are rationally allowed to do whatever we believe is necessary to preserve ourselves. From the second dictate of reason he concludes that we are rationally allowed to punish those who we believe have acted contrary to the second dictate of reason, to preserve others. Hobbes is correct in holding that all that reason requires us to do is to avoid harms to ourselves, and Locke is incorrect in claiming that reason requires that we seek to preserve others. But Locke is on to an important point; for reason allows us to help others even when this is contrary to our own preservation. Reason is not purely egocentric. Locke goes too far in saying that reason requires us to help others, and that it is rationally allowable to punish those whom we believe have violated the second dictate of reason, but he is correct in claiming that reason is not limited to a concern with oneself, which is what Hobbes often seems to be saying.

Although Hobbes admits that the sovereign can act immorally, he denies that the sovereign can be unjust, for only someone who has given up his right of nature can be unjust, and sovereigns never give up their right of nature. Because Hobbes allows punishment only for unjust actions, and not for anyone who has not submitted to the sovereign, it follows that the sovereign cannot be punished. Hobbes wants this conclusion because he wants to avoid legitimizing any actions that might lead to civil war. Locke allows that it is legitimate to punish the sovereign because he is not concerned with avoiding civil war. Hobbes's theory makes it very difficult to justify revolutions; Locke's theory makes it very easy to do so. Hobbes lived closer to the religious wars on the continent and the bloody civil wars in England, whereas Locke lived closer to the relatively bloodless Glorious Revolution of 1688.

It is not surprising that the founding fathers of the United States of America preferred Locke to Hobbes. For Locke provides them with a justification for the American Revolution, whereas Hobbes would correctly claim that it was unjustified. Although Hobbes would have regarded the English sovereign as behaving immorally and irrationally in the way it dealt with the American colonies, he would not have thought that the harms inflicted on the colonies were anywhere near serious enough to justify a revolution or civil war. The English sovereign did not threaten the lives of the colonists; at most, the sovereign may have imposed some taxation that violated the natural law dictating equity. There were no harms being inflicted that justified a war that would result in thousands dying, many more being injured, and extensive property damage. In fact, only one third of the population of the colonies endorsed the revolution, one third opposed it, and one third had no settled view on the matter.

Nevertheless, the American Revolution would not have surprised Hobbes, for although he would have held that reason did not support it, he knew that most people do not act on reason, but on their passions. After the success of the revolution, Hobbes would have favored obedience to the new sovereign, and he would even have favored creating the myths that portrayed the revolution as glorious and justified, because such myths made the new country more stable. But there is no question that, on Hobbes's political theory, the American Revolution was unjustified. This does not count at all against his political theory, because the revolution was in fact unjustified. The southern states had as much reason to secede from the United States as the United States had to secede from England, and Abraham Lincoln, who refused to let these states secede and so saved the country, is viewed as being as great, or greater, than George Washington, who led the secession from England and so created the country. It is important to realize that the American Civil War was not fought over slavery; it was fought in order to keep the country from splitting apart. Indeed, England had abolished slavery 30 years before the American Civil War, and it is quite likely that if there had been no revolution, slavery would have ended without a civil war.

Although Locke accepts Hobbes's view about human populations, he obscures this agreement by including in his definition of the state of nature that men act according to reason. But Locke knows that not all actual people do act according to reason and so the state of nature soon becomes a state of war, with similar characteristics to Hobbes's account of the state of war. Nonetheless, Locke uses the state of nature as he defines it, and which never existed, to justify limiting the power that people would grant to the sovereign. Rather than arguing that people form commonwealths in order to avoid being in the state of war, Locke argues that living in the fictitious state of nature is an alternative to living in a commonwealth. Given this illegitimate contrast, he holds that people would not be willing to give up so much of their right of nature to the sovereign. If people will not only survive in the state of nature, but even live a reasonably pleasant life, there is no reason for them to give up so much of their right to decide how to act in order to get out of that state. Hobbes presents a much more plausible contrast, and uses his concept of the state of nature more as a state that would result from a civil war than as that state from which commonwealths developed.

Locke says almost nothing about the harms that result from a civil war. This difference between him and Hobbes may be due to fact that Hobbes had experienced the horrendous religious wars on the continent and the bloody civil wars in England, whereas Locke's experience was primarily of the relatively bloodless Glorious Revolution of 1688. Locke intended to defend the limited sovereignty of the king brought about by the Glorious Revolution, and his account of the state of nature as if it might actually exist was used to support that form of government. Hobbes intended to defend the absolute authority of the sovereign, and his view of human populations without a common power to keep them all in awe was far more realistic than Locke's account of the state of nature. Hobbes's theory supported whatever government was in power, for he was primarily concerned with preventing civil war. The fact that Hobbes presented a copy of *Leviathan* to Cromwell shows that he knows that his political theory favors absolute authority no matter what form sovereignty takes.

Although Locke's rhetoric about the right of revolution seems to have popular appeal, no government allows citizens to decide when revolution is appropriate. Even in the most liberal democracies, governments allow only those changes that are made in accordance with the laws governing the making of changes. Just as Hobbes claims that all sovereigns, whether they are democracies, aristocracies, or monarchies, have absolute authority, all governments, whether they are democracies, aristocracies, or monarchies, claim absolute authority. Hobbes cannot be credited with influencing governments to claim absolute authority, for all governments, both before and after Hobbes, claim to have such authority. But Hobbes correctly describes the absolute authority of law that all governments claim. He realizes that no government is willing to accept that its citizens may rebel or revolt when they believe that the government is acting in what they consider to be unacceptable ways. However, he also realizes that citizens will rebel or revolt if enough of them are sufficiently dissatisfied with the way that the government is performing.

Hobbes's political theory takes account of the fact that people disagree on important moral and political matters and that, when dealing with a large number of people, there is no way to reach agreement other than giving one person or group the final authority to make decisions. One would have thought that Locke, who was so much more concerned with epistemological matters than Hobbes, would have realized that *"Want of a common Judge with Authority"* would immediately result in disagreements that would lead to the kind of state that Hobbes calls a state of war. Locke spends almost no time in his political theory considering how one is to settle disagreements; he simply ignores the problems that result from citizens challenging the sovereign's decision. Part of the reason for this is that Locke wants to allow the citizens to act on their own beliefs about whether the sovereign has violated the dictates of reason so that they have the right to punish the sovereign for his immoral behavior. This view is an invitation to anarchy. Hobbes's view is exactly the opposite. Since the absence of a common judge with authority inevitably leads to a state of war, which is worse than almost any civil state, Hobbes holds that only clear threats to the lives of the citizens gives them the right to disobey the sovereign. Hobbes states the way all governments view their relationship to citizens; Locke states the way citizens dissatisfied with their government view their relationship to it. Hobbes's view is far more likely to lead to a stable society than Locke's view, but Locke's view has far more rhetorical appeal.

Hobbes on Sovereignty

Hobbes holds that, insofar as they are rational, all people regard long-term survival as their primary goal and realize that their long-term survival depends on living in a secure civil society. They therefore agree to do whatever is necessary to create and maintain a secure civil society, and they realize that the only way to do this is to create a sovereign with sufficient power that fear of disobeying the sovereign keeps their irrational emotions in check. Creating such a power requires everyone to agree to obey the sovereign if their lives are not in immediate danger and never to aid anyone who does not obey the sovereign. For Hobbes, obeying the sovereign means obeying the law. This means that citizens agree not only never to do what the laws forbid them to do, but also never to assist anyone who has acted contrary to the law.

Citizens grant to the sovereign almost absolute authority and power. Not quite absolute, for they do not, indeed cannot, give up their right to defend themselves against an imminent threat to their lives. But they can and do give up their right to decide what is the best way to maintain their long-term survival. They realize that the best way for all of them to secure long-term survival is if they all give up this right to the sovereign. Reserving the right to self-defense is an almost insignificant limitation, for they agree that the sovereign has the final authority to decide if a person acts in self-defense. The granting of almost absolute authority and power to the sovereign is based on Hobbes's view that reason's primary goal is long-term survival and that the state of nature does not allow any man "(how strong or wise soever he be) of living out the time which nature ordinarily alloweth men to live" (*L.* XIV, 4).

Hobbes's support of the view that the sovereign has absolute authority has suffered unjustified criticism because it has been identified with his support of monarchy. His strong denunciation of the doctrine *"That the sovereign power may be divided"* by claiming that this doctrine goes "directly against the essence of a commonwealth" (*L.* XXIX, 12) has suffered more justified criticism. Hobbes is arguing against a situation like that which prevailed in England at the time at which he was writing, where there were two claimants to sovereign power, king and Parliament. Hobbes correctly sees that this kind of situation is not tenable. He thinks that it is inevitable that, when both sides have considerable support, a dispute between two claimants about who has what aspects of sovereign power will result in civil war. The situation that Hobbes confronted when writing *De Cive*, is similar to the situation that the United States confronted prior to the American Civil War when there were two claimants to sovereign power, the federal government and the state governments, and both had considerable support.

After the Civil War it was clear that the federal government, rather than the state governments, had the sovereign power, but within the federal government different branches – executive, judicial, and legislative – held different aspects of sovereignty. Hobbes did not envisage the enormous growth in the size and stability of democratic commonwealths whereby the different branches of government could control different aspects of sovereignty, but conflict between these different branches posed no serious threat of civil war. The stability of modern democracies is due to the acceptance by almost all of the population, including members of the government, of Hobbes's view that maintaining a peaceful civil society is more important than any other political goal. Hobbes's view is accepted by almost everyone in modern democratic states because of its intrinsic appeal, not because they know his arguments for it.

Hobbes is, however, the, strongest and most explicit defender of such a view.

The concept of sovereignty, as Hobbes thought of it, is now an anachronism. In fact, in the United States it is impossible to say who is the sovereign in any sense that would correspond to what Hobbes means by sovereignty. Hobbes could claim that the people are sovereign because there are set times to vote. However, the people cannot vote on who is in the judicial branch of government. Even with regard to the executive and legislative branches, for which they can vote, their votes do not all occur at the same times, so the people cannot bring about a complete change of government. The insignificance of the concept of the sovereign as Hobbes conceives it should be clear from the following. In the United State of America, if the legislatures of two-thirds of the states call for a convention at which constitutional amendments can be proposed, amendments proposed by the convention can be ratified by the legislatures of three-fourths of the states. There is no constitutional limitation on what changes can be made in this way; the entire structure of government can be changed. This should mean that the sovereign power lies in the legislatures of three-fourths of the states. However, no amendment to the constitution has ever been ratified in this way. Sovereign power when Hobbes was writing was an important political concept, but now it seems to be primarily a theoretical concept with little political significance.

Nonetheless, the point that Hobbes is making with regard to the absolute authority of the sovereign still holds when interpreted as the absolute authority of the law. Hobbes claims that except in extreme circumstances, e.g., when one's life is in immediate danger, the law must be obeyed regardless of one's view about whether it is a good law. No individual is allowed to decide whether or not a particular law should be obeyed, for that would result in anarchy. Even when, in the course of defending oneself against an attack, one kills the attacker, it is the government that decides whether the killing counts as an act of self-defense. If it agrees, then the person is deemed not to have committed a crime and receives no punishment. However, if the state decides that the killing does not count as self-defense, then the person can legitimately be punished even if he sincerely thought he was acting in self-defense. Hobbes may be misleading in regarding the laws as the commands of the sovereign, but even though there is now no clear idea of who is sovereign, all citizens are required to obey all the laws. Regardless of the lack of knowledge of who is sovereign, there is agreement about what the law is, or about who decides what the law is, and the law is still the ultimate authority governing the citizens' behavior.

Although Locke's rhetoric about the right of revolution seems to have popular appeal, no government allows citizens to decide when revolution is appropriate. Even in the most liberal democracies, governments allow only those changes that are made in accordance with the laws governing the making of changes. Just as Hobbes claimed that all sovereigns, no matter whether they are democracies, aristocracies, or monarchies, have absolute authority, so, even now, all governments, whether, democracies, aristocracies, or monarchies, claim absolute authority. Hobbes cannot be credited with influencing governments to claim absolute authority, for all governments, both before and after his time, claim to have such authority. But Hobbes correctly describes the absolute authority of law that all governments claim, realizing that no government accepts that it is not the final authority in deciding how people should behave.

What is almost universally neglected in Hobbes's political theory is his distinction between what is moral and what is legal. Hobbes claims that governments are the ultimate legal authority; he denies that they are the ultimate moral authority. He does not hold that sovereigns determine what counts as moral, although he does claim that it is almost always immoral to disobey the law. Hobbes acknowledges that sovereigns, like citizens, are subject to the laws of nature and so can act immorally, but he insists that citizens lack the authority to punish the government. Nonetheless, he realizes that if a government is to survive, it must act morally, i.e., act in the interests of the citizens, especially by protecting them from harm. If the government does not act to benefit the citizens, it will violate the law of nature requiring gratitude to the citizens for their obedience to the laws, and the citizens will, in turn, not only cease to obey the law but also may revolt against the government.

Hobbes makes four claims that may seem incompatible, but which are actually quite compatible: (1) citizens should always obey the law, (2) sovereigns should always act to further the interests of the citizens, (3) even if the sovereign does not act to further the interests of the citizens, they still should obey the law, and (4) if the sovereign does not act to further the interests of the citizens, they will cease to obey the law. Hobbes is aware that people, both those in governments as well as citizens, do not always behave in the way that they should. Although governments have the power to enforce obedience to the laws, they have that power only insofar as a substantial number of citizens choose to obey the law. Given that it is in the interests of both citizens and sovereigns to maintain a civil society, both citizens and sovereigns have prudential as well as moral reasons to act morally. For citizens this requires obeying the law, and for sovereigns this requires making good laws, that is, laws that further the interests of the citizens. Although Hobbes is not often cited as having an influence on the way that modern western democracies operate, he does, in fact, correctly describe the way they do operate. They teach patriotism and obedience to the law, and claim to act for the benefit of their citizens.

Aristotle, Hobbes, and Hume

Hobbes borrows from Aristotle without acknowledging that he is doing so. Leo Strauss has documented how closely Hobbes's account of the emotions follows Aristotle's account in the *Rhetoric*. Although Hobbes borrows from Aristotle without acknowledgment, he criticizes Aristotle by name. In a wonderful example of poetic justice in the history of philosophy, many later philosophers have explicitly criticized Hobbes, while borrowing from him without acknowledgment. Annette Baier, an admirer of Hume, has acknowledged (in personal conversation) how much Hume borrows from Hobbes in regard to his political philosophy. If one wants to find the places where Hume borrows from Hobbes, one should look for those instances where he provides a mistaken interpretation of Hobbes that he then criticizes; it can be seen that what he puts forward in those places as his view is actually a position held by Hobbes. However, apart from his political views, Hume differs from Hobbes in almost all of his basic philosophical positions. Hume is a phenomenalist; Hobbes is a materialist. Hume is a skeptic; Hobbes is not. Hume holds that reason has no ends of its own and that reason is and ought to be the slave of the passions; Hobbes holds that reason has its own ends and that people should follow reason rather than their passions. Hume holds that morality is based on sentiment and feeling; Hobbes holds that morality is derived from reason.

Consequentialism, Deontology, and Natural Law

The split between utilitarianism (consequentialism) and deontology, that is, between the view that morality is concerned solely with consequences and the view that acting morally involves acting in accordance with rules or virtues that are derived from reason, occurs after Hobbes's time, and both traditions seem to have been influenced by Hobbes. Here is what Hobbes says about breaking one's promise, or what he calls not abiding by the renouncing or transferring of one's right:

> So that *injury* or *injustice*, in the controversies of the world, is somewhat like to that which in the disputations of scholars is called absurdity. For as it is there called an *absurdity* to contradict what one maintained in the beginning, so in the world it is called injustice and injury voluntarily to undo that which from the beginning he had voluntarily done. (*L.* XIV, 7)

It should be obvious that Kant uses some similar sounding arguments in claiming that, by acting on those maxims that one cannot will to be universal laws, one is acting irrationally and immorally. Indeed, although Hobbes, unlike Kant, claims that reason has the goal of preserving one's life, Kant does hold that it is irrational to commit suicide. Like all natural law theorists, Hobbes holds the view, for which Kant is known, that acting immorally, i.e., contrary to any of the dictates of reason that are the moral laws, is acting irrationally.

Another similarity between Hobbes and Kant is their claim that morality is about intentions rather than actions: "The laws of nature oblige *in foro interno*, that is to say, they bind to a desire that they take place, but *in foro externo*, that is, putting them in act, not always" (*L.* XV, 36). That morality is concerned with intentions rather than actions comes out even more strongly in the following passage:

> And whatsoever laws bind *in foro interno* may be broken, not only by a fact contrary to the law, but also by a fact according to it, in case a man think it contrary. For though his action in this case be according to the law, yet his purpose was against the law, which, where the obligation is *in foro interno*, is a breach. (*L.* XV, 37)

This is in accord with Hobbes's claim that morality is about virtue and vice. "Now the science of virtue and vice is moral philosophy: and therefore the true doctrine of the laws of nature is the true moral philosophy" (*L.* XV, 40). Hobbes regards moral virtues both as those virtues dictated by the laws of nature dictating peace, and as those virtues that all people praise. These two methods determine the same moral virtues because it is the consequences of acting on the moral virtues, i.e., leading to and maintaining peace, which makes people praise them: "But the writers of moral philosophy, though they acknowledge the same virtues and vices, yet not seeing wherein consisted their goodness, nor that they come to be praised as the means of peaceable, sociable, and comfortable living, place them in a mediocrity of passions" (*L*. XV, 40).

Hobbes holds that reason dictates the moral virtues that are the means to achieving and maintaining peace because peace is a necessary means of avoiding death. This enables him to hold that it is irrational to act immorally and at the same time claim that acting contrary to the dictates of reason is immoral because such actions lead to bad consequences for all. His concern with consequences comes out clearly in the following passage: "The laws of nature are immutable and eternal; for injustice, ingratitude, arrogance, pride, iniquity, acception of persons, and the rest, can never be made lawful. For it can never be that war shall preserve life and peace destroy it" (*L*. XIV, 7). As this passage makes clear, Hobbes holds that the laws of nature are immutable and eternal. Thus he differs from contemporary consequentialists who claim that it is an empirical matter which moral rules actually lead to the best consequences. For Hobbes, it is universally true that the standard moral virtues have good consequences and the standard moral vices have bad consequences, because the only consequence that he regards as morally relevant is "peace for a means of the preservation of men in multitudes" (*L*. XV, 34). Hobbes's natural law account of morality combines deontological and consequentialist features because the laws of nature are the dictates of reason and reason has its own end, viz., the avoidance of an avoidable death. It may be that most commentators do not appreciate that Hobbes holds a natural law theory of morality, even though he explicitly claims to hold such a view, because God does not play an essential role in this account of morality.

Hobbes and Contemporary Political Philosophy: Rawls

Hobbes has significantly influenced a number of contemporary political philosophers, the most important being John Rawls. Rawls does not cite Hobbes as a significant influence, but it is clear that Hobbes did have a significant influence on the way in which Rawls develops his political theory. However, in Rawls's magisterial work, *A Theory of Justice*, the original position in which rational people decide on the two principles of justice resembles Locke's state of nature more than it does Hobbes's. Hobbes talks about the state of nature in several different ways, but he always maintains that the essential feature is that it is a state in which individuals or small families have no common power to keep them all in awe. For Hobbes, this state of nature can be an actual state, e.g., it can be the result of a protracted civil war, or it can be, as Hobbes thought, a primitive state where small families were always in danger of conflict with each other. But Hobbes also considered the state of nature as a theoretical concept, as shown by his remark, "Let us return to the state of nature, and consider men as if but even now sprung out of the earth, and suddenly, like mushrooms, come to full maturity, without all of kind of engagement to each other" (*D.C.* VIII, 1). Hobbes claims that nation-states are in an actual state of nature with regard to one another, as witnessed by how much they spend on the military. However, this is not his concern, nor is it Rawls's concern in *A Theory of Justice*. Both Hobbes and Rawls are concerned with the kinds of state or commonwealth that individuals should create.

Unlike Hobbes and like Locke, Rawls views the original position as a theoretical construct that is not peopled by actual persons. The only restriction that Hobbes puts on the people when he considers the state of nature as a purely theoretical state is that they not be engaged to each other in any way. Not only have they not given up or transferred any of their natural rights, they also do not have any friends or family ties, so that they might behave as psychological egoists. Rawls requires the people in the original position to behave as psychological egoists but, because they cannot have any beliefs about themselves that would enable them to distinguish themselves from any other person, the basic features of the state that they are creating are those that would be proposed by completely impartial persons. Hobbes allows rational people in the state of nature to have all beliefs about themselves that people normally have. For Rawls, it is rational to adopt any plan of life that will provide the best chance of being successfully pursued, but without any limits on the content of that plan of life. This is a version of the maximum satisfaction of desires view that most philosophers and social scientists seem to accept as their account of rationality. Because he adopts this modified Humean view of rationality, Rawls needs to severely limit the personal beliefs of rational persons in the original position in order to ensure that there will be agreement. As has been made clear throughout this book, Hobbes does not accept this view of rationality. He does not need to limit the beliefs of people in the state of nature because his account of rationality requires that the primary goal of rational people is to avoid death.

Hobbes allows rational people in the state of nature to have diverse desires and, apart from ranking avoiding death as their primary value, to rank their other values in quite diverse ways. Hobbes also holds that the state of nature is a state of war in which "there can be no security to any man (how strong or wise soever he be) of living out the time that nature ordinarily alloweth men to live" (L. XIV, 4). Because of this, Hobbes claims it is a dictate of reason that everyone "*be contented with so much liberty against other men, as, he would allow other men against himself*" (L. XIV, 5). (This is surprisingly similar to Rawls's first principle of justice.) This is because they know that otherwise they cannot form a commonwealth. They all believe that it is only possible to get out of the state of nature by setting up a secure commonwealth, and they believe this is possible only if the sovereign has enough power to keep them all in awe, thus they all agree to give the sovereign absolute power. Both Hobbes and Rawls require that when rational persons create a commonwealth, they do so impartially, that is, they do it without favoring any one individual over any other, but they obtain this impartiality in different ways. Hobbes obtains it by claiming that all rational persons know that no one can expect to live very long in the state of nature and that all rational persons value life above everything else; whereas Rawls gains it by taking away all beliefs and desires that enable any person to be distinguished from any other. Removing all individual differences from the people in the original position makes it impossible to favor any person or subgroup.

The basic characteristic of a commonwealth that all people in Hobbes's state of nature agree about is that it must be the most secure and stable possible. Because of their beliefs about human nature, they hold that creating a stable and secure commonwealth requires that the sovereign have enough power to keep them all in awe. The people in Rawls's original position, however, agree on all of the basic features of a commonwealth because Rawls eliminates all individual differences and so there is no basis for any disagreement at all. Rawls's method of obtaining impartiality results in complete uniformity of judgment about all the basic features of a commonwealth. However, Hobbes's method of obtaining impartiality results in agreement about morality, i.e., the laws of nature, but with regard to the nature of the commonwealth their basic agreement is only that the sovereign should have sufficient power to maintain a secure and stable commonwealth. Hobbes allows for people to disagree about whether a monarchy, aristocracy, or democracy is the best form of government. Their choice should be guided, according to Hobbes, solely by which form they believe would result in the most secure and stable commonwealth. Rawls has a far more detailed account of what people agree about, but in order to obtain this agreement, he not only has to limit the beliefs and desires of the people in unrealizable ways, he also has to rule out envy as a characteristic of the rational people in the original position.

A further important difference in their procedure for creating a commonwealth is that Hobbes considers punishment to be a critical feature in creating a commonwealth: who is subject to punishment and for what, as well as who is authorized to punish. Rawls does not consider punishment at all, but is concerned with setting up a commonwealth assuming full compliance, i.e., that all people will follow the basic rules of the society that they have set up. However, the features of the commonwealth that Rawls puts forward are those that it is up to the government to set up, and so punishment is not an issue. Punishment is also not an issue when Hobbes puts forwards those laws of nature that apply primarily to the sovereign, e.g., the laws requiring equity and gratitude and prohibiting cruelty. Although he holds that the sovereign is morally required to follow these laws, they are not subject to punishment if they do not. However, Hobbes also puts forward the law of nature concerning justice, which requires the citizens to obey the law. This law of nature is unique in that the citizens are subject to punishment if they violate it. So for Hobbes, it is important to distinguish between which moral violations are subject to punishment and which are not.

Hobbes is not concerned with guaranteeing citizens a role in deciding what laws will be enacted, for he has no objections to a monarchy. However, he is concerned about the content of the laws that any sovereign puts forward. He says:

> The office of the sovereign (be it monarch or an assembly) consisteth in the end for which he was trusted with the sovereign power, namely the procuration of the safety of the people, to which he is obliged by the law of nature. . . . But by safety here is not meant a bare preservation, but also all other contentments of life, which every man by lawful industry, without danger or hurt to the commonwealth, shall acquire to himself. (*L.* XXX, 1)

He reinforces this view later in the chapter, "A good law is that which is needful for the good of the people, and withal perspicuous" (*L.* XXX, 20). He then goes on to argue against laws that are not good. "A law that is not needful, having not the true end of a law, is not good . . . Unnecessary laws are not good laws" (*L.* XXX, 20). Hobbes is against taking away citizens' freedom unless doing so is necessary to promote the overall welfare of the citizens, but if promoting the overall welfare of the citizens requires limiting the freedom of the citizens, then Hobbes favors limiting that freedom. He does not give freedom the kind of special status that Rawls gives it. Given a choice between freedom and security, Hobbes picks security, whereas Rawls picks freedom. Rawls's position, like Locke's, has more rhetorical appeal than Hobbes's but, as political campaigns and the way people vote demonstrates, most citizens would side with Hobbes.

Hobbes and Contemporary Moral Philosophy: Gert

Hobbes has also had a significant influence on contemporary moral philosophers. David Gauthier, whose book on Hobbes, *The Logic of "Leviathan"*, interprets him as holding a Humean version of rationality, uses Hobbes in developing his moral theory in *Morals By Agreement*. Because Gauthier significantly misinterprets Hobbes, Gauthier's theory cannot be taken as a contemporary version of Hobbes's moral theory. One of the most prominent contemporary moral philosophers, Kurt Baier, explicitly acknowledges Hobbes's influence. His influential book, *The Moral Point of View*, makes use of many of Hobbes's insights. However, Baier is reluctant to reject the Humean account of reason, and adopts Hobbes's view that certain ends are irrational in a very tentative way. Partly as a result of failing to completely accept Hobbes's view that reason has ends of its own, he does not appreciate that Hobbes holds that the laws of nature that are the moral laws apply even in the state of nature. But he presents an ingenious way of achieving Hobbes's view that morality is universal. He realizes that the moral systems of all successful societies must have some important points in common and regards the moral system that contains all and only those features as the universal morality.

I am probably the contemporary moral philosopher who has been most influenced by Hobbes. I finished my PhD thesis on the moral philosophy of Thomas Hobbes in 1962 and have written about him in a dozen articles and in this book. I also edited, with a long introduction, *Man and Citizen*, first published in 1972, which contains the English translation of *De Cive* that was first published in 1651, the same year that *Leviathan* was published. It also contains the first and only English translation of the last six chapters of *De Homine* (published in 1658). Those chapters contain Hobbes's final account of human nature and make clear how well his account of human nature coheres with his moral and political theories. From the very beginning, I realized that Hobbes does not accept either psychological egoism or a Humean view of reason. This realization enabled me to take seriously Hobbes's explicit claim that he is putting forward a natural law version of morality, even though I knew that his natural law theory differed from the traditional natural law theories in that it did not depend on any beliefs about God. I did not appreciate the importance of Hobbes's distinction between justice and the rest of morality until much later, and until I did appreciate it, I was not able distinguish between Hobbes's natural law moral theory and his "social contract" political theory.

In a series of books, from *The Moral Rules: A New Rational Foundation for Morality* (1970; revised 1973 and 1975), to *Morality: A New Justification of the Moral Rules* (1988), to the revised edition of *Morality: Its Nature and Justification* (2005) and the paperback edition of *Common Morality: Deciding What to Do* (2007), I developed a moral theory that I consider to be a contemporary version of Hobbes's moral theory. This theory contains some revisions to the theory that Hobbes puts forward, but it is similar in its fundamental features. Indeed, studying Hobbes and working on my own theory were mutually reinforcing; studying Hobbes resulted in my seeing how I could incorporate his ideas into my own theory, and coming up with my own new ideas for my theory resulted in my seeing that Hobbes had already put forward very similar ideas. In what follows I shall point out the similarities and differences between Hobbes's moral theory and my own moral theory. I hope that this comparison will help readers to appreciate the power of Hobbes's moral theory.

The issues on which I agree with Hobbes are fundamental, significant, and numerous, but we differ on details because we have different purposes in providing our accounts of morality. Although I am more interested than most academic philosophers in trying to influence people's behavior, as an academic philosopher, I am less concerned than Hobbes with persuading people to act morally and more concerned than Hobbes with expressing my views with precision. We both agree that a moral theory should describe, explain, and justify our common morality, that is, the commonly accepted moral precepts, virtues, and vices, but we differ about which of these should be central in our description of morality. Hobbes, as was common in his time, starts with the commonly accepted moral virtues and vices; I start with the commonly accepted moral precepts. One result of this difference in starting points is that I regard actions, rather than traits of character, as the primary focus of morality. This allows me to talk about the immorality of careless, negligent, or thoughtless actions, about which Hobbes has very little to say. Hobbes has less concern with immoral actions of this kind because his primary concern is with intentional actions that are central to the virtues. He is trying to persuade citizens and sovereigns to act in those ways that are necessary to maintain a secure and stable commonwealth. Indeed, his explanation and justification of the standard moral virtues is that they lead to "peaceable, sociable, and comfortable living" (*L.* XV, 40).

Starting with precepts, I can distinguish far more easily than Hobbes between moral rules, which prohibit acting in ways that harm others, and moral ideals, which encourage helping those who are suffering harm. However, in *De Homine*, Hobbes makes a similar distinction among the virtues when he says that all virtues are contained in justice and charity, and claims that justice is measured by the civil law and charity only by the natural law. This has the result, with which I also agree, that failing to follow the moral rules makes one liable to punishment, but that failing to follow the moral ideals does not. But we both agree that a person can be subject to moral criticism for not following the moral ideals when one is in a situation that calls for following them. I also follow Hobbes when he makes a distinction between the moral virtue of justice, and the other three cardinal virtues of prudence, temperance, and courage, which he regards as personal rather than moral virtues. Hobbes regards virtues as moral virtues only if all rational persons praise them. The only virtues that all rational people praise are virtues that benefit them as much as the person who has the virtue, and only those virtues that lead to peace have that characteristic. Prudence, temperance, and courage benefit the person who has these virtues, but they need not be of benefit to anyone else.

I list ten moral rules: do not kill, do not cause pain, do not disable, do not deprive of freedom, and do not deprive of pleasure are the first five. The second five are: do not deceive, keep your promises, do not cheat, obey the law, and do your duty (what is required by your job or social role). I formulate these ten moral rules so that any immoral act can be regarded as a violation of one of these rules and no rule is redundant. However, I agree with Hobbes that the law decides what counts as a justified violation of one of these rules, e.g., whether this killing counts as killing in self-defense. I also agree with Hobbes that the law decides what counts as a violation of one of these rules, e.g., under what conditions turning off the ventilator of a ventilator-dependent patient counts as killing that patient. The law also decides what counts as violating any of the other moral rules, e.g., when an advertisement counts as deceptive. That the law decides these matters explains why Hobbes does not think there is any point in providing a list of the moral rules distinct from the moral requirement to obey the law. Whereas he derives the rule "obey the law" from his version of the rule "keep your promise," I regard all of the second five rules as being on a par. Nonetheless, I agree with Hobbes that "obey the law" is a universal moral rule. Even though different countries have different laws, it is a moral requirement for citizens in all countries to obey the law of their country.

Hobbes uses a negative version of the Golden Rule to summarize the laws of nature: "Do not that to another, which thou wouldst not have done to thyself" (*L.* XV, 35). This summary is another example of the importance of impartiality for Hobbes. This concern with impartiality is also shown by his formulation of the second law of nature in *Leviathan*, which includes the phrase "and be contented with so much liberty against other men, as he would allow other men against himself" (*L.* XIV, 4). In his discussion of this law he cites the Golden Rule again. The tenth law of nature, which is against arrogance, also concerns impartiality: "[N]o man require to reserve to himself any right which he is not content should be reserved to every one of the rest" (*L.* XV, 22; see also *D.C.* III, 14). Although the Golden Rule is often taken as a test of impartiality, it is not quite so common to regard the prohibition of arrogance as a requirement to be impartial. I agree with Hobbes that arrogance is the opposite of impartiality, but, like Kant, I do not think that the Golden Rule is a proper statement of the impartiality required by morality. Further, I regard impartiality as morally required only when a person is considering violating a moral rule. When a person violates a moral rule, he is acting impartially only if he is willing for everyone to know that they can violate the rule in the same circumstances. This statement resembles Hobbes's prohibition of arrogance more closely than it does either the Golden Rule or Kant's Categorical Imperative.

Hobbes does not put forward a procedure for a justified violation of a moral rule because for him it is the sovereign that decides when a violation is justified. I allow that a person can be morally justified in violating a moral rule even if the sovereign holds that he is not. But, in this situation, when people disagree about whether a violation is justified, I hold that the sovereign is justified in punishing the violator. Thus, although I allow for moral disagreement in situations where Hobbes does not, I agree with Hobbes that the sovereign can justifiably punish anyone whom he regards as having unjustifiably violated a moral rule. I also agree with Hobbes that when the sovereign determines which of two morally acceptable actions is legally required, that also makes it morally required. I am somewhat clearer than Hobbes about the distinction between moral and legal obligation, but I agree with Hobbes that in most cases a sovereign can make an action morally obligatory by making it legally required. Nonetheless Hobbes holds that the sovereign can act immorally, e.g., make immoral laws, and I agree with this. Hobbes seems to hold that, except when their own life is being threatened, citizens morally ought to obey bad laws. I have some reservations about this view and hold that when the law causes serious harm to innocent persons, e.g., as the slave laws of the southern states of the confederacy, people are not morally obliged to obey those laws.

I agree with Hobbes that avoiding and preventing harm is far more central to both morality and rationality than the promoting of benefits. The point of morality is not to increase benefits, but to avoid and relieve harms. I even use the following quote from Hobbes at the beginning of *Morality: Its Nature and Justification*: "The utility of moral and civil philosophy is to be estimated, not so much by the commodities we have by knowing these sciences, as by the calamities we receive by not knowing them" (*De Corpore*, I, 7). Hobbes's emphasis on the importance of avoiding harm results in an account of morality that is far closer to what we ordinarily regard as morality than the standard emphasis of philosophers on increasing goods. There is nothing morally questionable about being a pastry chef, but most people do not regard being a pastry chef as a moral vocation. However, it is common to regard being a physician as a moral vocation because medicine has as its primary goal the prevention and relief of harms.

The vast majority of philosophers disagree with Hobbes's account of rationality as being primarily concerned with avoiding harms, especially death, rather than with increasing goods. Most philosophers seem to accept some variation of the maximum satisfaction of desires account of rationality, with no limit on the content of those desires. Although Hobbes agrees that rational persons seek power, i.e., the ability to achieve future goals, and felicity, i.e., the continuing satisfaction of one's desires, he places limits on what counts as rational desires and goals. For Hobbes, in all normal circumstances reason requires avoiding death, pain, and disability, and any desires or goals that conflict with avoiding these harms are regarded by him as rationally unacceptable. Because Hobbes starts with what is irrational and defines what is rational as what is not irrational, he is far more tolerant of different ways of acting than most philosophers. As long as a person does not act so as to increase his risk of death, pain, and disability, Hobbes considers him to be acting rationally. This is in conflict with the standard philosophical method of providing a definition of rationality, and then claiming that any action that does not meet this definition is irrational. I agree completely with Hobbes on this point, pointing out that acting rationally need not mean doing what is rationally required, but can, and usually does, mean doing what is rationally allowed. This is a significant advance over the standard philosophical account of rationality. When Hobbes's account of rationality is combined with impartiality it results in an account of morality that is extremely close to our common morality. No variation of the Humean view of rationality as purely instrumental, even when combined with impartiality, results in anything resembling our common morality.

Hobbes's actual view of human nature, not the caricature of psychological egoism, is another area of agreement. I accept Hobbes's view that people differ from each other in significant ways not only with regard to the strength of their passions, but also with regard to which passions they have. For Hobbes, to talk about human nature is to talk about human populations. He makes no claims about how all human beings behave, for he knows that they behave in many different ways. He does hold that some passions, e.g., a disinterested love of all mankind, are exceedingly rare, and that some passions, e.g., fear of death, are exceedingly common, but it is only insofar as people are rational that they all have the same goals, the avoidance of death, pain, and disability. Although it is difficult to take seriously many of Hobbes's brief definitions of particular passions, his general point that emotions are best thought of as responses to present circumstances, or beliefs about these circumstances, seems correct. This is why the emotions often but not always conflict with reason, which is concerned with long-term consequences, especially long-term preservation. Hobbes is also right when he says that when people's emotions conflict with their reason, most people are more likely to act on their emotions than on their reason.

Because people are more likely to act for short-term gains even when they know that this is in conflict with their rational long-term goals, Hobbes is correct in claiming that the threat of punishment is essential to control people's behavior. The threat of immediate punishment, even if relatively mild, has more motive strength than the long-term threat of the breakdown of the commonwealth. The truth of this is shown by people who are not deterred from speeding recklessly by the thought that they are increasing their risk of dying or being seriously injured, but who slow down when they see a police car by the side of the road in order to avoid a speeding ticket. Hobbes was living at a time when people were prepared to risk civil war for religious reasons and he correctly saw that to prevent this kind of behavior requires a government with sufficient power to provide a threat plausible enough to keep people's emotions in check. Although civil wars fought in the name of religion are not as much of a threat as they used to be in England, they remain a possibility in some parts of the world. Hobbes realizes that unless religion is interpreted so that it never conflicts with morality, it is quite likely to lead people to act immorally, e.g., to discriminate against homosexuals.

Hobbes is certainly right that morality presupposes that the people to whom it applies are both vulnerable and fallible, but he insists that all human beings have these characteristics. He explicitly says that morality does not apply to God because God is neither vulnerable nor fallible. It is one of the classic errors of consequentialism to describe morality as if it applies to omniscient beings with no need for rules. Act consequentialists regard the inclusion of rules in morality to be a concession to fallible persons who need usable guides for acting. Hobbes accepts, as I do and consequentialists do not, the natural law position that all rational persons know what the system of morality prohibits, requires, discourages, encourages, and allows. He explains this universal knowledge as the result of morality being a system that all vulnerable and fallible human beings, insofar as they are rational, would put forward as necessary for large numbers of vulnerable and fallible people like themselves to live together in a peaceful society. With minor refinements, to avoid counter-examples,

I accept Hobbes's explanation of why all rational persons know what morality is.

Hobbes does not talk much about the value of freedom, but that is because he was concerned with citizens who thought that they were free to disobey any law that they did not agree with. Hobbes rightly holds that citizens do not have this kind of freedom. He holds that all people are free to do whatever is legally, morally, and rationally allowed, that is, allowed by the civil laws and the laws of nature. Because he is primarily concerned with the power of the sovereign to limit the freedom of citizens, he does not talk, as I do, of the loss of freedom as a harm that needs to be justified. However, Hobbes's condemnation of unnecessary laws, that is, laws that do not benefit the citizens, suggests that he regards depriving people of innocent liberty as a harm. Certainly, he would condemn as unjustified all unnecessary deprivation of freedom by the government.

Although Hobbes and I talk about morality in somewhat different terms, there are no significant disagreements between our views. As I said earlier, any disagreements that do exist are primarily due to differences in the goals we are trying to achieve. Hobbes was interested in providing arguments that would persuade people to act in those ways that would result in maintaining a secure and stable commonwealth. He was also interested in putting forward sound arguments, but he was not overly concerned with the kind of precision that academic philosophers like me regard as essential. He indulges in rhetorical excesses that have allowed academic philosophers to find inconsistencies and to justify attributing to him various absurd philosophical views. He talks about the laws of nature as the moral law, but says that the laws of nature also command prudence, temperance, and courage, even though he acknowledges that these virtues are not moral virtues. Further, only the first half of his list of the laws of nature have anything to do with any kind of virtue; the latter half require various political and judicial procedures that he regarded as necessary for maintaining a secure and stable commonwealth. He was not an academic philosopher and has suffered centuries of misinterpretation because academic philosophers have failed to see how cogent his account of moral and political philosophy is.

I also would like to persuade people to act morally and rationally, but I have taken more seriously than Hobbes his view that people's behavior is more influenced by their feelings than by arguments addressed to their reason. So I do not think that I am likely to persuade people to act either morally or rationally. But, like Hobbes, I hope to influence someone with the power to persuade people to act morally. In putting forward my own account of morality, I am primarily concerned with writing carefully and precisely, and avoiding any mistakes, so that if someone with power is influenced by my account of morality, this will not lead him to adopt immoral policies. This makes my books far less readable than Hobbes's. I have to admit that it is easier to read the very large *Leviathan* than even my little book *Common Morality*, which I wrote for a wider audience than merely philosophers. I have not written much on political philosophy, so I do not have the developed views that make it worthwhile to note the widespread agreement between Hobbes's views and my views. However, it may be worthwhile to note that when I take into account that Hobbes's political philosophy was addressed to two distinct audiences, I find that I agree far more with his political philosophy than I thought I would.

One audience that Hobbes is addressing consists of citizens of a functioning commonwealth. Hobbes is not addressing people in the state of nature, for there are no such people, and even if there were, they would not have the time or leisure to read his work. To citizens of any functioning commonwealth Hobbes is providing strong arguments for them to obey the laws of their commonwealth, even in those cases when they think that a particular law is a bad law. He provides both moral and prudential arguments for obeying all the laws. He does not say that citizens should not try, by lawful means, to get the laws changed, but he argues against any unlawful action that might threaten the stability of the commonwealth. However, when the commonwealth is secure and stable, I do not think that Hobbes provides any arguments against the kind of peaceful civil disobedience that, by accepting the punishments for such disobedience, acknowledges the authority of the commonwealth to make and enforce the laws. Unless the sovereign is clearly immoral and, as a result, there are some extraordinarily bad laws, these arguments for obedience seems to me to be correct.

However, we are now aware that sometimes there really are clearly immoral sovereigns who make and enforce extraordinarily bad laws. I am not talking merely about Nazi Germany and similar immoral dictatorships. From the founding of the United States of American up until about 150 years ago, the government of the United States, and of some of the individual states, were clearly immoral in making and enforcing some extraordinarily bad laws. Even after the Civil War ended the practice of slavery, some state

governments made and enforced extraordinarily bad laws discrimi-
nating against African Americans. Since the United States is a
democracy, it is clear that immoral sovereigns and extraordinarily
bad laws are not limited to monarchies or aristocracies. Hobbes's
political philosophy would clearly label such sovereigns as immoral,
for they violate the natural law requiring gratitude toward all those
who obey the law. Making and enforcing slavery is clearly not
showing gratitude toward law-abiding slaves. Hobbes acknowledges that there can be commonwealths in which some citizens are
no better off, and sometimes even worse off, than they would in the
state of nature. However, he has nothing to say about what other
citizens should do in this kind of situation. He thought that the
immorally treated citizens would revolt, and he does not condemn
revolution in such a situation, but he is so concerned with avoiding
a civil war that might arise from challenging the authority of the
sovereign that he never addresses the issue of what citizens should
do when the government acts immorally toward other citizens.

The other audience that Hobbes is addressing, and probably the
audience he thought it most important to persuade, are sovereigns,
either a monarch or members of a sovereign assembly. He could
even be addressing citizens in their role as members of a sovereign
democracy. Hobbes claims that all sovereigns have a duty to maintain the power that will keep all the citizens in awe, and not to let
it be divided in any way. Because of his belief that most citizens act
on their emotions rather than their reason, he holds that the sovereign should have so much power that none of the citizens would
even think of challenging its authority. He also recognizes that the
sovereign should leave no doubt about who is sovereign and what
the law is. Hobbes, however, realizes that the "terror of legal punishment" (*L.* XXX, 4) is not sufficient to maintain sovereign power,
for unless citizens, including members of the police and army,
understand the moral and prudential reasons for obeying the laws,
the sovereign will not be able to enforce the laws. Although Hobbes's talk about sovereignty no longer seems relevant, his claim that
any government must have the allegiance of the vast majority of its
citizens to maintain a secure and stable commonwealth, and that
acting in the interests of the citizens is the way to maintain that
allegiance, is correct.

Many schools teach what is often called civic education, seemingly agreeing with Hobbes that citizens must be taught about why
they must be good citizens and obey all the laws. I think that they,
and Hobbes, overestimate the importance of citizens understanding

the moral and prudential reasons for their obedience. Far more important is what Hobbes lists as the first duty of the sovereign, "namely, the procuration of the safety of the people. . . . But by safety here is not meant a bare preservation, but also all other contentments of life, which every man by lawful industry, without danger or hurt to the commonwealth, shall acquire to himself" (*L.* XXX, 1). By providing a commonwealth in which people feel safe and have all the contentments of life, citizens are much less likely to act in ways that challenge the government. This is why the western democracies are so stable; it is not that they are democracies, but that they are able to provide their citizens with security and the contentments of life. The stability of states does not depend directly on the form of sovereignty – monarchy, aristocracy, or democracy – but on whether the government is wealthy enough to provide the citizens with the contentments of life and smart enough to actually do so. It may be that democracies are more likely to be wealthy and more likely to act in the interests of all the citizens, but that is a complex question to which neither Hobbes nor I has any answer.

Hobbes seems to prefer a monarchy to the other forms of sovereignty, but he says that a democracy that elects a representative to govern them and leaves him alone between elections is as good as a monarchy. In the debates in the United States about whether the executive or the legislative branch should have more power, Hobbes would come out strongly in favor of the executive branch. The strongest objection to Hobbes's political philosophy is that he gives no preference to democracy over aristocracy or monarchy. He does not think it important that the people have a say in how they are governed; he thinks that what is important is simply how they are governed. In the United States, half of the people entitled to vote do not do so, and only when people are dissatisfied with the government is there likely to be a larger turnout. I think that Hobbes was mistaken in not seeing that democracies are better than other forms of government. His mistake was in not applying his account of human nature to those who are sovereigns. He knows that most people act on their emotions rather than on their reason, but does not seem to realize that this applies to sovereigns as well as to citizens. He regards the strength of the monarch as the strength of the commonwealth, so he thinks the monarch always acts for the benefit of the commonwealth. But that is clearly a mistake. In a democracy, the clash of emotions provides more room for reason to have influence.

In fact, Hobbes knew from personal experience that monarchs act on their emotions rather than on their reason, so it is surprising that he does not incorporate this fact into his political philosophy. It may be that, in contrast with the rest of his political philosophy, Hobbes's support of a monarchy, which he explicitly acknowledges is not part of his political theory, is explained by his loyalties to the monarch. When he is doing political philosophy he denies the divine right of kings, and when he talks about sovereignty by institution he explicitly says that it was originally a democracy. I do not claim that Hobbes was really a democrat, but it is interesting that he talks so much about a commonwealth by institution. He is quite clear that no actual commonwealths were formed by institution and that commonwealths by acquisition were the natural way for commonwealth to be formed. Even though sovereignty by acquisition is far more favorable to a monarchy, and even though he says, "the rights and consequences of sovereignty are the same in both" (*L.* XX, 3), Hobbes seems to regard a commonwealth by institution as more basic. He spends far more time and effort in describing and explaining how a commonwealth is instituted than in describing and explaining how a commonwealth is acquired by force.

Some of Hobbes's views on moral and political matters are mistaken. Some of these views are mistaken because Hobbes was too influenced by what was happening during the times in which he was writing. Some of his views are mistaken because his concern with persuading people led him to express himself with a rhetorical power that resulted in his not being as careful as he should have been. Hobbes often seems to realize when his moral and political views are influenced by his personal experience and biases and are not part of his systematic moral and political theory. His rhetorical flourishes are generally easily detected if one does not read him as if he were an academic philosopher, but as a political activist trying to influence the course of events. A sympathetic reading of his systematic moral and political theories reveals a philosopher with unusual ability to derive surprising conclusions from extremely plausible premises. Even an unsympathetic reading reveals an extremely powerful mind at work. So it is not surprising that after more than 350 years of being attacked and misinterpreted, he is still regarded as one of the greatest moral and political philosophers of all time.

Bibliography

Sharon Lloyd's excellent article, "Hobbes's Moral and Political Philosophy," in the Stanford Online Encyclopedia of Philosophy, has a bibliography of works about Hobbes's moral and political philosophy. She has graciously allowed me to use this as the foundation for my bibliography. I have added quite a few books to Lloyd's bibliography and have also eliminated many.

Works by Hobbes

Cropsey, J. (ed.) 1971. *Dialogue between a Philosopher and a Student of the Common Laws of England*. Chicago: University of Chicago Press.

Curley, E. (ed.) 1994. *Leviathan*. Indianapolis: Hackett Publishing Company. Inc.

Gert, B. (ed.) (1991) *Man and Citizen*. Indianapolis: Hackett Publishing Company. Inc. (orig. pub. by Doubleday and Co., 1972).

Holmes, S. (ed.) 1969. *Behemoth or the Long Parliament*. Chicago: University of Chicago Press.

Martinich, A. (ed.) 1981. *De Corpore*. Part 1. New York: Abaris Books.

Molesworth, W. (ed.) 1835–45. *English Works*, 11 vols; *Opera Latina*, 5 vols. London: John Bohn.

Tönnies, F. (ed.) 1928. *The Elements of Law. Natural and Politic*. Cambridge: Cambridge University Press.

Collections

Baumrin, B. H. (ed.) 1969. *Hobbes's Leviathan: Interpretation and Criticism*. Belmont, CA: Wadsworth Publishing Company. Inc.

Bertman, M. and Malherbe, M. 1989. *Thomas Hobbes: De la Metaphysique à la Politique*. Paris: Librarie Philosophique J. Vrin.

Brown, K. C. (ed.) 1965. *Hobbes Studies*. Cambridge, MA: Harvard University Press.

Caws, P. (ed.) 1989. *The Causes of Quarrel: Essays on Peace, War, and Thomas Hobbes*. Boston: Beacon Press.

Cranston, M. and Peters, R. 1972. *Hobbes and Rousseau: A Collection of Critical Essays*. New York: Anchor Doubleday.

Dick, O. L. 1962. *Aubrey's Brief Lives*. Ann Arbor: University of Michigan Press.

Dietz, M. (ed.) 1990. *Thomas Hobbes and Political Theory*. Lawrence: University of Kansas Press.

Finkelstein, C. (ed.) 2005. *Hobbes on Law*. Aldershot: Ashgate.

Foisneau, L. and Sorell, T. (eds.) 2004. *Leviathan after 350 Years*. Oxford: Oxford University Press.

Lloyd, S. A. (ed.) 2001. "Special Issue on Recent Work on the Moral and Political Philosophy of Thomas Hobbes." *Pacific Philosophical Quarterly* 82 (3&4).

Rogers, G. A. J. (ed.) 1995. *Leviathan: Contemporary Responses to the Political Theory of Thomas Hobbes*. Bristol: Thoemmes Press.

Rogers, G. A. J. and Ryan, A. (eds.) 1988. *Perspectives on Thomas Hobbes*. Oxford: Oxford University Press.

Shaver, R. (ed.) 1999. *Hobbes*. Hanover: Dartmouth Press.

Sorell, T. (ed.) 1996. *The Cambridge Companion to Hobbes*. Cambridge: Cambridge University Press.

Sorrell, T. and Rogers, G. A. J. (eds.) 2000. *Hobbes and History*. London: Routledge.

Springboard, P. (ed.) 2007. *The Cambridge Companion to Hobbes's Leviathan*. Cambridge: Cambridge University Press.

Books

Baumgold, D. 1988. *Hobbes's Political Thought*. Cambridge: Cambridge University Press.

Boonin-Vail, D. 1994. *Thomas Hobbes and the Science of Moral Virtue*. Cambridge: Cambridge University Press.

Brandt, F. 1928. *Thomas Hobbes' Mechanical Conception of Nature*. Copenhagen. Levin and Munksgaard

Collins, J. 2005. *The Allegiance of Thomas Hobbes*. Oxford: Oxford University Press.

Curley, E. (ed.) 1994. "Introduction to Hobbes's *Leviathan*". *Leviathan* with selected variants from the Latin edition of 1668. Indianapolis: Hackett Publishing Company. Inc.

Curley, E. 2007. *Reclaiming the Rights of Hobbesian Subjects*. Hampshire: Palgrave Macmillan.

Darwall, S. 1995. *The British Moralists and the Internal "Ought": 1640–1740.* Cambridge: Cambridge University Press.

Ewin, R. E. 1991. *Virtues and Rights: The Moral Philosophy of Thomas Hobbes.* Boulder: Westview Press.

Gauthier, D. 1969. *The Logic of "Leviathan": The Moral and Political Theory of Thomas Hobbes.* Oxford: Clarendon Press.

Gert, B. 1991. "Introduction to *Man and Citizen.*" In *Man and Citizen,* ed. B. Gert. Indianapolis: Hackett Publishing Company. Inc.

Goldsmith, M. M. 1966. *Hobbes's Science of Politics.* New York: Columbia University Press.

Hampton, J. 1986. *Hobbes and the Social Contract Tradition.* Cambridge: Cambridge University Press.

Hinant, C. H. 1977. *Thomas Hobbes.* Boston: Twayne Publishers.

Hinant, C. H. 1980. *Thomas Hobbes: A Reference Guide.* Boston: G. K. Hall & Co.

Hood, E. C. 1964. *The Divine Politics of Thomas Hobbes.* Oxford: Clarendon Press.

Johnston. D. 1986. *The Rhetoric of "Leviathan": Thomas Hobbes and the Politics of Cultural Transformation.* Princeton: Princeton University Press.

Kavka, G. 1986. *Hobbesian Moral and Political Theory.* Princeton: Princeton University Press.

Lloyd, S. A. 1992. *Ideals as Interests in Hobbes's "Leviathan": The Power of Mind Over Matter.* Cambridge: Cambridge University Press.

Lloyd, S. A. 2009. *Morality in the Philosophy of Thomas Hobbes: Cases in the Law of Nature.* Cambridge: Cambridge University Press.

Macdonald, H. and Hargreaves, M. 1952. *Thomas Hobbes: A Bibliography.* London: The Bibliographical Society.

Macpherson, C. B. 1962. *The Political Theory of Possessive Individualism: Hobbes to Locke.* Oxford: Oxford University Press.

Malcolm, N. 2002. *Aspects of Hobbes.* Oxford: Oxford University Press.

Martinich, A. P. 1992. *The Two Gods of Leviathan: Thomas Hobbes on Religion and Politics.* Cambridge: Cambridge University Press.

Martinich, A. P. 1995. *A Hobbes Dictionary.* Oxford: Blackwell.

Martinich, A. P. 1999. *Hobbes: A Biography.* Cambridge: Cambridge University Press.

Martinich, A. P. 2005. *Hobbes.* New York: Routledge.

McNeilly, F. S. 1968. *The Anatomy of Leviathan.* New York: St Martin's Press.

Mintz, S. I. 1970. *The Hunting of Leviathan.* Cambridge: Cambridge University Press.

Oakeshott, M. 1975. *Hobbes on Civil Association.* Oxford: Oxford University Press.

Peter, R. 1956. *Hobbes.* London: Penguin Books

Raphael, D. D. 1977. *Hobbes: Morals and Politics.* London: Routledge Press.

Reik, M. M. 1977. *The Golden Lands of Thomas Hobbes.* Detroit: Wayne State University Press.

Robertson, G. C. 1886. *Hobbes*. Edinburgh: Edinburgh University Press.
Rogow, A. A. *Thomas Hobbes: Radical in the Service of Reaction*. New York: W. W. Norton & Company.
Schneewind, J. B. 1997. *The Invention of Autonomy: History of Modern Moral Philosophy*. Cambridge: Cambridge University Press.
Skinner, Q. 1996. *Reason and Rhetoric in the Philosophy of Hobbes*. Cambridge: Cambridge University Press.
Skinner, Q. 2002. *Visions of Politics. Volume 3: Hobbes and Civil Science*. Cambridge: Cambridge University Press.
Skinner, Q. 2008. *Hobbes and Republican Liberty*. Cambridge: Cambridge University Press.
Sommerville, J. 1992. *Thomas Hobbes: Political Ideas in Historical Context*. London: Macmillan.
Sorell, T. 1986. *Hobbes*. London: Routledge and Kegan Paul.
Spragens, T. A. Jr. 1973. *The Politics of Motion. The World of Thomas Hobbes*. Lexington: University Press of Kentucky.
Strauss, L. 1936. *The Political Philosophy of Hobbes: Its Basis and Genesis*. Oxford: Oxford University Press.
Taylor, A. E. 1908. *Thomas Hobbes*. London: Kennicat Press
Tuck, R. 1979. *Natural Rights Theories: Their Origin and Development*. Cambridge: Cambridge University Press.
Tuck, R. 1989. *Hobbes*. Oxford: Oxford University Press.
Tuck, R. 1993. *Philosophy and Government 1572–1651*. Cambridge: Cambridge University Press.
Warrender, H. 1957. *The Political Philosophy of Hobbes: His Theory of Obligation*. Oxford: Oxford University Press.
Watkins, J. W. N. 1965. *Hobbes's System of Ideas*. London: Hutchison and Co.

Further works

This is a list of philosophy books that may have influenced, or may have been influenced by, Hobbes.

Aristotle. *c.* 350 BCE. *Nicomachean Ethics*.
Aristotle. *c.* 330 BCE. *Politics*.
Aristotle. *c.* 330 BCE. *Rhetoric*.
Baier, K. 1965.*The Moral Point of View*, abridged and rev. edn.
Gauthier, David. 1999. *Morals by Agreement*, paperback edn.
Gert, B. 2005. *Morality: Its Nature and Justification*, rev. edn.
Gert, B. 2007. *Common Morality: Deciding What To Do*, paperback edn.
Grotius, H. 1625. *Law of War and Peace*.
Hume, D. 1739–40. *A Treatise of Human Nature*.
Hume, D. 1748. *An Enquiry Concerning Human Understanding*.

Hume, D. 1751. *An Enquiry Concerning the Principles of Morals.*
Hume, D. 1779. *Dialogues Concerning Natural Religion.*
Kant, I. 1785. *Groundwork for the Metaphysics of Morals.*
Kant, I. 1788. *Critique of Practical Reason.*
Kant, I. 1797. *The Metaphysics of Morals.*
Locke, J. 1688. *Two Treatises of Government.*
Locke, J. 1689. *A Letter Concerning Toleration.*
Mill, J. S. 1859. *On Liberty.*
Mill, J. S. 1862. *Considerations on Representative Government.*
Mill, J. S. 1863. *Utilitarianism.*
Plato. *c.* 360 BCE. *Republic.*
Plato. *c.* 360 BCE. *Statesman.*
Plato. *c.* 360 BCE. *Laws.*
Rawls, J. 1971. *A Theory of Justice.*
Rawls, J. 1993. *Political Liberalism.*
Rawls, J. 1999. *The Law of Peoples.*
Rawls, J. 2001. *Justice as Fairness: A Restatement.*
Spinoza, B. 1670. *Tractatus Theologico-Politicus.*
Spinoza, B. 1677. *Ethics.*

Index